Also by Ursula K. Le Guin

NOVELS

THE BOOKS OF EARTHSEA

A Wizard of Earthsea
The Tombs of Atuan
The Farthest Shore
Tehanu
Tales from Earthsea
The Other Wind

OTHER NOVELS

The Lathe of Heaven
Very Far Away from Anywhere Else
Malafrena
The Beginning Place
The Eye of Heron
Always Coming Home
Lavinia
The Complete Orsinia: Malafrena/Stories and Songs

NOVELS OF THE EKUMEN

Worlds of Exile and Illusion:
City of Illusions, Planet of Exile, and Rocannon's World
The Left Hand of Darkness
The Dispossessed: An Ambiguous Utopia
The Word for World Is Forest
The Telling

THE ANNALS OF THE WESTERN SHORE

Powers
Voices
Gifts

POETRY

Wild Angels
Hard Words and Other Poems

THE LANGUAGE OF THE NIGHT

ESSAYS ON WRITING, SCIENCE FICTION, AND FANTASY

URSULA K. Le GUIN

SCRIBNER

New York   London   Toronto   Sydney   New Delhi

Scribner
An Imprint of Simon & Schuster, LLC
1230 Avenue of the Americas
New York, NY 10020

For information about special discounts for bulk purchases, please contact
Simon & Schuster Special Sales at 1-866-506-1949 or
business@simonandschuster.com.

The Simon & Schuster Speakers Bureau can bring authors to your live event. For
more information or to book an event, contact the Simon & Schuster Speakers
Bureau at 1-866-248-3049 or visit our website at www.simonspeakers.com.

Interior design by Erika R. Genova

Illustration by Jim Tierney

Manufactured in the United States of America

1   3   5   7   9   10   8   6   4   2

Library of Congress Cataloging-in-Publication Data is available.

ISBN 978-1-6680-3490-3
ISBN 978-1-6680-3505-4 (ebook)

Page 263 constitutes an extension of this copyright page.

CONTENTS

THE LANGUAGE
OF THE NIGHT

INTRODUCTION TO *THE LANGUAGE OF THE NIGHT*

**by Ken Liu
(2024)**

More than any other value, Ursula K. Le Guin stands for *liberty*. In her 1977 introduction to *The Word for World Is Forest* (which is collected in this volume), Le Guin asks the question: Why do artists bother creating art at all? Like all important questions, it's as relevant today as it was in 1977, in 1907, and in 907 BCE.

In her usual mordant style, Le Guin begins by noting Freud's theory, which she considers both "funny" and "comforting," that artists are solely motivated by the desire for "honor, power, riches, fame, and the love of women." (Like modern AI chatbots, Freud could always be counted on to confidently opine on any topic about which he knew nothing.) Le Guin then turns to someone with rather more authority to speak on the subject, Emily Brontë:

> *Riches I hold in light esteem*
> *And Love I laugh to scorn*

And lust of Fame was but a dream
That vanished with the morn—

And if I pray, the only prayer
That moves my lips for me
Is—"Leave the heart that now I bear
And give me liberty."

I could stop right here. Brontë's poem serves as the perfect introduction to this collection of essays (and for that matter, to the entirety of Le Guin's body of work as critic, poet, novelist, translator, short story writer, and more). You are perfectly justified to skip over the rest of my intro and get to Le Guin's essays if you wish.

Still here?

There is *one* good reason to read an introduction to a monumental classic—a book of criticism so influential that it has become a work of art itself, which is to converse with a fellow reader who also admires that classic. In the Daoist framework to which Le Guin subscribed, our understanding grows ever deeper when it is in motion, like a living river, and that requires speaking as well as listening, leading to discourse, communion, gathering (referring to the Indo-European root of "logos").

When reading, we don't converse only with the writer, but also with our fellow readers. As much as we in the West have emphasized the sovereignty of the individual, the good life isn't lived alone, but in flowing conversation—and Le Guin's conception of liberty is, in particular, not solitary, static, or stable, but communitarian, dynamic, anarchic.

You can see some of this in the way Le Guin has, over the years, conversed with herself in the footnotes to these essays upon the publication of new editions. *The Language of the Night* is her first collection of criticism, and some of the essays were written decades ago. Over the years, some of the ideas she relied on proved to be false or exaggerated (e.g., the work on Senoi Dream Theory), she changed her mind on a number of issues (e.g., using or refusing to use certain pronouns, and the significance thereof), and some of the things she once said she later preferred to say differently. And so she corrects herself, pushes herself, forgives herself—this is what a living understanding looks like, instead of dead dogma. We should all be so willing to collaborate with our old selves throughout our life journey.

For Le Guin, "the pursuit of art . . . by artist or audience, is the pursuit of liberty."* However, this liberty is not mere license to do whatever seizes one's fancy: frame a can of soup, push a button on Poem-O-Matic, photocopy a photocopy, and scribble your initial on it. Indeed, the sort of pseudo-liberty defined by the "almost limitless freedom of form available to the modern artist" is, for Le Guin, a "trivialization of art."† And trivialization can be even worse than outright oppression. (Likewise trivial, I would argue, is the also almost limitless freedom of forms of consumption for the modern audience.) The kind of emphasis on "self-expression" that leads to "cover[ing] a cliff with six acres of plastic film" presumes and accepts deep entanglement with the mechanisms of capitalism; requires riches, fame, power, status (if not honor), and maybe even love of a sort; but is ultimately devoid of moral significance. However, when "art is taken seriously by its creators or consumers, that total permissiveness disappears, and the possibility of the truly revolutionary reappears."‡

Le Guin's emphasis on liberty, serious liberty, demands much

---

* "Introduction to *The Word for World Is Forest*."
† "The Stalin in the Soul."
‡ Ibid.

of the artist as well as the audience. Throughout her life, she never stopped pushing for the audience to be more discriminating, to not settle for mere recycled "adventures," to push fantasy and science fiction—long dismissed as puerile make-believe by outsiders and often defiantly defended as such by fans—to fulfill their true potential. Le Guin has no patience or kind words for cowardly audiences who refuse to take responsibility for tolerating bad art. "Within the SF ghetto, many people don't want their books, or their favorite writers' books, judged as literature. They want junk, and they bitterly resent aesthetic judgment of it."* Similarly, she pushed herself and her fellow artists to work harder, to explore and go beyond the known boundaries, to always do (not merely try) their best. "In art, the best is the standard."† For an artist, "there are just two ways to go: to push toward the limit of your capacity, or to sit back and emit garbage."‡ She turned Sturgeon's law, which states that 95 percent of anything is trash, from an ironic acceptance of mediocrity into a rallying cry for renewed artistic commitment: "The Quest for Perfection fails at least 95 percent of the time, but the Search for Garbage never fails."§

For Le Guin, aesthetics *is* ethics. In order for art to be free, it must be moral, a constant revolution.

This insistence on a moral imperative for art pits Le Guin against the dominant ideology of our Western modernity: the sacrosanct "will" of the market. Under this view, the artist is a producer no different from a baker of cakes or digger of ditches, and the audience is no different than any other kind of consumer, free

---

*   "Escape Routes."
†   "From Elfland to Poughkeepsie."
‡   "The Stone Ax and the Muskoxen."
§   Ibid.

to vote with their money for what gives them the most pleasure. Art—now renamed "Entertainment"—is justified by the degree to which it adds to the GDP. As Le Guin puts it, "[O]ur businessman might allow himself to read a bestseller now and then: not because it is a good book, but because it is a bestseller—it is a success, it has made money."* Since everyone is acting in the most rational manner in this little drama, revealing their entertainment preferences with their dollars, how can the market not be free? Isn't this the very definition of liberty?

Well, no. When artists depend on the whims of the market for their next meal, for that room of one's own, for self-respect, Le Guin astutely observes that they are also subjected to a different kind of censorship. Not the overt kind practiced in totalitarian societies where disobedience is met with imprisonment or death; not the kind of book-banning and library-cleansing led by petty demagogues backed by insecure mobs wishing to exert power over marginalized groups; not even the sort of collective censure that has been pejoratively termed "identity politics" or "cancel culture"; but censorship by "the idols of the marketplace: . . . a form of censorship [that] is unusually fluid and changeable; one should never feel sure one has defined it. Suppressions occur before one is aware of them; they occur behind one's eyes."†

This form of censorship is particularly dangerous to artists in a democracy because it's invisible and never talked about. It feels simply like the inevitable way things work out. Le Guin speaks of artists like Yevgeny Ivanovich Zamyatin, who risked everything in his ceaseless pursuit of liberty and who ultimately succeeded in escaping the Soviet

---

* "Why Are Americans Afraid of Dragons?"
† Ibid.

censors even if his novel *We,* which Le Guin considered the best single work of science fiction yet written, could not be published in his homeland. His life was a tragedy. In contrast, Le Guin also writes of another artist, unnamed, in our land of the free, who put the great novel that he dreamed of writing on hold because he needed to eat; he wanted to have money; he wanted to be famous—or at least he believed he wanted those things. He wrote books like *Deep Armpit* and scripts for Hollywood, wrote "for the market," and then he died, without having published his greatest novel in his homeland, because he never wrote it. His life was a farce. "He accepted, unquestioning, the values of his society. And the price of unquestioning acceptance is silence."*

When success in art is defined as success in the market, the pursuit of liberty is corrupted by the pursuit of *Will this sell?* The relentless pressure to be commoditized—rather comically reframed as the drive to be "professional"—pervades every aspect of the contemporary practice of art. Since writers are paid by the word, we boast to each other of our "productivity," evidenced by the number of words we write each day, as though we are miners digging for ore. We envy those who have gotten big advances or sold a million copies, as though these arbitrary indicia of commerce confer some incontrovertible validation of artistic worth. If movies make more money than books and are consumed by more people, then it necessarily follows that movies are superior as art, and if your work hasn't been elevated by a screen adaptation, you must be a failure. I have seen writers speak with pride of the "business" of writing as though it is of the same importance or even more important than writing itself. By submitting to the judgment of the market, we debase ourselves into hacks, all the while perversely claiming that selling out is ennobling

---

* "The Stalin in the Soul."

because we have captured the taste of an equally debased audience.

> Genuine newness, genuine originality, is suspect. Unless it's
> something familiar rewarmed, or something experimental in
> form but clearly trivial or cynical in content, it is unsafe. And it
> must be safe. It mustn't hurt the consumers. It mustn't change
> the consumers. Shock them, *épater le bourgeois,* certainly,
> that's been done for a hundred and fifty years now, that's the
> oldest game going. Shock them, jolt them, titillate them, make
> them writhe and squeal—but do not make them think. If they
> think, they may not come back to buy the next can of soup.[*]

I would add to this that the audience has been taught to not expect
much from art. If we say that we want more than giant alien robots
shooting lasers at villainous prehistoric sharks while the heroes—all
beautiful, all young, all so rich, famous, and powerful—reassure us
that the answer to everything is Love, Recycling, and Violence (because it's the American Way), we're laughed at for daring to expect
Hollywood to be better than it is. Why should we hold such low
expectations? Is it not just an excuse for our continuing mediocrity
as artists and as an audience? Shame on us.

"To sell" has never been the purpose of art, no more than a price
tag has ever been of any use in ascertaining the value of something.
More than any other modern critic, Le Guin articulates with conviction and clarity the moral imperative of art as fantasy, as the pursuit
of liberty. Drawing on Tolkien, Le Guin affirms fantasy as an "escape" from the oppressive structures of the so-called "Real World":

> Yes, he said, fantasy is escapist, and that is its glory. If a
> soldier is imprisoned by the enemy, don't we consider it his

---

[*]   "The Stalin in the Soul."

duty to escape? The moneylenders, the know-nothings, the authoritarians have us all in prison; if we value the freedom of the mind and soul, if we're partisans of liberty, then it's our plain duty to escape, and to take as many people with us as we can.[*]

In this act of defiant escape—for the artist and the audience— the Real World is revealed to consist of nothing more than our own mental constructs, walls and shackles fashioned out of anti-imagination (what is money but a collective hallucination, a lie repeated so often it begins to sound like truth?).

(Not coincidentally, fantasy's power to break us free from the shackles of oppressive reality also demolishes the supposed incompatibility between Art [intentionally capitalized] and "fun." Those fans who react with defensive rage to Le Guin's admonishment that they're tolerating bad science fiction and bad art call her elitist and claim that she wants to drive "fun" out of their beloved genre. But to qualify as an escape, the prisoners must get to somewhere better than their prison, somewhere more desirable, more true, more fun. "[W]e're escaping a world that consists of *Newsweek*, *Pravda*, and *the Stock Market Report*, and asserting the existence of a primary, vivid world, an intenser reality where joy, tragedy, and morality exist."[†] The purported dichotomy between "fun" and "Art" is nonsense. "To imply that Art is something heavy and solemn and dull, and Entertainment is modest but jolly and popular, is neo-Victorian idiocy at its worst."[‡])

How can artists effectuate an entertaining and moral escape, an

---

[*] "Escape Routes." I should note that Le Guin is not quoting Tolkien here, but summarizing and expanding on some of the points he made in "On Fairy-Stories," and then adding in insights entirely her own.

[†] Ibid.

[‡] "The Stone Ax and the Muskoxen."

escape worthy of being called Art? Answers to this question form the backbone of every essay in this volume. An artist who chooses to work in the ancient empire of fantasy, and more specifically science fiction, which is that empire's newest province, full of untamed metaphors and wild dreams uniquely suited to our cyborg present and posthuman futures, must go beyond the phony, trivial escapes of SF's pulp past (the "Golden Age" of square-jawed starship captains saving honey-tressed damsels from little green barbarian aliens with slanted eyes, the spirit of which age lives on in our blockbuster films that require us to turn off our brains); must go beyond the equally false (but confident and simple, and therefore attractive) escapes offered by "ideologies," which Le Guin dismisses as "the reactionary, easy-answer schools of SF, the technocrats, scientologists, 'libertarians,' and so on, . . . [as well as] the chic nihilism affected by many talented American and English writers of my generation";* and embrace, instead, the only escape that is mythic, eternal, and real: the journey inside our collective unconscious.

> The great fantasies, myths, and tales are indeed like dreams: they speak from the unconscious to the unconscious, in the language of the unconscious—symbol and archetype. Though they use words, they work the way music does: they short-circuit verbal reasoning, and go straight to the thoughts that lie too deep to utter.†

This is the language of the night. To speak it requires the artist to go on a harrowing journey toward the interior, where the wordless dreams and voiceless music that have been with us since the caves

---

* "Escape Routes."
† "The Child and the Shadow."

of Lascaux, since Kakadu and Maros-Pangkep, still reign supreme; where our shared evolutionary history allows us to understand one another without speech; where we step into the dream time of the Athsheans in *The Word for World Is Forest*; where we recognize that there is one collective Jungian Self shared by all humanity; where we immerse ourselves in the language beneath the language, and the soul finds no partition between imago and ego.

"Human beings all look roughly alike; they also think and feel alike. And they are all part of the universe."* This is the truth to be rediscovered each time we journey inside, the revelation that propels us out of our rational solitude and into communion with all in the time before time, "where we all meet . . . the source of true community; of felt religion; of art, grace, spontaneity, and love."†

As Le Guin notes, this "sounds mystical, and it is, but it's also exact and practical."‡ This is the source of the power of art. Imprisoned in our skulls, isolated in our quirky cells of semi-rationality, how can any single mind, no matter how capacious, discern a true and beautiful escape route applicable to any other mind? The answer is obvious: we share that boundless interior; there is only one Self. Artists explore that vast terra incognita of our shared inner world, and then try, as Laozi and Zhuangzi both note, to paint that which cannot be caught with pigments, to sing that which cannot be confined by words, to dance down the path—the Dao, the escape hatch—that cannot be walked. "The novelist says in words what cannot be said in words."§

Those who would try to do this, the artists, essentially, must

---

* Ibid.
† Ibid.
‡ Ibid.
§ "Introduction to *The Left Hand of Darkness*."

have the courage as well as the imagination to seek answers to the hardest questions—about justice, love, mercy, faith, pain, evil, and so on. The answers require poetry.

> [I]f you want to enter the House of Poetry, you have to enter it in the flesh, the solid, imperfect, unwieldy body, which has corns and colds and greeds and passions, the body that casts a shadow . . . [I]f the artist tries to ignore evil, he will never enter into the House of Light.*

There it is. The problem of evil. Every attempt at progress leaves behind a shadow. Even in *The Word for World Is Forest*, where Le Guin's anger at the American war in Vietnam causes her to come close to writing a moralizing story instead of a moral story ("I knew, because of the compulsive quality of the composition, that it was likely to become a preachment, and I struggled against this"†), she manages to recognize the evil within every noble heart, the shadow cast by every act of resistance, the death that darkens the pursuit of liberty. The truth is complicated, paradoxical, dialectical, and slips from too firm a grasp—just like the yin-yang fish.

Compared to the deep answers, those myths and symbols of fantasy, the answers from ideologues are laughably shallow. This is because ideologies, by their nature, refuse to recognize the existence of shadows, of the evil within themselves. At most they come up with some allegory but no myth, which requires facing one's own darkness. The "easy-answer schools" that Le Guin dismisses dare not go inward; they'll never be inside the House of Poetry. ("I am a petty-bourgeois anarchist, and an internal emigrée," says Le Guin,

---

*   "The Child and the Shadow."
†   "Introduction to *The Word for World Is Forest*."

contemptuous of ideological labels. Elsewhere, she calls herself "an unconsistent Taoist and a consistent un-Christian,"* playfully but also seriously. I love these social media–ready bios.)

The slipperiness and irreducible complexity of true myths are why Le Guin despised allegorical and biographical readings of fantasy and science fiction (and of her own work in particular). Allegorical readings ("The girl mechanic is obviously the Virgin Mary, while the leader of the alien robots is a Christ figure, just like Gollum—or was it Frodo?") have the virtue of CliffsNotes and model standardized test answers: they simplify and crush dreams into neatly labeled boxes in the service of a game of intellectual self-admiration. Just like pinning a butterfly, the practice kills (Le Guin calls allegory "dead equivalence"†). But the symbols of fantasy are living—trails of a dragon beyond mortal ken, echoes of a truth too deep to be heard. The biographical reading, on the other hand, mostly serves to make the critic-reader feel superior, as though they're Freud confidently telling the story of the author on the couch. Readers who try to map the art to details in the writer's life are asking all the wrong questions, forgoing all that is eternal, deep, lasting; the author has already placed all that matters of herself, her soul, into the work. ("And then people read them and call up and say, But who are you? tell us about yourself! And we say, But I have. It's all there, in the book. All that matters."‡) These lazy forms of reading, like the fannish defense of bad art, prevent the reader from going deep within themselves, from reaching the interior Self, where the language of the night reigns, where the escape hatch opened by the artist is found.

---

*   Sources for these quotes are in Susan Wood's Introduction.
†   "Myth and Archetype in Science Fiction."
‡   "Dreams Must Explain Themselves."

Le Guin should have the last word. The fantasist, the guide who probes for an escape route into a world that is more real than Reality, must speak in the language of the night in the pursuit of liberty. The "adults" who fear fantasy know that "its truth challenges, even threatens, all that is false, all that is phony, unnecessary, and trivial in the life they have let themselves be forced into living. They are afraid of dragons, because they are afraid of freedom."*

---

*   "Why Are Americans Afraid of Dragons?"

PREFACE

by Ursula K. Le Guin
(1989)

The Language of the Night was first published in the United States in 1979. When the idea of a collection of my talks and essays was first proposed, I begged off from the job of getting the stuff sorted out and edited, as I wanted to get on with my fiction, and was too lazy to face the awful tangle in the file folder marked "Non Fic." Susan Wood, whom I had known when we visited Australia, a generous, brilliant woman and a scholar at the beginning of a notable career, undertook the task. She found directions in the tangle and made a whole out of all the bits and pieces. The book's shape is hers. I wish with all my heart that she had lived to enjoy its success. I hope—I'm fairly sure—that she'd have approved of the revisions I did for this new edition.

In general, I feel that revising published work is taboo. You took the risk then, you can't play safe now . . . And also, what about the readers of the first version—do they have to trot out loyally and buy the recension, or else feel that they've been cheated of something? It seems most unfair to them. All the same, I have in this case broken my taboo. The changes I wanted to make were not aesthetic improvements, but had a moral and intellectual urgency to me. I excuse them to myself by saying that since this is the only British appearance of the book it has no Old English Readers to be unfair to.

The changes in the text are rare, mostly omissions of a word or sentence or corrections of my own or a typesetter's errors. The principal revision involves the so-called "generic pronoun" *he*. It has been changed, following context, euphony, or whim, to *they*, *she*, *one*, *I*, *you*, or *we*. This is, of course, a political change (just as the substitution of *he* for *they* as the "correct" written form of the singular generic pronoun—see the *OED*—was a political act). Having resistingly, reluctantly, but finally admitted that *he* means *he*, no more, no less, I can't let it stand in these essays, because it misleads. When I wrote in the early seventies about "the artist who works from the center of his own being," I did not intend to refer to male artists only, still less to imply that artists are, or should be, male; but that is what the words say and imply. The existence of women artists is not (in the grammarians' cute phrase) "embraced" by the male pronoun; it is (in the non-cute Argentinean usage) "disappeared" by it. I was in fact disappearing myself in my own writing—just like a woman. Well, no more of that.

In making these pronoun changes, especially if I was replacing *he* with *I*, *we*, or *you*, I found that they often led me to take what I said in a more engaged way, to be wary of glibness, to be certain that I or we or you might really do or think what he could so easily be said to do or to think, since he wasn't really there at all . . .

The essay that confronts the whole matter directly is the one about my novel *The Left Hand of Darkness*, called "Is Gender Necessary?" This 1976 piece has been quoted from a good deal, often to my intense embarrassment. Within a few years I came to disagree completely with some of the things I said in it, but there they were in print, and all I could do was writhe in deserved misery as the feminists told me off and the masculinists patted my head. Clearly it would have been unethical to rewrite the 1976 text, to disappear it; so it appears here, complete, but with remarks and annotations and self-recriminations from later years. I do hope I don't have to do this again in the nineties.

Elsewhere in preparing the text for this edition I have added notes at the foot of the page, commenting, enlarging, updating, grumbling, or clarifying.

The response to the American editions of the book has come largely from people interested in the process of writing because they write, or want to write, or teach writing, or want to know how artists' minds work. And it has always had readers among people capable of taking science fiction seriously as an interesting variety of modern fiction.

When I read the last paragraphs of the book, the end of a talk at the World Science Fiction Convention in Melbourne in 1975, I feel a bit sad. At that time I thought there was a real chance that the genrification/devaluation of science fiction and fantasy by critics and academics and its self-ghettoizing by publishers and many writers was giving way to a sane recognition of science fiction as literature, with all the privileges and obligations thereto pertaining. I was perhaps more hopeful than wise. In the thirteen years since, some very fine works of English literature have been published as science fiction; several gallant risk-takers, including Doris Lessing and Margaret Atwood, have published and identified new novels as science fiction; the study and teaching of the field in schools and universities has increased its scope and refined its methods. But that is all. The Canoneers of Literature still refuse to admit that genrification is a political tactic and that the type of fiction they distinguish as serious, mainstream, literary, etc., is itself a genre without inherent superiority to any other. Reviews of imaginative literature in most journals are still segregated into a column or section of "Sci Fi"; real criticism of any popular literature is almost entirely segregated into specialist journals, not the prestigious ones. And within the science fiction community of conventions, conferences, journals, and reviews, while the crossover novelists have been mostly ignored, possibly through xenophobia, many successful writers have been content to stay within the safe parameters of the predictable, substituting cyberjargon for engineering jargon and sexual athletes for virtuous heroes, but taking no risks and going nowhere we haven't all been before. That the reactionary mood of the Reagan-Thatcher years should be reflected in the reality-sensitive imagery of science fiction isn't surprising, and the reflection is mutual—as in the name and nature of SDI, "Star Wars," an undertaking which is, as they say, pure science fiction.

Competition for big advances, the bestseller mentality, a kind of degraded professionalism, the reduction of book to product or commodity, the replacement of editors by PR teams, has demoralized many writers in the past decade, and science fiction writers seem particularly vulnerable. Now that it's possible to "be a success," that is, to make real money, as a science fiction writer, there's a temptation to make success the criterion of excellence—and so to regard quality, literary excellence, as something foreign and possibly subversive. I used to be told by people who knew nothing about science fiction that I didn't write science fiction, because what I wrote had literary merit; nowadays I am told by people in science fiction that I have repudiated science fiction—partly because I don't (I never did) write only science fiction, but also, apparently, because what I write has, or strives for, literary merit. This is tiresome. I am afraid that such accusations of apostasy, and the failure of much of the science fiction community to recognize innovative writing within its own confines or such great cognate movements as the magical realists of South America, reveal a failure of self-respect—an assumption that science fiction has only commercial value and is artistically a dead end. I disagree passionately.

Also passionately, I dislike the misogyny—a kind of cozy misogyny—which often accompanies this self-denigration of science fiction. Doris Lessing, Margaret Atwood, Carolyn See, Patricia Geary, and many others including myself, who have been crossing over into or settling down in or coming in and out of science fiction freely and easily—we don't just happen to be women. Our refusal to accept rules we don't make and boundaries that make no sense to us is a direct expression of our being women writers in the ninth decade of the twentieth century. We aren't "writing like men" anymore, if we ever did, and therefore are used to the fact that a good many male supremacists, both men and women, will not understand what we're doing, and that some of them will resent and denounce our refusal to play games we have no interest in winning by rules we never agreed to. One such game is the Old Boys' Club game, including the SF Old Boys' Club. That another is the Literature Game, played by academics and critics, and that its rules include the Canon of Literature (no science fiction, no fantasy, and no women authors except two or three dead virgins)—this doesn't seem to occur to these vigilantes; they're too busy shooting at their own feet. It's too bad. Their defensiveness can only delay the recognition and celebration of science fiction as one of the central fictional modes of our century.

May 1989

INTRODUCTION

by Susan Wood
(1979)

Those who refuse to listen to dragons are probably doomed to spend their lives acting out the nightmares of politicians. We like to think we live in daylight, but half the world is always dark; and fantasy, like poetry, speaks the language of the night.

This warning, a reminder of the need for balance, comes from a poet, a fantasy writer, and a creator of dragons: Ursula K. Le Guin. In a brief article, "Fantasy, Like Poetry, Speaks the Language of the Night," published in *World* (the magazine supplement of the *San Francisco Sunday Examiner and Chronicle*, November 21, 1976), Le Guin discusses "the particular process of fantasy" which she calls "translation." We dream, she points out, in nonverbal images, which can be translated into word-symbols and "understood" by the conscious mind. She continues:

In much the same way, though with the universality proper to art, written fantasy translates into verbal images and coherent narrative forms the intuitions and perceptions of the unconscious mind—body language, dreamstuff, primary process thinking. This idiom, for all its intense privacy, is one we all seem to share, whether we speak English or Urdu, whether we're five or eighty-five. The witch, the dragon, the hero; the night journey, the helpful animal, the hidden treasure . . . we all know them, we recognize them (because, if Jung is right, they represent profound and essential modes of thought). Modern fantasy attempts to translate them into modern words.

The essays reprinted here are also translations, explanations of dreams. In them Ursula Le Guin, one of the best contemporary science fiction and fantasy writers, discusses and analyzes her craft. In so doing, she clarifies what fantasy, and its modern offshoot science fiction, are and can be. These essays are critical in the most creative sense. They work from practical experience to formulate theories; they use those theories to suggest the potential that individual works, and the genre as a whole, can reach. They are "critical" in the sense of making judgments when writers ignore the possibilities open to them in favor of easy formulas. Watching Le Guin as critic fairly but firmly dissecting Le Guin as writer is a particularly valuable experience for anyone who cares about writing well.

We tend, in North America at least, to think of the artist and the critic as separate and perhaps mutually hostile people. Science fiction, however, here and in Europe, has a tradition of writer-critics concerned with the whys and hows of their particular mode of telling the truth. As Le Guin says in her autobiographical essay "A Citizen of Mondath," writing science fiction and fantasy has been for her "a matter of keeping on pushing out toward the limits—my

own, and those of the medium" in a field which, by its lack of definitions and standards, offers the most challenging freedom of all:
the freedom to set one's own boundaries.

This border country on the frontiers of the best work possible,
which Le Guin points toward in essays like "Do-It-Yourself Cosmology," is a territory she shares with such contemporary writer-
critics as Brian Aldiss, the late James Blish, Joanna Russ, Samuel R.
Delany, Alexei and Cory Panshin, Damon Knight, George Turner,
A. J. Budrys, and Stanislaw Lem, among many others. They have,
of course, widely different views of and approaches to the limits of
science fiction. In essays like "American SF and The Other" and
"Is Gender Necessary?" Le Guin shares with Russ a concern with
breaking down the social and sexual stereotypes common to all formula fiction. She shares with Lem, in particular, a concern with the
political and ethical aspects of art, expressed most directly here in
"The Stalin in the Soul" and evident in such articles and reviews for
Science-Fiction Studies as her contribution to the debate on "Change,
SF and Marxism" in issue 2 (Fall 1973) and her review entitled "European SF: Rottensteiner's Anthology, the Strugatskys, and Lem" in
issue 3 (Spring 1974). Indeed, Le Guin has been particularly active
in calling the attention of the North American science fiction community to the works and ideas of Eastern European writers.

Le Guin does not, however, write fiction or criticism from any
particular political viewpoint. In "A Response to the Le Guin Issue" in
Science-Fiction Studies 8 (March 1976) she comments: "I do not like
to see the word 'liberal' used as a smear-word. That's mere newspeak. If
people must call names, I cheerfully accept Lenin's anathemata as suitable: I am a petty-bourgeois anarchist, and an internal emigrée." (In
Science-Fiction Studies 6, July 1975, commenting on David Ketterer's
New Worlds for Old, she describes herself as "an unconsistent Taoist

and a consistent un-Christian" who rejects the Apocalypse.) Le Guin admires such Soviet writers as Zamyatin, Lem, and the Strugatskys as writers who work within "the open universe" and speak for the essential freedom of the individual mind. Thus in "European SF . . ." she praises Lem's *The Invincible* because, while it presents a "terrifyingly open universe" not comprehensible to human beings, it does so in such a way that "the human scale is not destroyed—it is not even shaken. For no matter whether we understand the how, the why, or even the what, we have to act, and our acts retain, in the very depths of the abyss, their unalterable moral value. The center of gravity of Lem's books is ethics." This is Le Guin's highest praise; and it establishes the central values of her fiction, and her criticism.

Science fiction, then, like all art, deals with important human concerns, and should be taken seriously. Uniting the writer-critics is a general view of the creative process as one which can, and should, explain itself: a view of reading, writing, and thinking about literature as complementary and supremely enjoyable activities.

Le Guin's background, as she explains in "A Citizen of Mondath," introduced her to a wide variety of cultures: those her parents, anthropologist A. L. Kroeber and author Theodora Kroeber, studied and wrote about; and those she encountered in the "saurian ooze" of SF and pulp magazines, in myths and legends and in her own imagination. Her own academic training was in the study of literature, specifically the formalized world of French and Italian Renaissance literature. *Science-Fiction Studies* 7 (November 1975) is a special Le Guin issue, containing several critical articles analyzing her work, and her own essay "American SF and the Other." The following issue (March 1976) contains Le Guin's own response to the critics in which she comments, tongue in cheek, on their failure to reap the harvest of "this rich field of inquiry, the Le Guin theses"—

and then goes on to discuss those critical essays not written in her "language," those which are preoccupied with ideas and intellectual concepts. These essays, she writes,

> gave me the impression that I have written about nothing but ideas, and I was enormously impressed with myself. By God! Did I really think all that?—The answer is, No. I didn't. I did think some of it. The rest of it I felt, or guessed, or stole, or faked, or intuited; in any case achieved, not deliberately and not through use of the frontal lobes, but through humbler and obscurer means, involving (among others) imagery, metaphors, characters, landscapes, the sound of English words, the restrictions of English syntax, the rests and rhythms of narrative paragraphs . . . At times ideas alone are discussed, as if the books existed through and for their ideas; and this involves a process of *translation* with which I am a bit uncomfortable. Somehow the point has been lost in translation. It's as if one should discuss the ideas expressed by St. Paul's Cathedral without ever observing what the walls are built of or how the dome is supported. But it wasn't Wren's ideas that kept that dome standing through the bombings of 1940. It was the way he used the stone he built with. This is the artist's, the artisan's view; it is a meaner, humbler view than the philosopher's or ideologue's. But all the same, what makes a novel a novel is something nonintellectual, though not simple; something visceral, not cerebral . . . ; something that rises from touch not thought, from sounds, rests, rhythms . . . It involves ideas, of course, and ideas issue from it, the splendid affirmation of the dome rises above the terror and the rubble and the smoke . . . but all

the thinking in the world won't hold that dome up. Theory is not enough. There must be stones.

You see what I mean about my language. I can't even think one stupid platitude without dragging in a mess of images and metaphors, domes, stones, rubble. What is Christopher Wren doing here? This lamentable concreteness of the mental processes is supposed, by some, to be a feminine trait. If so, all artists are women. And/or vice versa.

The key word here, as in "The Language of the Night," is "translation." Le Guin as critic attempts to make an intuitive process comprehensible in intellectual terms, to translate a dream into word-symbols. In doing so, she draws on her own practice, exploring and describing fantasy worlds. In the 1960s and 1970s, she published a notable body of SF and fantasy fiction. She received awards: four Hugo Awards of the World Science Fiction Convention, three Nebula Awards from the Science Fiction Writers of America, the Jupiter Award, the 1969 *Boston Globe–Horn Book Award*, a Newbery Honor Book citation for *The Tombs of Atuan*, and the National Book Award for *The Farthest Shore*. (Her acceptance speech is reprinted in this collection.) While pleased by this recognition, she has retained her senses of humor and of perspective (which are much the same thing), as is evident in an interview conducted by Jonathan Ward, published in *Algol* 24 (Summer 1975):

Ward: Which would you rather have, a National Book Award or a Hugo?

Le Guin: Oh, a Nobel, of course.

Ward: They don't give Nobel Prize awards in fantasy.

Le Guin: Maybe I can do something for peace.

With recognition have come requests: please discuss your work. Le Guin emphasizes the futility of asking writers to analyze their creative processes in an early essay, "The View In," published in the Australian fanzine *Scythrop* 22 (April 1971), edited by John Bangsund. It begins:

> People in my line of work are forever being asked three questions: What name do you write under? Where do you get your ideas? Why do you write science fiction?
>
> To the first I answer, What name do you beat your wife under? To the second, Out of my head. That is, I would make these answers if I didn't always remember them several hours later. To the third I have never had a satisfactory answer even several hours later. I shall attempt now to produce an unsatisfactory answer . . .
>
> I write science fiction because that is what publishers call my books. Left to myself, I should call them novels.

As the 1978 introduction to the first hardcover edition of *Planet of Exile* reveals, Le Guin still has no pat answers to questions like "Where do you get your ideas?" Yet such questions seem to interest her as much as they do her readers. Since 1971, she has written a number of essays about her craft and her art, essays that complement her writing of fiction. Several, notably "Dreams Must Explain Themselves," draw upon and analyze her experiences in discovering fictional worlds. The "Le Guin on Le Guin" group are retrospective self-criticisms, candidly discussing early work. Many essays here began as talks on SF, fantasy, and writing; for example, the piece I have entitled "Talking about Writing" is a previously unpublished speech from 1976/77. Even those which did not begin as speeches are informal and immediate. Le Guin seems, even on this page, to be sitting with an unlit pipe in a circle of new writers at a workshop, or on a panel at a science fiction convention, having a conversation with other people who care about good writing. This immediacy draws you into well-developed and passionate arguments, exploring and testing ideas: the importance of ethical values in art, the place of fantasy as an art in society, the necessity that readers *demand* the best from their favorite authors.

The essays reprinted here are arranged thematically rather than chronologically. They overlap and complement each other, reexamining and developing certain key ideas. These include the view of fantasy and science fiction as different branches of the same form of writing, as is clear in "A Citizen of Mondath," the introduction of the 1977 edition of *Rocannon's World*, and especially the National Book Award acceptance speech, which speaks of both genres as offering new "metaphors for the human condition." Fantasy and SF provide Le Guin with a distancing technique, as she discusses in "A Citizen of Mondath" and other essays, notably "Is Gender Necessary?"—a way of providing new perspectives on everyday human situations. This distancing is clearly related to the view of fantasy and SF as "translations" of an intuitive process, of an interior journey, into words; the writer finds within herself patterns and archetypes common and meaningful to humanity as a whole. (It is interesting to note here how many of Le Guin's novels and stories, from *Rocannon's World* through *The Left Hand of Darkness* and *A Wizard of Earthsea* to *The Dispossessed*, are structured as physical journeys, often circular or spiral journeys, which lead to self-knowledge.)

Another central idea is that expressed in "Why Are Americans

Afraid of Dragons?" and the essays that follow it: the *necessity* for the internal exploration, provided by fantasy, to produce a whole, integrated human being. Two important aspects of this journey are the acceptance of the subconscious and the collective unconscious (as discussed in "Dreams Must Explain Themselves"); and the acceptance and discipline of the imagination. If the imagination is suppressed, Le Guin writes in "Dragons," humans will mature physically, but will remain at worst "eggplants" and at best stunted and unhappy people afraid of anything "childish" or "untrue." If the imagination is nurtured, however, each person can become a truly mature adult: "not a dead child, but a child who survived."

A third major idea is that underlying all the essays, but expressed most clearly in "Escape Routes," "The Stalin in the Soul," and "The Stone Ax and the Muskoxen": a concern with the ethics and aesthetics of art. Indeed, these are inseparable. As Le Guin says in "From Elfland to Poughkeepsie": "In art, the best is the standard." As Tolkien comments in his essay "On Fairy-Stories," the word *spell* "means both a story told, and a formula of power over living men." A wizard of Earthsea, if he casts a true spell, possesses such power; his whole study is to use it rightly or not at all, and to understand "the Balance and the Pattern which the true wizard knows and serves." The Earthsea trilogy, like *The Lathe of Heaven* and Le Guin's more overtly "political" novels like *The Dispossessed* and *The Eye of the Heron*, is a profoundly moral work. As Le Guin points out in "Dreams Must Explain Themselves," in one sense her tale of wizards is "about art, the creative experience, the creative process." The function of art, as she discusses it in her essays and practices it in fiction and poetry, is to find the truth, and express it as clearly and beautifully as possible.

Le Guin also demonstrates that true art is more than concepts, symbols, stones, or any of its parts. These essays express powerful ideas; and their impact is increased by Le Guin's skill in casting word-spells. The essays are direct, clear, and free from unnecessary jargon. More: they sometimes—often—flash into beauty, so that the cadences of the language and the aptness of the images work with the idea to make a statement unforgettable. In "From Elfland to Poughkeepsie" Le Guin comments: "Style is how you as a writer see and speak. It is how you see: your vision, your understanding of the world, your voice." As writer and critic, she has helped to emphasize the importance of style in science fiction. The voice in this book of essays, like the voice in the novels and poems, is that of an artist who uses her tool, language, with skill and with delight.

Assembling this collection, I have shared in that delight. As editor, I would like to thank several people for help, encouragement, and ideas: Jim Bittner, Terry Carr, Eli Cohen, Ryszard Dubanski, David Hartwell of Berkley Publishing Corporation (whose idea this was in the first place), Virginia Kidd, Elizabeth A. Lynn—and especially Ursula Le Guin, for her patience and cooperation.

—Susan Wood
University of British Columbia

I
LE GUIN INTRODUCES LE GUIN

Ethics flourishes in the timeless soil of Fantasy, where ideologies wither on the vine.

from "European SF . . . ," *Science-Fiction Studies* 3
(Spring 1974)

Distancing, the pulling back from "reality" in order to see it better, is perhaps the essential gesture of SF. It is by distancing that SF achieves aesthetic joy, tragic tension, and moral cogency.

from "On Norman Spinrad's *The Iron Dream*,"
Science-Fiction Studies 1 (Spring 1973)

INTRODUCTION

Why do you write science fiction?
Ursula Le Guin has answered that question in many different ways over the past decade. The first "answer," in "The View In," was to see science fiction as a publisher's category for a certain kind of novel: interesting but inferior to the "absolute novel" tradition of Dickens and Tolstoy, which attempts to imitate the "coherent complexity" of life. If she reads such a novel, she says,

> I know what I am going to experience is reality, as expressed
> and transfigured through art. Reality translated to a higher plane,
> a more passionate intensity, than most of us can experience
> at all without the help of art or religion or profound emotion;
> but reality. The shared world, the scene of our mortality.

If she reads science fiction or fantasy (and the two overlap so closely "as to render any effort at exclusive definition useless"), however,

> I know that I am going to meet a personal variation on
> reality; a scene *less* real than the world around us, a partial
> view of reality.

But I know that by that partiality, that independence, that distancing from the shared experience, it will be new: a revelation. It will be a vision, a more or less powerful or haunting dream. A view in, not out. A space-voyage through somebody else's psychic abysses. It will fall short of tragedy, because tragedy is the truth, and truth is what the very great artists, the absolute novelists, tell. It will not be truth; but it will be imagination.

Truth is best. For it encompasses tragedy, and partakes of the eternal joy. But very few of us know it; the best we can do is recognize it. Imagination—to me—is next best. For it partakes of Creation, which is one aspect of the eternal joy.

And all the rest is either Politics or Pedantry, or Mainstream Fiction, may it rest in peace.

This 1971 essay is interesting as an early statement of Le Guin's view of fantasy as "a view in" to the psyche. It is also interesting to see how quickly her own experience, discovering universal truths in that inner land, led her to modify and even discard the view of fantasy as a form that must necessarily fall short of greatness. For example, in *Science-Fiction Studies* 3 (Spring 1974) she reviews the English translation of the Russian SF novel *Hard to Be a God*, and praises its authors, Arkady and Boris Strugatsky:

They write not only like SF novelists, but like "Russian novelists." There is a sureness of touch, a perceptiveness to their psychology, an easy, unrestrained realism about human behavior, which is admirable, and seldom met with in SF.

Finally, in the essays reprinted here, most notably "Why Are Americans Afraid of Dragons?" Le Guin asserts that fantasy, like any other art responsibly created, can present both truth *and* the joy of the imagination.

"A Citizen of Mondath" appeared in July 1973 in issue 4 of the British critical journal *Foundation* edited by Peter Nicholls, in the magazine's series on "the development of a science fiction writer." Most readers are fascinated by "inside" stories: How did a writer begin to write, and to be published? (As Le Guin's account reminds us, the two are not synonymous at all.) Le Guin, unlike many North American SF writers, didn't begin with an exclusive addiction to the genre and activity in the fan community. Rather, she followed both the practical need to find a commercial market and the personal desire to explore imaginative worlds: the Inner Lands. This reference to Dunsany points toward a major theme in her essays: the exploration of the inner world, and its embodiment in an envisioned world created both to delight an audience and to express a truth.

Science fiction and fantasy offer more than "great spaces"; they offer necessary "limits," too. The second major concern in "A Citizen of Mondath" is quality. Le Guin gave up reading SF in the late 1940s, she says, because "it seemed to be all about hardware and soldiers," a criticism she repeats in essays like "American SF and The Other" and "Science Fiction and Mrs. Brown." One of the motives behind the writing of all these essays, it seems, is the ethical one stated here: the desire to establish high standards for the genre, to inspire readers to intelligent responses, and to awaken writers to a "sense of responsibility."

Some of the short stories mentioned in this essay were published by Harper & Row in 1976 as *Orsinian Tales*; the collection was nominated for a National Book Award for Fiction. *The Dispossessed* was published in 1974 by Harper & Row. Far from eliciting "cries of dismay," it received praise within the SF field, and won the 1975 Hugo Award for Best Novel at the 33rd World Science Fiction Convention in Melbourne, at which Le Guin was guest of honor. It has also attracted significant attention outside the SF community as a Utopian novel.

A CITIZEN OF MONDATH

One evening when I was about twelve I was looking through the living room bookshelves for something to read, and pulled out a little Modern Library book, in the old limp leather binding; it had a queer title, *A Dreamer's Tales*. I opened it, standing beside the battered green armchair by the lamp; the moment is perfectly vivid to me now. I read:

> Toldees, Mondath, Arizim, these are the Inner Lands, the lands whose sentinels upon their borders do not behold the sea. Beyond them to the east there lies a desert, for ever untroubled by man: all yellow it is, and spotted with shadows of stones, and Death is in it, like a leopard lying in the sun. To the south they are bounded by magic, to the west by a mountain.

I don't entirely understand why Dunsany came to me as a revelation, why that moment was so decisive. I read a lot, and a lot of my reading was myth, legend, fairy tale; first-rate versions, too, such as Padraic Colum, Asbjørnsen, etc. I had also heard my father tell

Indian legends aloud, just as he had heard them from informants, only translated into a rather slow, impressive English; and they were impressive and mysterious stories. What I hadn't realized, I guess, is that people were still making up myths. One made up stories oneself, of course; but here was a grown-up doing it, for grown-ups, without a single apology to common sense, without an explanation, just dropping us straight into the Inner Lands. Whatever the reason, the moment was decisive. I had discovered my native country.

The book belonged to my father, a scientist, and was a favorite of his; in fact he had a large appetite for fantasy. I have wondered if there isn't some real connection between a certain kind of scientific-mindedness (the explorative, synthesizing kind) and fantasy-mindedness. Perhaps "science fiction" really isn't such a bad name for our genre after all. Those who dislike fantasy are very often equally bored or repelled by science. They don't like either hobbits or quasars; they don't feel at home with them; they don't want complexities, remoteness. If there is any such connection, I'll bet that it is basically an aesthetic one.

I wonder what would have happened if I had been born in 1939 instead of 1929, and had first read Tolkien in my teens, instead of in my twenties. That achievement might have overwhelmed me. I am glad I had some sense of my own direction before I read Tolkien. Dunsany's influence was wholly benign, and I never tried much to imitate him in my prolific and derivative adolescent scribblings. I must have known already that this sort of thing is inimitable. He was not a model to me, but a liberator, a guide.

However, I was headed toward the Inner Lands before I ever heard of them. I still have my first completed short story, written at age nine. It is about a man persecuted by evil elves. People think he is mad, but the evil elves finally slither in through the keyhole and get him. At ten or eleven I wrote my first science fiction story. It involved time travel and the origin of life on Earth, and was very breezy in style. I submitted it to *Amazing Stories*. There's another vivid memory, my brother Karl on the stairs, looking up at me on the landing and saying very reluctantly, "I'm afraid this is your story come back." I don't remember being very downcast, rather flattered by a real rejection slip. I never submitted anything else to anybody till I was twenty-one, but I think that was less cowardice than wisdom.

We kids read science fiction in the early forties: *Thrilling Wonder*, and *Astounding* in that giant format it had for a while, and so on. I liked "Lewis Padgett" best, and looked for his stories, but we looked for the trashiest magazines, mostly, because we *liked* trash. I recall one story that began "In the beginning was the Bird." We really dug that bird. And the closing line from another (or the same?)—"Back to the saurian ooze from whence it sprung!" Karl made that into a useful chant: The saurian ooze from which it sprung / Unwept, unhonor'd, and unsung. I wonder how many hack writers who think they are writing down to "naive kids" and "teenagers" realize the *kind* of pleasure they sometimes give their readers. If they did, they would sink back into the saurian ooze from whence they sprung.

I never read only science fiction, as some kids do. I read everything I could get my hands on, which was limitless; there was a house full of books, and a good public library. I got off science fiction some time in the late forties. It seemed to be all about hardware and soldiers. Besides, I was busy with Tolstoy and things. I did not read any science fiction at all for about fifteen years, just about that period which people now call The Golden Age of Science Fiction. I almost totally missed Heinlein, et al. If I glanced at a magazine, it still seemed to be all about starship captains in black with lean rugged faces and a lot of fancy artillery. Possibly I would never have gone back to reading science fiction, and thence to writing it, if it hadn't been for a friend of ours in Portland in 1960 and 1961 who had a small collection and lent me whatever I glommed on to. One of the things he lent me was a copy of *Fantasy and Science Fiction* containing a story called "Alpha Ralpha Boulevard," by Cordwainer Smith.

I don't really remember what I thought when I read it; but what I think now I ought to have thought when I read it is *My God! It can be done!*

After that I read a good deal of science fiction, looking for "that kind" of writing; and found some, here and there. Presently it seemed that since there was so little of it, why not do some myself?

No, that is not true. It is much more complicated, and boring.

To put it briefly, I had been writing all my life, and it was becoming a case of publish or perish. You cannot keep filling up the attic with mss. Art, like sex, cannot be carried on indefinitely solo; after all, they have the same enemy, sterility. I had had a number of poems published, and one short story, in little magazines; but this wasn't enough, considering that I had written five novels in the last ten years. I had either to take off or give up.

One of the novels was set in contemporary San Francisco, but the others were set in an invented though nonfantastic Central European country, as were the best short stories I had done. They were not science fiction, they were not fantasy, yet they were not realistic. Alfred Knopf said (in 1951) that he would have published the first of them, ten years earlier, but he'd lose too much money on it now. Viking and other publishers merely remarked that "this material seems remote." It was remote. It was meant to be. Searching for a technique of distancing, I had come on this one. Unfortunately it was not a technique used by anybody else at the moment, it was not fashionable, it did not fit into any of the categories. You must either fit a category or "have a name" to publish a book in America. As the only way I was ever going to achieve Namehood was *by* writing, I was reduced to fitting a category. Therefore my first efforts to write science fiction were motivated by a pretty distinct wish to get published: nothing higher or lower. The stories reflect this extrinsic motivation. They are kind of amiable, but not very good, not serious, essentially slick. They were published by Cele Goldsmith Lalli, the kindly and outrageous editor of *Amazing* and *Fantastic*, in the early sixties.

The shift from the kind of writing I had done before to categorizable "fantasy" and "science fiction" was not a big one, but I had a good deal to learn all the same. Also I was pretty ignorant of science, and was just beginning to educate myself (a hopeless job, but one which I continue to enjoy immensely). At first I knew too little science to use it as the framework, as part of the essential theme of a story, and so wrote fairy tales decked out in space suits. If anything gives these merit, it would be my long apprenticeship in poetry and in the psychologically realistic kind of novel.

The first science fiction story I wrote that begins to break from the trivial became the source, and prologue, of the little novel *Rocannon's World*. I was beginning to get the feel of the medium. In the next books I kept on pushing at my own limitations and at the limits of science fiction. That is what the practice of an art is, you keep looking for the outside edge. When you find it you make a whole, solid, real, and beautiful thing; anything less is incomplete. These books were certainly incomplete, especially *City of Illusions*, which I should not have published as it stands. It has some good bits, but is only half thought out. I was getting vain and hasty.

That is a real danger when you write science fiction. There is so little real criticism that, despite the very delightful and heartening feedback from and connection with the fans, the writer is almost her only critic. Second-rate stuff will be bought just as fast, maybe faster sometimes, by the publishers, and the fans will buy it because it is science fiction. Only the writer's conscience remains to insist that she try *not* to be second-rate. Nobody else seems much to care.

Of course, this is basically true of the practice of all writing, and all art; but it is exaggerated in science fiction. And equally, of course, it is not true in the long run of science fiction or any other form. But it is an awfully long run. One can trust in the verdict of posterity, but it's not a handy tool to apply in specific instances. What almost all of us need is some genuine, serious, literate criticism: some standards. I don't mean pedantry and fancy academic theorizing. I mean just the kind of standards which any musician, for instance, has to meet. Whether she plays rock on the electric piccolo or Bach on the cello, she is listened to by informed, profoundly interested people, and if she's second-rate she will be told so; ditto if she's good. In science fiction, sometimes it seems that so long as it's science fiction at all, the fans will love it—briefly; therefore the publishers will put it in print—briefly; therefore the writer is likely to settle for doing much less than her best. The mediocre and the excellent are praised alike by aficionados, and ignored alike by outsiders. In such a situation it is simply amazing that writers like Philip K. Dick continue in excellence. It is not at all amazing, though very sad, that writers like Roger Zelazny may be forced into a long period of floundering and groping, after initial sureness. After all, writing is not only an originative act, it is a responsive one. The lack of genuine response, and therefore the lack of the sense of responsibility, is painfully clear in those writers who simply go on and on imitating themselves—or others.

I think the standards are rising, however. In fact, I know they are, when I think back to the saurian ooze from whence we sprung.

Along in 1967–68 I finally got my pure fantasy vein separated off from my science fiction vein, by writing *A Wizard of Earthsea* and then *The Left Hand of Darkness*, and the separation marked a very large advance in both skill and content. Since then I have gone on writing, as it were, with both the left and the right hands; and it has been a matter of keeping on pushing out toward the limits—my own, and those of the medium. Very much the largest push was made in my last (not yet published) novel, *The Dispossessed.* I hope rending sounds and cries of dismay are not heard when it comes out. Meanwhile, people keep predicting that I will bolt science fiction and fling myself madly into the Mainstream. I don't know why. The limits, and the great spaces of fantasy and science fiction are precisely what my imagination needs. Outer Space, and the Inner Lands, are still, and always will be, my country.

II
ON FANTASY AND SCIENCE FICTION

The story—from Rumpelstiltskin *to* War and Peace—*is one of the basic tools invented by the human mind, for the purpose of gaining understanding. There have been great societies that did not use the wheel, but there have been no societies that did not tell stories.*

from "Prophets and Mirrors: Science Fiction as a
Way of Seeing," *The Living Light* 7, no. 3 (Fall 1970)

I don't think SF writers merely play with scientific or other ideas, merely speculate or extrapolate; I think—if they're doing their job—they get very involved with them. They take them personally, which is precisely what scientists must forbid themselves to do. They try to hook them in with the rest of existence. Writers' ability to find a genuine theme (and the great writers' ability to develop profound and complex themes out of very simple materials) seems to be a function of the capacity to see implications, to make connections.

from "On Theme," in *Those Who Can*, ed. Robin Scott Wilson
(New York: NAL Mentor, 1973)

INTRODUCTION

The essays on science fiction and fantasy that follow are not arranged chronologically. They begin with "Why Are Americans Afraid of Dragons?"—a defense of fantasy outlining some of the reasons for reading and writing it. From there, the essays follow what is, for Le Guin, the necessary journey inward, with the immediate and personal "Dreams Must Explain Themselves." Then they proceed outward to the more general aspects of fantasy as a way of finding and expressing psychological truths. Following these theoretical discussions are essays dealing with specifics, with matters of technique: style and language, characterization and stereotypes, plausibility.

"Why Are Americans Afraid of Dragons?" began as a talk at the 1973 Pacific Northwest Library Association conference in Portland, and was published in *PNLA Quarterly* 38 (Winter 1974). It was reprinted, with some slight changes to British idiom, under the title "This Fear of Dragons" in *The Thorny Paradise*, edited by Edward Blishen (Harmondsworth: Kestrel, 1975), an anthology of essays by writers of children's books on their craft. Many of these writers, like Le Guin, stress the intuitive, self-exploratory nature of fantasy writing.

In "Dreams Must Explain Themselves," Le Guin develops this idea clearly and with her characteristic humor, drawing specifically on her experiences "discovering" Earthsea. The article was first published in *Algol* 21 (November 1973), a magazine about science fiction edited by Andrew Porter. It was followed immediately (as it is here) by the acceptance speech Le Guin delivered on winning the 1973 National Book Award for Children's Books for *The Farthest Shore*, the third volume of the Earthsea trilogy.

"The Child and the Shadow" also develops the idea that "most of the great works of fantasy are about that journey" down into the subconscious and the collective unconscious, and up again "to self-knowledge, to adulthood, to the light." This article, based on a lecture presented at the Library of Congress on November 11, 1974, in observance of National Children's Book Week, was published in the *Quarterly Journal of the Library of Congress* 32, no. 2 (April 1975). Like "Myth and Archetype in Science Fiction," published in *Parabola* 1, no. 4 (Fall 1976), it reveals the importance of C. G. Jung's writings in helping Le Guin to articulate her own intuitive processes in creating fantasy. It is important to note that Jung's theories did not "influence" Le Guin in her *writing* of fiction, any more than did Tolkien's *Lord of the Rings* and his essay "On Fairy-Stories," to which she alludes in "The Child and the Shadow." As "Is Gender Necessary?" indicates, Le Guin had not read Jung when she wrote *The Left Hand of Darkness*. In "A Response to the Le Guin Issue" in *Science-Fiction Studies* 8 (March 1976), she comments that any Freudian critic exploring Earthsea will find only "Jung's Shadow! (As I found it: having never read a word of Jung when I wrote the book.)" An orthodox Marxist, she continues, will meet only "a bourgeois preoccupation with ethics." Yet these books go beyond doctrine and dogma, and are "my best books, as art; why?

Ideas will not explain it. Theory is not enough." As "Dreams Must Explain Themselves" makes clear, Earthsea, dragons and all, owes its power to the fact that Le Guin discovered her truths exactly as Jung discovered his—by making the journey to the Inner Lands.

Nevertheless, Jungian terminology has proved useful to Le Guin in discussing critical theory. In replying to David Ketterer's criticisms of *The Left Hand of Darkness* in his book *New Worlds for Old* (Bloomington: Indiana University Press, 1974), Le Guin writes, in *Science-Fiction Studies* 6 (July 1975):

> To me a myth is a living element, a symbolic constellation, in Jung's terms, within my own psyche; and my job as an artist is to create a way, a thoroughfare, to and from it, by means of my art, so that both the image and some sense of its meaning can come up into consciousness and be communicated to other consciousnesses. I fully accept Jung's definition: "The symbol differs essentially from sign or symptom, and should be understood as the expression of an intuitive perception which can as yet neither be apprehended better, nor expressed differently."

As Le Guin makes clear in "Myth and Archetype in Science Fiction," in her reply to the Le Guin issue of *Science-Fiction Studies*, and elsewhere, works of art are far more than assemblages of myths, or burrows of scared gerbils. They are attempts to discover and tell a whole truth. Some of the ways of approaching truth are indicated in essays like "From Elfland to Poughkeepsie," with its emphasis on the need for an appropriate style and language, "the genuine Elfland accent." This essay, too, originated as a talk given to the second Science Fiction Writers' Workshop (the Clarion West workshop) at the University of Washington in 1972. It was published as a chapbook by Pendragon Press of Portland, Oregon, in June of 1973, and to date has gone through three printings, reflecting its importance as a germinal essay on fantasy. Its origins may perhaps be seen in a letter from Le Guin, dated July 20, 1971, published in the Australian fanzine *SF Commentary* 23 (September 1971), edited by Bruce Gillespie. Le Guin discusses her admiration for the British writer D. G. Compton, and the lack of "the recognition he deserves" in North America. She comments:

> I think several things are involved, and one of them is his Britishness. Of tone, setting, language, mood, everything. I personally like it, and prefer it vastly to the Instant American style and locale used by some English writers; but Americans (as is seldom noticed by non-Americans) vary; and quite a lot of them are simply confused, alienated, by a genuinely foreign style. "If he writes my language why doesn't he write it like I would?" is what it comes down to. It is funny. A lot of people can take Proxima Centauri in their stride, but only if they feel that all the while they have a toehold in Poughkeepsie—as it were.

"American SF and the Other" began as Le Guin's contribution to a panel of women in SF at a science fiction convention in Bellingham, Washington, in 1973; it was first published in *Science-Fiction Studies* 7 (November 1975), the special Le Guin issue. It deals succinctly with the ethical and artistic issues raised by "the low status of women" and of people in general in most science fiction. These issues are dealt with more fully in "Science Fiction and Mrs. Brown," a speech which Le Guin gave in London in January 1975, reprinted with other papers in the series in *Science Fiction at Large*, edited by Peter Nicholls (London: Gollancz, 1976). Nicholls, in his introduction, says of Le Guin's speech: "Standing perfectly still at the lectern, even though she was reading her prepared script word for word, she nevertheless seemed to speak directly to the audience as individuals." The novel, as she defines it and as she tries to create it, also speaks to, and of, the individual. Thus it is important, because "in its stubborn assertion of human personality and human morality, [it] does seem even now to affirm the existence of hope."

Finally, in "Do-It-Yourself Cosmology," published in *Parabola* II, no. 3 (1977), Le Guin deals again with the creation of a believable world for fictional individuals to inhabit. (As she has pointed out since, the essay itself embodies a minor inconsistency. First she ask readers to "turn from science fiction to fantasy," as if these were separate genres; then she removes this separation by calling science fiction "a modern, intellectualized, extroverted form of fantasy." This association seems more consistent with her general use of these terms.)

The original article by Poul Anderson which Le Guin cites appeared in the *Bulletin* of the Science Fiction Writers of America for November 1966; it was reprinted in the SFWA *Handbook*, and an expanded version, "The Creation of Imaginary Worlds," appeared in *Science Fiction, Today and Tomorrow*, edited by Reginald Bretnor (New York: Harper & Row, 1974). Science fiction writers enthusiastically attest to the practical value of Anderson's scientific point, as Le Guin mentions. Yet her concern, here as elsewhere, is with something beyond the physical plausibility of the invented external world: the truth of the internal world. With this essay we return full circle to the discovery of dragons, and the journey to the stars and home again.

WHY ARE AMERICANS AFRAID OF DRAGONS?

(1974)

This was to be a talk about fantasy. But I have not been feeling very fanciful lately, and could not decide what to say; so I have been going about picking people's brains for ideas. "What about fantasy? Tell me something about fantasy." And one friend of mine said, "All right, I'll tell you something fantastic. Ten years ago, I went to the children's room of the library of such-and-such a city, and asked for *The Hobbit*; and the librarian told me, 'Oh, we keep that only in the adult collection; we don't feel that escapism is good for children.'"

My friend and I had a good laugh and shudder over that, and we agreed that things have changed a great deal in these past ten years. That kind of moralistic censorship of works of fantasy is very uncommon now in the children's libraries. But the fact that the children's libraries have become oases in the desert doesn't mean that there isn't still a desert. The point of view from which that librarian spoke still exists. She was merely reflecting, in perfect good faith, something that goes very deep in the American character: a moral disapproval of fantasy, a disapproval so intense, and often so aggressive, that I cannot help but see it as arising, fundamentally, from fear.

So: Why are Americans afraid of dragons?

Before I try to answer my question, let me say that it isn't only Americans who are afraid of dragons. I suspect that almost all very highly technological peoples are more or less anti-fantasy. There are several national literatures which, like ours, have had no tradition of adult fantasy for the past several hundred years: the French, for instance. But then you have the Germans, who have a good deal; and the English, who have it, and love it, and do it better than anyone else. So this fear of dragons is not merely a Western, or a technological, phenomenon. But I do not want to get into these vast historical questions; I will speak of modern Americans, the only people I know well enough to talk about.

In wondering why Americans are afraid of dragons, I began to realize that a great many Americans are not only anti-fantasy, but altogether anti-fiction. We tend, as a people, to look upon all works of the imagination either as suspect or as contemptible.

"My wife reads novels. I haven't got the time."

"I used to read that science fiction stuff when I was a teenager, but of course I don't now."

"Fairy stories are for kids. I live in the real world."

Who speaks so? Who is it that dismisses *War and Peace*, *The Time Machine*, and *A Midsummer Night's Dream* with this perfect self-assurance? It is, I fear, the man in the street—the hardworking, over-thirty American male—the men who run this country.

Such a rejection of the entire art of fiction is related to several American characteristics: our Puritanism, our work ethic, our profit-mindedness, and even our sexual mores.

To read *War and Peace* or *The Lord of the Rings* plainly is not "work"—you do it for pleasure. And if it cannot be justified as "educational" or as "self-improvement," then, in the Puritan value system, it can only be self-indulgence or escapism. For pleasure is not a value to the Puritan; on the contrary, it is a sin.

Equally, in the businessman's value system, if an act does not bring in an immediate, tangible profit, it has no justification at all. Thus the only person who has an excuse to read Tolstoy or Tolkien is the English teacher, who gets paid for it. But our businessman might allow himself to read a bestseller now and then: not because it is a good book, but because it is a bestseller—it is a success, it has made money. To the strangely mystical mind of the money changer, this justifies its existence; and by reading it he may participate, a little, in the power and mana of its success. If this is not magic, by the way, I don't know what it is.

The last element, the sexual one, is more complex. I hope I will not be understood as being sexist if I say that, within our culture, I believe that this anti-fiction attitude is basically a male one. The American boy and man is very commonly forced to define his maleness by rejecting certain traits, certain human gifts and potentialities, which our culture defines as "womanish" or "childish." And one of these traits or potentialities is, in cold sober fact, the absolutely essential human faculty of imagination.

Having got this far, I went quickly to the dictionary.

The *Shorter Oxford Dictionary* says: "Imagination. 1. The action of imagining, or forming a mental concept of what is not actually present to the senses; 2. The mental consideration of actions or events not yet in existence."

Very well; I certainly can let "absolutely essential human faculty" stand. But I must narrow the definition to fit our present subject. By "imagination," then, I personally mean the free play of the mind, both intellectual and sensory. By "play" I mean recreation, re-creation, the recombination of what is known into what is new. By "free" I mean that the action is done without an immediate object of profit—spontaneously. That does not mean, however, that there may not be a purpose behind the free play of the mind, a goal; and the goal may be a very serious object indeed. Children's imaginative play is clearly a practicing at the acts and emotions of adulthood; a child who did not play would not become mature. As for the free play of an adult mind, its result may be *War and Peace*, or the theory of relativity.

To be free, after all, is not to be undisciplined. I should say that the discipline of the imagination may in fact be the essential method or technique of both art and science. It is our Puritanism, insisting that discipline means repression or punishment, which confuses the subject. To discipline something, in the proper sense of the word, does not mean to repress it, but to train it—to encourage it to grow, and act, and be fruitful, whether it is a peach tree or a human mind.

I think that a great many American men have been taught just the opposite. They have learned to repress their imagination, to reject it as something childish or effeminate, unprofitable, and probably sinful.

They have learned to fear it. But they have never learned to discipline it at all.

Now, I doubt that the imagination can be suppressed. If you truly eradicated it in a child, that child would grow up to be an eggplant. Like all our evil propensities, the imagination will out. But if it is rejected and despised, it will grow into wild and weedy shapes; it will be deformed. At its best, it will be mere ego-centered daydreaming; at its worst, it will be wishful thinking, which is a very dangerous occupation when it is taken seriously. Where literature is concerned, in the old, truly Puritan days, the only permitted reading was the Bible. Nowadays, with our secular Puritanism, the man who refuses to read novels because it's unmanly to do so, or because they aren't true, will most likely end up watching bloody detective thrillers on the television, or reading hack Westerns or sports stories, or going in for pornography, from *Playboy* on down. It is his starved imagination, craving nourishment, that forces him to do so. But he can rationalize such entertainment by saying that it is realistic— after all, sex exists, and there are criminals, and there are baseball players, and there used to be cowboys—and also by saying that it is virile, by which he means that it doesn't interest most women.

That all these genres are sterile, hopelessly sterile, is a reassurance to him, rather than a defect. If they were genuinely realistic, which is to say genuinely imagined and imaginative, he would be afraid of them. Fake realism is the escapist literature of our time. And probably the ultimate escapist reading is that masterpiece of total unreality, the daily stock market report.

Now, what about our man's wife? She probably wasn't required to squelch her private imagination in order to play her expected role in life, but she hasn't been trained to discipline it, either. She is allowed to read novels, and even fantasies. But, lacking training and encouragement, her fancy is likely to glom on to very sickly fodder, such things as soap operas, and "true romances," and nursy novels, and historico-sentimental novels, and all the rest of the baloney ground out to replace genuine imaginative works by the artistic sweatshops of a society that is profoundly distrustful of the uses of the imagination.

What, then, are the uses of imagination?

You see, I think we have a terrible thing here: a hardworking, upright, responsible citizen, a full-grown, educated person, who is afraid of dragons, and afraid of hobbits, and scared to death of fairies. It's funny, but it's also terrible. Something has gone very wrong. I don't know what to do about it but to try and give an honest answer to that person's question, even though he often asks it in an aggressive and contemptuous tone of voice. "What's the good of it all?" he says. "Dragons and hobbits and little green men—what's the *use* of it?"

The truest answer, unfortunately, he won't even listen to. He won't hear it. The truest answer is "The use of it is to give you pleasure and delight."

"I haven't got the time," he snaps, swallowing a Maalox pill for his ulcer and rushing off to the golf course.

So we try the next-to-truest answer. It probably won't go down much better, but it must be said: "The use of imaginative fiction is to deepen your understanding of your world, and your fellow men, and your own feelings, and your destiny."

To which I fear he will retort, "Look, I got a raise last year, and I'm giving my family the best of everything, we've got two cars and a color TV. I understand enough of the world!"

And he is right, unanswerably right, if that is what he wants, and all he wants.

The kind of thing you learn from reading about the problems of a hobbit who is trying to drop a magic ring into an imaginary volcano has very little to do with your social status, or material success, or income. Indeed, if there is any relationship, it is a negative one. There is an inverse correlation between fantasy and money. That is a law, known to economists as Le Guin's Law. If you want a striking example of Le Guin's Law, just give a lift to one of those people along the roads who own nothing but a backpack, a guitar, a fine head of hair, a smile, and a thumb. Time and again, you will find that these waifs have read *The Lord of the Rings*—some of them can practically recite it. But now take Aristotle Onassis or J. Paul Getty: Could you believe that those men ever had anything to do, at any age, under any circumstances, with a hobbit?

But, to carry my example a little further, and out of the realm of economics, did you ever notice how very gloomy Mr. Onassis and Mr. Getty and all those billionaires look in their photographs? They have this strange, pinched look, as if they were hungry. As if they were hungry for something, as if they had lost something and were trying to think where it could be, or perhaps what it could be, what it was they've lost.

Could it be their childhood?

So I arrive at my personal defense of the uses of the imagination, especially in fiction, and most especially in fairy tale, legend, fantasy, science fiction, and the rest of the lunatic fringe. I believe that maturity is not an outgrowing, but a growing up: that an adult is not a dead child, but a child who survived. I believe that all the best faculties of a mature human being exist in the child, and that if these faculties are encouraged in youth they will act well and wisely in the adult, but if they are repressed and denied in the child they will stunt and cripple the adult personality. And finally, I believe that one of the most deeply human, and humane, of these faculties is the power of imagination: so that it is our pleasant duty, as librarians, or teachers, or parents, or writers, or simply as grown-ups, to encourage that faculty of imagination in our children, to encourage it to grow freely, to flourish like the green bay tree, by giving it the best, absolutely the best and purest, nourishment that it can absorb. And never, under any circumstances, to squelch it, or sneer at it, or imply that it is childish, or unmanly, or untrue.

For fantasy is true, of course. It isn't factual, but it is true. Children know that. Adults know it, too, and that is precisely why many of them are afraid of fantasy. They know that its truth challenges, even threatens, all that is false, all that is phony, unnecessary, and trivial in the life they have let themselves be forced into living. They are afraid of dragons because they are afraid of freedom.

So I believe that we should trust our children. Normal children do not confuse reality and fantasy—they confuse them much less often than we adults do (as a certain great fantasist pointed out in a story called "The Emperor's New Clothes"). Children know perfectly well that unicorns aren't real, but they also know that books about unicorns, if they are good books, are true books. All too often, that's more than Mummy and Daddy know; for, in denying their childhood, the adults have denied half their knowledge, and are left with the sad, sterile little fact: "Unicorns aren't real." And that fact is one that never got anybody anywhere (except in the story "The Unicorn in the Garden," by another great fantasist, in which it is shown that a devotion to the unreality of unicorns may get you straight into the loony bin). It is by such statements as "Once upon a time there was a dragon," or "In a hole in the ground there lived a hobbit"—it is by such beautiful nonfacts that we fantastic human beings may arrive, in our peculiar fashion, at the truth.

DREAMS MUST
EXPLAIN THEMSELVES

(1973)

Andy Porter called from New York earlier this year to try and tell me what he hoped I'd write for *Algol*. The conversation was pleasant, though disarranged by a bad connection, several explosive intrusions by a person at this end who wanted some cookies and attention, and a slight degree of misunderstanding. Andy kept saying things like "Tell the readers about yourself," and I kept saying things like "How? Why?"

Some people can talk on the telephone. They must really believe in the thing. For me the telephone is for making appointments with the doctor with and canceling appointments with the dentist with. It is not a medium of human communication. I can't stand there in the hall with the child and the cat both circling around my legs, frisking and purring and demanding cookies and cat food, and explain to a disembodied voice in my ear that the Jungian spectrum of introvert/extravert can usefully be applied not only to human beings but also to authors. That is, that there are some authors who want and need to tell about themselves, you know, like Norman Mailer, and there are others who want and need privacy. Privacy! What an elitist, Victorian concept. These days it sounds almost as quaint as modesty. But I can't say all that on the telephone; it just won't come out. Nor can I say (although I made a feeble effort to, about the time the connection failed entirely, probably because the cat, in despair, had settled for chewing on the telephone cord) that the problem of communication is a complex one, and that some of us introverts have solved it in a curious, not wholly satisfactory, but interesting way: we communicate (with all but a very few persons) in writing, but indirectly in writing. As if we were deaf and dumb. And not just in writing, but indirectly in writing. We write stories about imaginary people in imaginary situations. Then we publish them (because they are, in their strange way, acts of communication—addressed to others). And then people read them and call up and say, But who are you? Tell us about yourself! And we say, But I have. It's all there, in the book. All that matters—But you made all that up!—Out of what?

Where Andy and I temporarily misunderstood each other was at this point. Wanting me to write about the Earthsea trilogy, the background of it, he said (excuse me, Andy, for misquoting) something like "People would be interested in knowing things like how you planned the Earthsea world, and how you developed the languages, and how you keep lists of places and characters and so on." To which I returned some kind of garble-garble, of which I recall only one sentence, "But I didn't plan anything, I found it."

Andy (not unnaturally): "Where?"

Me: "In my subconscious."

Now as I think about it, perhaps this is worth talking about a little. Andy and I surprised each other because we had different unexamined notions of how writing is done; and they were so different that their collision produced a slight shock. Both of them are completely valid; they're just different methodologies. As mine is the one not talked about in writers' manuals, however, perhaps it needs some explanation.

All my life I have written, and all my life I have (without conscious decision) avoided reading how-to-write things. The *Shorter Oxford Dictionary* and Follett's and Fowler's manuals of usage are my entire arsenal of tools.* However, in reading and teaching and talking with other writers, one does arrive at a certain consciousness of technique. The most different technique from my own, the one that starts from the point furthest removed, is just this one of preliminary plans and lists and descriptions. The technique of keeping a notebook and describing all the characters in it before the story is begun: how much William weighs and where he went to school and how his hair is cut and what his dominant traits are.

I do have notebooks, in which I worry at plot ideas as if they were old bones, growling and snarling and frequently burying them and digging them up again. Also, during the writing of a piece, I often make notes concerning a character, particularly if it's a novel. My memory is very poor, and if there's something I just noticed about the character, but this is not the right point to put it into the book, then I make a note for future reference. Something like:

W. d not appr H's ing.—Repr!!

---

* Note (1989). I use Fowler and Follett rarely now, finding them authoritarian. Strunk and White's *Elements of Style*, corrected and supplemented by Miller and Swift's *Words and Women*, are my road atlas to English, and have never led me astray. A secondhand copy of the small-print *Oxford English Dictionary* in two volumes has been an infinite source of learning and pleasure, but the *Shorter Oxford* is still good for a quick fix.

Then I lose the note.

But I don't write out descriptions beforehand, and would indeed feel ridiculous, even ashamed, to do so. If the character isn't so clear to me that I know all *that* about him, what am I doing writing about him? What right have I to describe what William did when Helen bit his knee if I don't even know what he looks like, and his past, and his psyche, inside and out, as well as I know myself? Because after all he is myself. Part of myself.

If William is a character worthy of being written about, then he exists. He exists, inside my head to be sure, but in his own right, with his own vitality. All I have to do is look at him. I don't plan him, compose him of bits and pieces, inventory him. I find him.

There he is, and Helen is biting his knee, and he says with a little cough, "I really don't think this is relevant, Helen." What else, being William, could he say?

This attitude toward action, creation, is evidently a basic one, the same root from which the interest in the *I Ching* and Taoist philosophy evident in most of my books arises. The Taoist world is orderly, not chaotic, but its order is not one imposed by man or by a personal or humane deity. The true laws—ethical and aesthetic, as surely as scientific—are not imposed from above by any authority, but exist in things and are to be found—discovered.

To return circuitously to Earthsea: this anti-ideological, pragmatic technique applies to places as well as people. I did not deliberately invent Earthsea. I did not think, "Hey wow—islands are archetypes and archipelagoes are superarchetypes and let's build us an archipelago!" I am not an engineer but an explorer. I discovered Earthsea.

Plans are likely to be made, if well made, inclusively; discoveries are made bit by bit. Planning negates time. Discovery is a temporal process. It may take years and years. People are still exploring Antarctica.

The history of the discovery of Earthsea is something like this:

In 1964 I wrote a story called "The Word of Unbinding" about a wizard. Cele Goldsmith Lalli bought it for *Fantastic*. (Cele Lalli gave me and a lot of other people their start in SF; she was one of the most sensitive and audacious editors the field has ever had.) I don't recall now whether the fact is made much of in the story, but it was perfectly clear in my mind that it took place on an island, one among many islands. I did not give much attention to the setting, as it was (as William would say) not relevant, and developed only such rules of magic as were germane to the very small point the very minor story made.

Soon after, I wrote a story, "The Rule of Names," in which both the islands and the rules of magic were considerably more developed (Cele published it, too). This story was lighthearted (the other one was glum), and I had fun playing around a bit with the scenery, and with the old island ladies drinking rushwash tea, and so on. It was set on an island called Sattins, which I knew to be one of an outlying group east of the main archipelago. The main character, a dragon known first as Mr. Underhill and then, when his nature is revealed, by his true name Yevaud, came from a westerly isle called Pendor.

I did not much bother with all the islands that I knew lay between Sattins and Pendor, and north and south of them. They weren't involved. I had the distinct feeling, however, that the island of "Word of Unbinding" lay up north of Pendor. I am not now sure which island it actually is, that one I first landed on. Later voyages of discovery have so complicated the map that the first landfall, like that of the Norsemen in the New World, is hard to pin down for certain. Sattins, however, is on the map, high in the East Reach between Yore and Vemish.

Along in 1965 or 1966 I wrote a longish story about a prince who travels down through the archipelago from its central island, Havnor, in search of the Ultimate. He goes southwest out into the open sea, beyond all islands, and finds there a people who live on rafts all their lives long. He ties his boat to a raft and settles down with them, content with this as the Ultimate, until he realizes that out past the farthest journey of the drifting raft-colony there are sea-people, living in the sea itself. He joins them. I think the implication was that (not being a merman) he'll wear out eventually, and sink, and find the ultimate Ultimate. This story wasn't submitted for publication, as it never worked itself out at all well; but I felt strongly that the basic image—the raft-colony—was a lulu, and would find itself its home somewhere eventually. It did, in the last of the Earthsea books, *The Farthest Shore.*

I explored Earthsea no further until 1967, when the publisher of Parnassus Press, Herman Schein, asked me if I'd like to try writing a book for him. He wanted something for older kids; till then Parnassus had been mainly a young-juvenile publisher, putting out the handsomest and best-made picture books in America. He gave me complete freedom as to subject and approach. Nobody until then had ever asked me to write anything. I had just done so, relentlessly. To be asked to do it was a great boon. The exhilaration carried me over my apprehensions about writing "for young people," something I had never seriously tried. For some weeks or months I let my imagination go groping around in search of what was wanted, in the dark. It stumbled over the Islands, and the magic employed there. Serious consideration of magic, and of writing for kids, combined to make me wonder about wizards. Wizards are usually elderly or ageless Gandalfs, quite rightly and archetypically. But what were they before they had white beards? How did they learn what is obviously an erudite and dangerous art? Are there colleges for young wizards? And so on.

The story of the book is essentially a voyage, a pattern in the form of a long spiral. I began to see the places where the young wizard would go. Eventually I drew a map. Now that I knew where everything was, now was the time for cartography. Of course, a great deal of it only appeared above water, as it were, in drawing the map.

Three small islands are named for my children, their baby names; one gets a little jovial and irresponsible, given the freedom to create a world out of nothing at all. (Power corrupts.) None of the other names "mean" anything that I know of, though their sound is more or less meaningful to me.

People often ask how I think of names in fantasies, and again I have to answer that I find them, that I hear them. This is an important subject in this context. From that first story on, *naming* has been the essence of the art-magic as practiced in Earthsea. For me, as for the wizards, to know the name of an island or a character is to know the island or the person. Usually the name comes of itself, but sometimes one must be very careful: as I was with the protagonist, whose true name is Ged. I worked (in collaboration with a wizard named Ogion) for a long time trying to "listen for" his name, and making certain it really was his name. This all sounds very mystical, and indeed there are aspects of it I do not understand, but it is a pragmatic business, too, since if the name had been wrong the character would have been wrong—misbegotten, misunderstood.

A man who read the ms. for Parnassus thought "Ged" was meant to suggest "God." That shook me badly. I considered changing the name in case there were other such ingenious minds waiting to pounce. But I couldn't do so. The fellow's name was Ged and no two ways about it.

It isn't pronounced Jed, by the way. That sounds like a mountain moonshiner to me. I thought the analogy with "get" would make it clear, but a lot of people have asked. One place I do exert deliberate control in name-inventing is in the area of pronounceability. I try to spell them so they don't look too formidable (unless, like Kurremkarmerruk, they're meant to look formidable), and they can be pronounced either with the English or the Italian vowels. I don't care which.

Much the same holds for the bits of invented languages in the text of the trilogy.

There are words, like rushwash tea, for which I can offer no explanation. They simply drink rushwash tea there; that's what it's called, like Lapsang souchong or Lipton's here. Rushwash is a Hardic word, of course. If you press me, I will explain that it comes from the rushwash bush, which grows both wild and cultivated everywhere south of Enlad, and bears a small round leaf which when dried and steeped yields a pleasant brownish tea. I did not know this before I wrote the foregoing sentence. Or did I know it, and simply never thought about it? What's in a name? A lot, that's what.

There are more formal examples of foreign languages in the trilogy; in *The Farthest Shore* there are several whole sentences in the Language of the Making, as dragons will not speak anything else. These arrived, spelling (formidable) and all, and I wrote them down without question. No use trying to make a lexicon of Hardic or of the True Speech; there's not enough in the books. It's not like Tolkien, who in one sense wrote *The Lord of the Rings* to give his invented languages somebody to speak them. That is lovely, that is the Creator Spirit working absolutely unhindered—making the word flesh. But Tolkien is a linguist as well as a great creator.

(In other books I have taken the invented languages further. I knew enough Karhidish, when I was writing *The Left Hand of Darkness*, to write a couple of short poems in it. I couldn't do so now. I made no methodical lexicon or grammar, only a word list for my own reference.)

I said that to know the true name is to know the thing, for me, and for the wizards. This implies a good deal about the "meaning" of the trilogy, and about me. The trilogy is, in one aspect, about the artist. The artist as magician. The Trickster. Prospero. That is the only truly allegorical aspect it has of which I am conscious. If there are other allegories in it, please don't tell me; I hate allegories. A is "really" B, and a hawk is "really" a handsaw—bah. Humbug. Any creation, primary or secondary, with any vitality to it, can "really" be a dozen mutually exclusive things at once, before breakfast.

Wizardy is artistry. The trilogy is then, in this sense, about art, the creative experience, the creative process. There is always this circularity in fantasy. The snake devours its tail. Dreams must explain themselves.

What I wanted to send Andy Porter was a long passionate article about the status of "children's books." He wanted something more personal. But as an SF writer I resent being low paid in comparison to dreck-writers; and if SF writers think they're low-paid, they should look at writers for children. I am not complaining personally. Atheneum, who now publish my children's books, have treated me well, and with great personal civility; the same goes for Gollancz in England; and both firms have given me splendid (woman) editors. What is wrong is the whole scale—all the publishers' budgets for their children's books. There is seldom big quick money in kiddylit, but a successful kids' book has an unusually long life. It sells to schools, to libraries, and to gift-giving adults, and it goes on selling, and making money, for years and years and years. This is not reflected in the advances or the royalties. It is a very badly paid field, in general.

But the economic discrimination is only an element, as usual, of the real problem: a reflection of a prejudice. The real trouble isn't the money, it's the adult chauvinist piggery.

"You're a juvenile writer, aren't you?"

Yeth, Mummy.

"I love your books—the real ones, I mean, I haven't read the ones for children, of course!"

Of courthe not, Daddy.

"It must be relaxing to write *simple* things for a change."

Sure it's simple, writing for kids. Just as simple as bringing them up.

All you do is take all the sex out, and use little short words, and little dumb ideas, and don't be too scary, and be sure there's a happy ending. Right? Nothing to it. Write down. Right on.

If you do all that, you might even write *Jonathan Livingston Seagull* and make twenty billion dollars and have every adult in America reading your book.

But you won't have every kid in America reading your book. They will look at it, and they will see straight through it, with their clear, cold, beady little eyes, and they will put it down, and they will go away. Kids will devour vast amounts of garbage (and it is good for them), but they are not like adults: they have not yet learned to eat plastic.

The British seem not to believe publishers' categorizations of "juvenile," "teenage," "young adult," etc., so devoutly as we do. It's interesting that, for instance, Andre Norton is often reviewed with complete respect by English papers, including the *Times Literary*

Supplement. No pats, no sniggers, no put-downs. They seem to be aware that fantasy is the great age-equalizer; if it's good when you're twelve, it's quite likely to be just as good, or better, when you're thirty-six.

Most of my letters about the Earthsea books from American readers are from people between sixteen and twenty-five. The English who write me tend to be, as well as I can guess, over thirty, and more predominantly male. (Several of them are Anglican clergymen. As a congenital non-Christian I find this a little startling; but the letters are terrific.) One might interpret this age difference to mean that the English are more childish than the Americans, but I see it the other way. The English readers are grown-up enough not to be defensive about being grown up.

The most childish thing about *A Wizard of Earthsea*, I expect, is its subject: coming-of-age.

Coming-of-age is a process that took me many years; I finished it, so far as I ever will, at about age thirty-one; and so I feel rather deeply about it. So do most adolescents. It's their main occupation, in fact.

The subject of *The Tombs of Atuan* is, if I had to put it in one word, sex. There's a lot of symbolism in the book, most of which I did not, of course, analyze consciously while writing; the symbols can all be read as sexual. More exactly, you could call it a feminine coming-of-age. Birth, rebirth, destruction, freedom are the themes.

The Farthest Shore is about death. That's why it is a less well-built, less sound, and complete book than the others. They were about things I had already lived through and survived. *The Farthest Shore* is about the thing you do not live through and survive. It seemed an absolutely suitable subject to me for young readers since, in a way, one can say that the hour when a child realizes, not that death exists—children are intensely aware of death—but that he/she, personally, is mortal, will die, is the hour when childhood ends and the new life begins. Coming-of-age again, but in a larger context.

In any case I had little choice about the subject. Ged, who was always very strong-minded, always saying things that surprised me and doing things he wasn't supposed to do, took over completely in this book. He was determined to show me how his life must end, and why. I tried to keep up with him, but he was always ahead. I rewrote the book more times than I want to remember, trying to keep him under some kind of control. I thought it was all done when it was printed here, but the English edition differs in three long passages from the earlier American one: my editor at Gollancz said, "Ged is talking too much," and she was quite right, and I shut him up three times, much to the improvement of the whole. If you insist upon discovering instead of planning, this kind of trouble is inevitable. It is a most uneconomical way to write. The book is still the most imperfect of the three, but it is the one I like best. It is the end of the trilogy, but it is the dream I have not stopped dreaming.*

---

*   (1989) Nor have I yet stopped dreaming it.
It was a pleasant surprise to me to discover that Ged was in fact quite mistaken about how his life must end, and that the person who would guide me through the last book of Earthsea was Tenar. That last book—*Tehanu*—though I longed to call it *Better Late Than Never*—is to be published soon.

NATIONAL BOOK AWARD
ACCEPTANCE SPEECH

(1972)

I am very pleased, very proud, and very startled to accept the National Book Award in children's literature for my novel *The Farthest Shore.*

Nothing could give me greater joy than to share that honor, as it should be shared, with the people whose work and patience and constant trust were essential to the writing and publication of the book: the people at Atheneum Press, especially my editor, Jean Karl, and illustrator, Gail Garraty; and my literary agent, Virginia Kidd; and—last of all and first of all—my husband and our children.

And I also rejoice in the privilege of sharing this honor, if I may, with my fellow writers, not only in the field of children's books, but in that even less respectable field, science fiction. For I am not only a fantasist but a science fiction writer, and odd though it may seem, I am proud to be both.

We who hobnob with hobbits and tell tall tales about little green men are quite used to being dismissed as mere entertainers, or sternly disapproved of as escapists. But I think that perhaps the categories are changing, like the times. Sophisticated readers are accepting the fact that an improbable and unmanageable world is going to produce an improbable and hypothetical art. At this point, realism is perhaps the least adequate means of understanding or portraying the incredible realities of our existence. A scientist who creates a monster in the laboratory; a librarian in the library of Babel; a wizard unable to cast a spell; a spaceship having trouble in getting to Alpha Centauri: all these may be precise and profound metaphors of the human condition. Fantasists, whether they use the ancient archetypes of myth and legend or the younger ones of science and technology, may be talking as seriously as any sociologist—and a good deal more directly—about human life as it is lived, and as it might be lived, and as it ought to be lived. For after all, as great scientists have said and as all children know, it is above all by the imagination that we achieve perception, and compassion, and hope.

THE CHILD AND
THE SHADOW

(1974)

Once upon a time, says Hans Christian Andersen, there was a kind, shy, learned young man from the North, who came south to visit the hot countries, where the sun shines fiercely and all shadows are very black.

Now, across the street from the young man's window is a house, where he once glimpses a beautiful girl tending beautiful flowers on the balcony. The young man longs to go speak to her, but he's too shy. One night, while his candle is burning behind him, casting his shadow onto the balcony across the way, he "jokingly" tells his shadow to go ahead, go on into that house. And it does. It enters the house across the street and leaves him.

The young man's a bit surprised, naturally, but he doesn't do anything about it. He presently grows a new shadow and goes back home. And he grows older, and more learned; but he's not a success. He talks about beauty and goodness, but nobody listens to him.

Then one day when he's a middle-aged man, his shadow

comes back to him—very thin and rather swarthy, but elegantly dressed. "Did you go into the house across the street?" the man asks him, first thing; and the shadow says, "Oh, yes, certainly." He claims that he saw everything, but he's just boasting. The man knows what to ask. "Were the rooms like the starry sky when one stands on the mountaintops?" he asks, and all the shadow can say is "Oh, yes, everything was there." He doesn't know how to answer. He never got in any farther than the anteroom, being, after all, only a shadow. "I should have been annihilated by that flood of light had I penetrated into the room where the maiden lived," he says.

He is, however, good at blackmail and such arts; he is a strong, unscrupulous fellow, and he dominates the man completely. They go traveling, the shadow as master and the man as servant. They meet a princess, who suffers "because she sees too clearly." She sees that the shadow casts no shadow and distrusts him, until he explains that the man is really his shadow, which he allows to walk about by itself, a peculiar arrangement, but logical; the princess accepts it. When she and the shadow engage to marry, the man rebels at last. He tries to tell the princess the truth, but the shadow gets there first, with explanations: "The poor fellow is crazy, he thinks he's a man and I'm his shadow!"—"How dreadful," says the princess. A mercy killing is definitely in order. And while the shadow and the princess get married, the man is executed.

Now, that is an extraordinary, cruel story. A story about insanity ending in humiliation and death.

Is it a story for children? Yes, it is. It's a story for anybody who's listening.

If you listen, what do you hear?

The house across the street is the House of Beauty, and the

maiden is the Muse of Poetry; the shadow tells us that straight out. And that the princess who sees too clearly is pure, cold reason is plain enough. But who are the man and the shadow? That's not so plain. They aren't allegorical figures. They are symbolic or archetypal figures, like those in a dream. Their significance is multiple, inexhaustible. I can only hint at the little I'm able to see of it.

The man is all that is civilized—learned, kindly, idealistic, decent. The shadow is all that gets suppressed in the process of becoming a decent, civilized adult. The shadow is the man's thwarted selfishness, his unadmitted desires, the swear words he never spoke, the murders he didn't commit. The shadow is the dark side of his soul, the unadmitted, the inadmissible.

And what Andersen is saying is that this monster is an integral part of the man and cannot be denied—not if the man wants to enter the House of Poetry.

The man's mistake is in not following his shadow. It goes ahead of him, as he sits there at his window, and he cuts it off from himself, telling it, "jokingly," to go on without him. And it does. It goes on into the House of Poetry, the source of all creativity—leaving him outside, on the surface of reality.

So, good and learned as he is, he can't do any good, can't act, because he has cut himself off at the roots. And the shadow is equally helpless; it can't get past the shadowy anteroom to the light. Neither of them, without the other, can approach the truth.

When the shadow returns to the man in middle life, he has a second chance. But he misses it, too. He confronts his dark self at last, but instead of asserting equality or mastery, he lets it master him. He gives in. He does, in fact, become the shadow's shadow, and his fate, then, is inevitable. The Princess Reason is cruel in having him executed, and yet she is just.

Part of Andersen's cruelty is the cruelty of reason—of psychological realism, radical honesty, the willingness to see and accept the consequences of an act or a failure to act. There is a sadistic, depressive streak in Andersen also, which is his own shadow; it's there, it's part of him, but not all of him, nor is he ruled by it. His strength, his subtlety, his creative genius, come precisely from his acceptance of and cooperation with the dark side of his own soul. That's why Andersen the fabulist is one of the great realists of literature.

Now I stand here, like the princess herself, and tell you what the story of the shadow means to me at age forty-five. But what did it mean to me when I first read it, at age ten or eleven? What does it mean to children? Do they "understand" it? Is it "good" for them—this bitter, complex study of a moral failure?

I don't know. I hated it when I was a kid. I hated all the Andersen stories with unhappy endings. That didn't stop me from reading them, and rereading them. Or from remembering them . . . so that after a gap of over thirty years, when I was pondering this talk, a little voice suddenly said inside my left ear, "You'd better dig out that Andersen story, you know, about the shadow."

At age ten I certainly wouldn't have gone on about reason and repression and all that. I had no critical equipment, no detachment, and even less power of sustained thought than I have now. I had a somewhat less conscious mind than I have now. But I had as much, or more, of an unconscious mind, and was perhaps in better touch with it than I am now. And it was to that, to the unknown depths in me, that the story spoke; and it was the depths which responded to it and, nonverbally, irrationally, understood it, and learned from it.

The great fantasies, myths, and tales are indeed like dreams:

they speak *from* the unconscious *to* the unconscious, in the *language* of the unconscious—symbol and archetype. Though they use words, they work the way music does: they short-circuit verbal reasoning, and go straight to the thoughts that lie too deep to utter. They cannot be translated fully into the language of reason, but only a Logical Positivist, who also finds Beethoven's Ninth Symphony meaningless, would claim that they are therefore meaningless. They are profoundly meaningful, and usable—practical—in terms of ethics; of insight; of growth.

Reduced to the language of daylight, Andersen's story says that a man who will not confront and accept his shadow is a lost soul. It also says something specifically about itself, about art. It says that if you want to enter the House of Poetry, you have to enter it in the flesh, the solid, imperfect, unwieldy body, which has corns and colds and greeds and passions, the body that casts a shadow. It says that if the artist tries to ignore evil, he will never enter into the House of Light.

That's what one great artist said to me about shadows. Now if I may move our candle and throw the shadows in a different direction, I'd like to interrogate a great psychologist on the same subject. Art has spoken, let's hear what science has to say. Since art is the subject, let it be the psychologist whose ideas on art are the most meaningful to most artists, Carl Gustav Jung.

Jung's terminology is notoriously difficult, as he kept changing meanings the way a growing tree changes leaves. I will try to define a few of the key terms in an amateurish way without totally misrepresenting them. Very roughly, then, Jung saw the ego, what we usually call the self, as only a part of the Self, the part of it which we are consciously aware of. The ego "revolves around the Self as the earth around the Sun," he says. The Self is transcendent, much larger than the ego; it is not a private possession, but collective—that is, we share it with all other human beings, and perhaps with all beings. It may indeed be our link with what is called God. Now, this sounds mystical, and it is, but it's also exact and practical. All Jung is saying is that we are fundamentally alike; we all have the same general tendencies and configurations in our psyche, just as we all have the same general kind of lungs and bones in our body. Human beings all look roughly alike; they also think and feel alike. And they are all part of the universe.

The ego, the little private individual consciousness, knows this, and it knows that if it's not to be trapped in the hopeless silence of autism it must identify with something outside itself, beyond itself, larger than itself. If it's weak, or if it's offered nothing better, what it does is identify with the "collective consciousness." That is Jung's term for a kind of lowest common denominator of all the little egos added together, the mass mind, which consists of such things as cults, creeds, fads, fashions, status-seeking, conventions, received beliefs, advertising, popcult, all the isms, all the ideologies, all the hollow forms of communication and "togetherness" that lack real communion or real sharing. The ego, accepting these empty forms, becomes a member of the "lonely crowd." To avoid this, to attain real community, it must turn inward, away from the crowd to the source: it must identify with *its own* deeper regions, the great unexplored regions of the Self. These regions of the psyche Jung calls the "collective unconscious," and it is in them, where we all meet, that he sees the source of true community; of felt religion; of art, grace, spontaneity, and love.

How do you get there? How do you find your own private entrance to the collective unconscious? Well, the first step is often the most important, and Jung says that the first step is to turn around and follow your own shadow.

Jung saw the psyche as populated with a group of fascinating figures, much livelier than Freud's grim trio of Id, Ego, Superego; they're all worth meeting. The one we're concerned with is the shadow.

The shadow is on the other side of our psyche, the dark brother of the conscious mind. It is Cain, Caliban, Frankenstein's monster, Mr. Hyde. It is Vergil who guided Dante through hell, Gilgamesh's friend Enkidu, Frodo's enemy Gollum. It is the Doppelgänger. It is Mowgli's Gray Brother; the werewolf; the wolf, the bear, the tiger of a thousand folktales; it is the serpent Lucifer. The shadow stands on the threshold between the conscious and the unconscious mind, and we meet it in our dreams, as sister, brother, friend, beast, monster, enemy, guide. It is all we don't want to, can't, admit into our conscious self, all the qualities and tendencies within us which have been repressed, denied, or not used. In describing Jung's psychology, Jolande Jacobi wrote that "the development of the shadow runs parallel to that of the ego; qualities which the ego does not need or cannot make use of are set aside or repressed, and thus they play little or no part in the conscious life of the individual. Accordingly, a child has no real shadow, but his shadow becomes more pronounced as his ego grows in stability and range."[1] Jung himself said, "Everyone carries a shadow, and the less it is embodied in the individual's conscious life, the blacker and denser it is."[2] The less you look at it, in other words, the stronger it grows, until it can become a menace, an intolerable load, a threat within the soul.

Unadmitted to consciousness, the shadow is projected outward, onto others. There's nothing wrong with me—it's *them*. I'm not a monster, other people are monsters. All foreigners are evil. All communists are evil. All capitalists are evil. It was the cat that made me kick him, Mummy.

If I want to live in the real world, I must withdraw my projections; I must admit that the hateful, the evil, exists within myself. This isn't easy. It is very hard not to be able to blame anybody else. But it may be worth it. If the individual, says Jung, "only learns to deal with his own shadow he has done something real for the world. He has succeeded in shouldering at least an infinitesimal part of the gigantic, unsolved social problems of our day."[3]

Moreover, that individual has grown toward true community, and self-knowledge, and creativity. For the shadow stands on the threshold. We can let it bar the way to the creative depths of the unconscious, or we can let it lead us to them. For the shadow is not simply evil. It is inferior, primitive, awkward, animal-like, child-like; powerful, vital, spontaneous. It's not weak and decent, like the learned young man from the North; it's dark and hairy and unseemly; but, without it, the person is nothing. What is a body that casts no shadow? Nothing, a formlessness, two-dimensional, a comic strip character. If I deny my own profound relationship with evil I deny my own reality. I cannot do, or make; I can only undo, unmake.

Jung was especially interested in the second half of life, when this conscious confrontation with a shadow that's been growing for thirty or forty years can become imperative—as it did for the poor fellow in the Andersen story. As Jung says, the child's ego and shadow are both still ill-defined; children are likely to find their ego in a ladybug, and their shadow lurking horribly under the bed. But I think that when in preadolescence and adolescence the conscious sense of self emerges, often quite overwhelmingly the shadow darkens right with it. The normal adolescent ceases to project so blithely as the little child did, realizing that you can't blame everything on the bad guys with black Stetsons. The adolescent begins to take responsibility for his or her acts and feelings. And with the responsibility may come a terrible load of guilt. The adolescent shadow often appears as much blacker, more wholly evil, than it is. The only way for a youngster to get past the paralyzing self-blame and self-disgust of this stage is really to look at that shadow, to face it, warts and fangs and pimples and claws and all—to accept it as the self—as *part* of the self. The ugliest part, but not the weakest. For the shadow is the guide. The guide inward and out again; downward and up again; there, as Bilbo the Hobbit said, and back again. The guide of the journey of self-knowledge, to adulthood, to the light.

"Lucifer" means the one who carries the light.

It seems to me that Jung described, as the individual's imperative need and duty, that journey which Andersen's learned young man failed to make.

It also seems to me that most of the great works of fantasy are about that journey; and that fantasy is the medium best suited to a description of that journey, its perils and rewards. The events of a voyage into the unconscious are not describable in the language of rational daily life: only the symbolic language of the deeper psyche will fit them without trivializing them.

Moreover, the journey seems to be not only a psychic one, but a moral one. Most great fantasies contain a very strong, striking moral dialectic, often expressed as a struggle between the Darkness and the Light. But that makes it sound simple, and the ethics of the unconscious—of the dream, the fantasy, the fairy tale—are not simple at all. They are, indeed, very strange.

Take the ethics of the fairy tale, where the shadow figure is often played by an animal—horse, wolf, bear, snake, raven, fish. In her article "The Problem of Evil in Fairytales," Marie Louise von Franz—a Jungian—points out the real strangeness of morality in folktales. There *is no right way* to act when you're the hero or heroine of a fairy tale. There is no system of conduct, there are no standards of what a nice prince does and what a good little girl doesn't do. I mean, do good little girls usually push old ladies into baking ovens, and get rewarded for it? Not in what we call "real life," they don't. But in dreams and fairy tales they do. And to judge Gretel by the standards of conscious, daylight virtue is a complete and ridiculous mistake.

In the fairy tale, though there is no "right" and "wrong," there is a different standard, which is perhaps best called "appropriateness." Under no conditions can we say that it is morally right and ethically virtuous to push an old lady into a baking oven. But, under the conditions of fairy tale, in the language of the archetypes, we can say with perfect conviction that it may be *appropriate* to do so. Because, in those terms, the witch is not an old lady, nor is Gretel a little girl. Both are psychic factors, elements of the complex soul. Gretel is the archaic child-soul, innocent, defenseless; the witch is the archaic crone, the possessor and destroyer, the mother who feeds you cookies and who must be destroyed before she eats you like a cookie, so that you can grow up and be a mother, too. And so on and so on. All explanations are partial. The archetype is inexhaustible. And children understand it as fully and surely as adults do—often more fully, because they haven't got minds stuffed full of the one-sided, shadowless half-truths and conventional moralities of the collective consciousness.

Evil, then, appears in the fairy tale not as something diametrically opposed to good, but as inextricably involved with it, as in the yang-yin symbol. Neither is greater than the other, nor can human reason and virtue separate one from the other and choose between them. The hero or heroine is the one who sees what is appropriate to be done, because he or she sees the *whole*, which is greater than either evil or good. Their heroism is, in fact, their certainty. They do not act by rules; they simply know the way to go.

In this labyrinth, where it seems one must trust to blind instinct, there is, von Franz points out, one—only one—consistent rule or "ethic": "Anyone who earns the gratitude of animals, or whom they help for any reason, invariably wins out. This is the only unfailing rule that I have been able to find."

Our instinct, in other words, is not blind. The animal does not reason, but it sees. And it acts with certainty; it acts "rightly," appropriately. That is why all animals are beautiful. It is the animal who knows the way, the way home. It is the animal within us, the primitive, the dark brother, the shadow soul, who is the guide.

There is often a queer twist to this in folktales, a kind of final secret. The helpful animal, often a horse or a wolf, says to the hero, "When you have done such-and-so with my help, then you must kill me, cut off my head." And the hero must trust his animal guide so wholly that he is willing to do so. Apparently the meaning of this is that when you have followed the animal instincts far enough, then they must be sacrificed, so that the true self, the whole person, may step forth from the body of the animal, reborn. That is von Franz's explanation, and it sounds fair enough; I am glad to have any explanation of that strange episode in so many tales, which has always shocked me. But I doubt that that's all there is to it—or that any Jungian would pretend it was. Neither rational thought nor rational ethics can "explain" these deep strange levels of the imagining mind. Even in merely reading a fairy tale, we must let go our daylight convictions and trust ourselves to be guided by dark figures, in silence; and when we come back, it may be very hard to describe where we have been.

In many fantasy tales of the nineteenth and twentieth centuries the tension between good and evil, light and dark, is drawn absolutely clearly, as a battle, the good guys on one side and the bad guys on the other, cops and robbers, Christians and heathens, heroes and villains. In such fantasies I believe the author has tried to force reason to lead where reason cannot go, and has abandoned the faithful and frightening guide, the shadow. These are false fantasies, rationalized fantasies. They are not the real thing. Let me, by way of exhibiting the real thing, which is always much more interesting than the fake one, discuss *The Lord of the Rings* for a minute.

Critics have been hard on Tolkien for his "simplisticness," his division of the inhabitants of Middle Earth into the good people and the evil people. And indeed he does this, and his good people tend to be entirely good, though with endearing frailties, while his Orcs and other villains are altogether nasty. But all this is a judgment by daylight ethics, by conventional standards of virtue and vice. When you look at the story as a psychic journey, you see something quite different, and very strange. You see then a group of bright figures, each one with its black shadow. Against the Elves, the Orcs. Against Aragorn, the Black Rider. Against Gandalf, Saruman. And above all, against Frodo, Gollum. Against him—and with him.

It is truly complex, because both the figures are clearly doubled. Sam is, in part, Frodo's shadow, his "inferior" part. Gollum is two people, too, in a more direct, schizophrenic sense; he's always talking to himself, Slinker talking to Stinker, Sam calls it. Sam understands Gollum very well, though he won't admit it and won't accept

Gollum as Frodo does, letting Gollum be their guide, trusting him. Frodo and Gollum are not only both hobbits; they are the same person—and Frodo knows it. Frodo and Sam are the bright side, Smeagol-Gollum the shadow side. In the end Sam and Smeagol, the lesser figures, drop away, and all that is left is Frodo and Gollum, at the end of the long quest. And it is Frodo the good who fails, who at the last moment claims the Ring of Power for himself; and it is Gollum the evil who achieves the quest, destroying the Ring, and himself with it. The Ring, the archetype of the Integrative Function, the creative-destructive, returns to the volcano, the eternal source of creation and destruction, the primal fire. When you look at it that way, can you call it a simple story? I suppose so. *Oedipus Rex* is a fairly simple story, too. But it is not simplistic. It is the kind of story that can be told only by one who has turned and faced his shadow and looked into the dark.

That it is told in the language of fantasy is not an accident, or because Tolkien was an escapist, or because he was writing for children. It is a fantasy because fantasy is the natural, the appropriate language for the recounting of the spiritual journey and the struggle of good and evil in the soul.

That has been said before—by Tolkien himself, for one—but it needs repeating. It needs lots of repeating, because there is still, in this country, a deep puritanical distrust of fantasy, which comes out often among people truly and seriously concerned about the ethical education of children. Fantasy, to them, is escapism. They see no difference between the Batmen and Supermen of the commercial dope-factories and the timeless archetypes of the collective unconscious. They confuse fantasy, which in the psychological sense is a universal and essential faculty of the human mind, with infantilism and pathological regression. They seem to think that shadows are something that we can simply do away with, if we can only turn on enough electric lights. And so they see the irrationality and cruelty and strange amoralities of fairy tale, and they say: "But this is very bad for children, we must teach children right from wrong, with realistic books, books that are true to life!"

I agree that children need to be—and usually want very much to be—taught right from wrong. But I believe that realistic fiction for children is one of the very hardest media in which to do it. It's hard not to get entangled in the superficialities of the collective consciousness, in simplistic moralism, in projections of various kinds, so that you end up with the baddies and goodies all over again. Or you get that business about "there's a little bit of bad in the best of us and a little bit of good in the worst of us," a dangerous banalization of the fact, which is that there is incredible potential for good and for evil in every one of us. Or writers are encouraged to merely capitalize on sensationalism, upsetting the child reader without themselves being really involved in the violence of the story, which is shameful. Or you get the "problem books." The problem of drugs, of divorce, of race prejudice, of unmarried pregnancy, and so on— as if evil were a problem, something that can be solved, that has an answer, like a problem in fifth-grade arithmetic. If you want the answer, you just look in the back of the book.

That is escapism, that posing evil as a "problem," instead of what it is: all the pain and suffering and waste and loss and injustice we will meet all our lives long, and must face and cope with over and over and over, and admit, and live with, in order to live human lives at all.

But what, then, are the naturalistic writers for children to do? Can they represent the child with evil as an *insoluble* problem— something neither the child nor any adult can do anything about at all? To give the child a picture of the gas chambers of Dachau, or the famines of India, or the cruelties of a psychotic parent, and say, "Well, baby, this is how it is, what are you going to make of it?"—that is surely unethical. If you suggest that there is a "solution" to these monstrous facts, you are lying to the child. But to unload adult despair onto one too young to cope with it is itself a psychotic act.

The young creature does need protection and shelter. But it also needs the truth. It seems to me that the way you can speak absolutely honestly and factually to children about good and evil is to talk about the self—the inner, the deepest self. That is something children can and do cope with; indeed, our job in growing up is to become ourselves. We can't do this if we feel the task is hopeless, nor if we're led to think there isn't any work to it. Growth will be stunted or perverted if a child is forced to despair or encouraged in false security, terrified or coddled. What we need to grow up is reality, the wholeness which exceeds human virtue and vice. We need knowledge; we need self-knowledge. We need to see ourselves and the shadows we cast. For we can face our own shadow; we can learn to control it and to be guided by it; so that when we grow into our strength and responsibility as adults in society, we will be less inclined, perhaps, either to give up in despair or to deny what we see, when we must face the evil that is done in the world, and the injustices and grief and suffering that we all must bear, and the final shadow at the end of all.

Fantasy is the language of the inner self. I will claim no more for fantasy than to say that I personally find it the appropriate language in which to tell stories to children—and others. But I say that with some confidence, having behind me the authority of a very great poet, who put it much more boldly. "The great instrument of moral good," Shelley said, "is the imagination."

NOTES

1. Jolande Jacobi, *The Psychology of C. G. Jung* (New Haven: Yale University Press, 1962), 107.

2. Carl Gustav Jung, *Psychology and Religion: West and East*, Bollingen Series XX, *The Collected Works of C. G. Jung*, vol. 11 (New York: Pantheon Books, 1958), 76.

3. Jung, *Psychology and Religion*, 83.

MYTH AND ARCHETYPE
IN SCIENCE FICTION

(1976)

"Science fiction is the mythology of the modern world." It's a good slogan, and a useful one when you're faced with people ignorant and contemptuous of science fiction, for it makes them stop and think. But like all slogans it's a half-truth, and when used carelessly, as a whole truth, can cause all kinds of confusion.

Where care must be taken is with that complex word "mythology." What is a myth?

"Myth is an attempt to explain, in rational terms, facts not yet rationally understood." That is the definition provided by the reductive, scientistic mentality of the first half of the twentieth century and still accepted by many. According to this definition, the god Apollo "is merely" an inadequate effort made by primitive minds to explain and systematize the nature and behavior of the Sun. As soon as the Sun is rationally understood to be a ball of fire much larger than the Earth, and its behavior has been described by a system of scientific laws, the old mythological pseudo-explanation is left empty. The fiery horses and the golden chariot vanish, the god is dethroned, and his exploits remain only a pretty tale for children. According to this view, the advance of science is a progressive draining dry of the content of mythology.[1] And, insofar as the content of myth is rational and the function of myth is explanatory, this definition is suitable. However, the rational and explanatory is only one function of the myth. Myth is an expression of one of the several ways the human being, body/psyche, perceives, understands, and relates to the world. Like science, it is a product of a basic human mode of apprehension. To pretend that it can be replaced by abstract or quantitative cognition is to assert that the human being is, potentially or ideally, a creature of pure reason, a disembodied Mind. It might indeed be nice if we were all little bubbles of pure reason floating on the stream of time; but we aren't. We are rational beings, but we are also sensual, emotional, appetitive, ethical beings, driven by needs and reaching out for satisfactions which the intellect alone cannot provide. Where these other modes of being and doing are inadequate, the intellect should prevail. Where the intellect fails, and must always fail, unless we become disembodied bubbles, then one of the other modes must take over. The myth, mythological insight, is one of these. Supremely effective in its area of function, it needs no replacement. Only the schizoid arrogance of modern scientism pretends that it ought to be replaced, and that pretension is pretty easily deflated. For example, does our scientific understanding of the nature and behavior of the Sun explain (let alone explain away) Apollo's remarkable sex life, or his role as the god of music and of the divine harmony? No, it has nothing whatever to do with all that; it has nothing to do with sex, or music, or harmony, or divinity; nor *as science* did it ever pretend to—only scientism made the claim.

Apollo is not the Sun, and never was. The Sun, in fact, "is merely" one of the names of Apollo.

Reductionism cuts both ways, after all.

So long, then, as we don't claim, either, that the science in science fiction replaces the "old, false" mythologies, or that the fiction in science fiction is a mere attempt to explain what science hasn't yet got around to explaining, we can use the slogan. Science fiction is the mythology of the modern world—or one of its mythologies— even though it is a highly intellectual form of art, and mythology is a nonintellectual mode of apprehension. For science fiction does use the mythmaking faculty to apprehend the world we live in, a world profoundly shaped and changed by science and technology, and its originality is that it uses the mythmaking faculty on new material.

But there's another catch to look out for. The presence of mythic material in a story does not mean that the mythmaking faculty is being used.

Here is a science fiction story: its plot is modeled directly upon that of an ancient myth, or there are characters in it modeled upon certain gods or heroes of legend. Is it, therefore, a myth? Not necessarily; in fact, probably not. No mythmaking is involved: just theft.

Theft is an integral function of a healthy literature. It's much easier to steal a good plot from some old book than to invent one. Anyhow, after you've sweated to invent an original plot, it very often turns out to be a perfect parallel to one of the old stories (more on this curious fact later). And since there are beautiful and powerful stories all through world legendry, and since stories need retelling from generation to generation, why not steal them? I'm certainly not the one to condemn the practice; parts of my first novel were lifted wholesale from the Norse mythos (Brisingamen, Freya's necklace, and episodes in the life of Odin). My version isn't a patch on the original, of course, but I think I did the gods of Asgard no harm, and they did my book some good. This sort of pilfering goes on all the time, and produces many pleasant works of art, though it does not lead to any truly new creations or cognitions.

There is a more self-conscious form of thievery which is both more destructive and more self-destructive. In many college English courses the words "myth" and "symbol" are given a tremendous charge of significance. You just ain't no good unless you can see a symbol hiding, like a scared gerbil, under every page. And in many creative writing courses the little beasts multiply, the place swarms with them. What does this Mean? What does that Symbolize? What is the Underlying Mythos? Kids come lurching out of such courses with a brain full of gerbils. And they sit down and write a lot of empty pomposity, under the impression that that's how Melville did it.*

Even when they begin to realize that art is not something produced for critics, but for other human beings, some of them retain the overintellectualizing bent. They still do not realize that a symbol is not a sign of something known, but an indicator of something not known and not expressible otherwise than symbolically. They mistake symbol (living meaning) for allegory (dead equivalence). So they use mythology in an arrogant fashion, rationalizing it, condescending to it. They take plots and characters from it, not in the healthily furtive fashion of the literary sneak thief, but in a posturing, showy way. Such use of myth does real disservice to the original, by trivializing it, and no good at all to the story. The shallowness of its origin is often betrayed either by an elaborate vocabulary and

---

* Note (1989). In fact, part of the time, he did. A good deal of Melville is pompously self-conscious.

ostentatiously cryptic style, or by a kind of jocose, chatty discomfort in the tone. Watch me up here on Olympus, you peasants, being fresh with Aphrodite. Look at me juggling symbols, folks! We sophisticates, we know how to handle these old archetypes.

But Zeus always gets 'em. ZAP!

So far I have been talking as if all mythologies the writer might use were dead—that is, not believed in with some degree of emotion, other than aesthetic appreciation, by the writer and his community. Of course, this is far from being the case. It's easy to get fresh with Aphrodite. Who believes in some old Greek goddess, anyhow? But there are living mythologies, after all. Consider the Virgin Mary; or the State.

For an example of the use in science fiction of a living religious mythos one may turn to the work of Cordwainer Smith, whose Christian beliefs are evident, I think, all through his work, in such motifs as the savior, the martyr, rebirth, the "underpeople." Whether or not one is a Christian, one may admire wholeheartedly the strength and passion given the works by the author's living belief. In general, however, I think the critics' search for Christian themes in science fiction is sterile and misleading. For the majority of science fiction writers, the themes of Christianity are dead signs, not living symbols, and those who use them do so all too often in order to get an easy emotional charge without working for it. They take a free ride on the crucifix, just as many now cash in cynically on the current occultist fad. The difference between this sort of thing and the genuine, naïve mysticism of an Arthur Clarke, struggling to express his own, living symbol of rebirth, is all the difference in the world.

Beyond and beneath the great living mythologies of religion and power there is another region into which science fiction enters.

I would call it the area of Submyth: by which I mean those images, figures, and motifs which have no religious resonance and no intellectual or aesthetic value, but which are vigorously alive and powerful, so that they cannot be dismissed as mere stereotypes. They are shared by all of us; they are genuinely collective. Superman is a submyth. His father was Nietzsche and his mother was a funny book, and he is alive and well in the mind of every ten-year-old—and millions of others. Other science-fictional submyths are the blond heroes of sword and sorcery, with their unusual weapons; insane or self-deifying computers; mad scientists; benevolent dictators; detectives who find out who done it; capitalists who buy and sell galaxies; brave starship captains and/or troopers; evil aliens; good aliens; and every pointy-breasted brainless young woman who was ever rescued from monsters, lectured to, patronized or, in recent years, raped, by one of the aforementioned heroes.

It hurts to call these creatures mythological. It is a noble word, and they are so grotty. But they are alive, in books, magazines, pictures, movies, advertising, and our own minds. Their roots are the roots of myth, are in our unconscious—that vast dim region of the psyche and perhaps beyond the psyche, which Jung called "collective" because it is similar in all of us, just as our bodies are basically similar. The vigor comes from there, and so they cannot be dismissed as unimportant. Not when they can help motivate a world movement such as fascism!—But neither can they furnish materials useful to art. They have no element of the true myth except its emotive, irrational "thereness." Writers who deliberately submit to them have forfeited the right to call their work science fiction; they're just popcultists cashing in.

True myth may serve for thousands of years as an inexhaustible source of intellectual speculation, religious joy, ethical inquiry, and artistic renewal. The real mystery is not destroyed by reason. The fake one is. You look at it and it vanishes. You look at the Blond Hero—really look—and he turns into a gerbil. But you look at Apollo, and he looks back at you.

The poet Rilke looked at a statue of Apollo about fifty years ago, and Apollo spoke to him. "You must change your life," he said.

When the genuine myth rises into consciousness, that is always its message. You must change your life.

The way of art, after all, is neither to cut adrift from the emotions, the senses, the body, etc., and sail off into the void of pure meaning, nor to blind the mind's eye and wallow in irrational, amoral meaninglessness—but to keep open the tenuous, difficult, essential connections between the two extremes. To connect. To connect the idea with value, sensation with intuition, cortex with cerebellum.

The true myth is precisely one of these connections.

Like all artists, we science fiction writers are trying to make and use such a connection or bridge between the conscious and the unconscious—so that our readers can make the journey, too. If the only tool we use is the intellect, we will produce only lifeless copies or parodies of the archetypes that live in our own deeper mind and in the great works of art and mythology. If we abandon intellect, we're likely to submerge our own personality and talent in a stew of mindless submyths, themselves coarse, feeble parodies of their archetypal origins. The only way to the truly collective, to the image that is alive and meaningful in all of us, seems to be through the truly personal. Not the impersonality of pure reason; not the impersonality of "the masses"; but the irreducibly personal—the self. To reach the others, artists go into the self. Using reason, they deliberately enter the irrational. The farther they go into the self, the closer they come to the other.

If this seems a paradox it is only because our culture overvalues abstraction and extraversion. Pain, for instance, can work the same way. Nothing is more personal, more unshareable, than pain; the worst thing about suffering is that you suffer alone. Yet those who have not suffered, or will not admit that they suffer, are those who are cut off in cold isolation from their fellow men. Pain, the loneliest experience, gives rise to sympathy, to love: the bridge between self and other, the means of communion. So with art. The artist who goes inward most deeply—and it is a painful journey—is the artist who touches us most closely, speaks to us most clearly.

Of all the great psychologists, Jung best explains this process, by stressing the existence, not of an isolated "id," but a "collective unconscious." He reminds us that the region of the mind/body that lies beyond the narrow, brightly lit domain of consciousness is very much the same in all of us. This does not imply a devaluing of consciousness or of reason. The achievement of individual consciousness, which Jung calls "differentiation," is to him a great achievement, civilization's highest achievement, the hope of our future. But the tree grows only from deep roots.

So it would seem that true myth arises only in the process of connecting the conscious and the unconscious realms. I won't find a living archetype in my bookcase or my television set. I will find it only in myself: in that core of individuality lying in the heart of the common darkness. Only the individual can get up and go to the window, and draw back the curtains, and look out into the dark.

Sometimes it takes considerable courage to do that. When you open curtains you don't know what may be out there in the night. Maybe starlight; maybe dragons; maybe the secret police. Maybe the grace of God; maybe the horror of death. They're all there. For all of us.

Writers who draw not upon the words and thoughts of others but upon their own thoughts and their own deep being will inevitably hit upon common material. The more original the work, the more imperiously *recognizable* it will be. "Yes, of course!" say I, the reader recognizing myself, my dreams, my nightmares. The characters, figures, images, motifs, plots, events of the story may be obvious parallels, even seemingly reproductions, of the material of myth and legend. There will be—openly in fantasy, covertly in naturalism—dragons, heroes, quests, objects of power, voyages at night and under sea, and so forth. In narrative, as in painting, certain familiar patterns will become visible.

This again is no paradox, if Jung is right, and we all have the same kind of dragons in our psyche, just as we all have the same kind of heart and lungs in our body. It does imply that nobody can invent an archetype by taking thought, any more than we can invent a new organ in our body. But this is no loss; rather a gain. It means that we can communicate, that alienation isn't the final human condition, since there is a vast common ground on which we can meet, not only rationally, but aesthetically, intuitively, emotionally.

A dragon, not a dragon cleverly copied or mass-produced, but a creature of evil who crawls up, threatening and inexplicable, out of the artist's own unconscious, is alive: terribly alive. It frightens little children, and the artist, and the rest of us. It frightens us because it is part of us, and the artist forces us to admit it. We have met the enemy, as Pogo remarked, and he is us.

"What do you mean? There aren't any dragons in my living room, dragons are extinct, dragons aren't real . . ."

"Look out the window . . . Look into the mirror . . ."

The artist who works from the center of being will find

archetypal images and release them into consciousness. The first science fiction writer to do so was Mary Shelley. She let Frankenstein's monster loose. Nobody has been able to shut him out again, either. There he is, sitting in the corner of our lovely modern glass and plastic living room, right on the tubular steel contour chair, big as life and twice as ugly. Edgar Rice Burroughs did it, though with infinitely less power and originality—Tarzan is a true myth-figure, though not a particularly relevant one to modern ethical/emotional dilemmas, as Frankenstein's monster is. Čapek did it, largely by *naming* something (a very important aspect of archetypizing): "Robots," he called them. They have walked among us ever since. Tolkien did it; he found a ring, a ring which we keep trying to lose . . .

Scholars can have great fun, and can strengthen the effect of such figures, by showing their relationship to other manifestations of the archetype in myth, legend, dogma and art.[2] These linkages can be highly illuminating. Frankenstein's monster is related to the Golem; to Jesus; to Prometheus. Tarzan is a direct descendant of the Wolfchild/Noble Savage on one side, and every child's fantasy of the Orphan-of-High-Estate on the other. The robot may be seen as the modern ego's fear of the body, after the crippling division of "mind" and "body," "ghost" and "machine," enforced by post-Renaissance mechanistic thought. In *The Time Machine* there is one of the great visions of the End, an archetype of eschatology comparable to any religious vision of the day of judgment. In "Nightfall" there is the fundamental opposition of dark and light, playing on the fear of darkness that we share with our cousins the great apes. Through Philip K. Dick's work one can follow an exploration of the ancient themes of identity and alienation, and the sense of the fragmentation of the ego. In Stanislaw Lem's works there seems to be a similarly complex and subtle exploration of the archetypal Other, the alien.

Such myths, symbols, images do not disappear under the scrutiny of the intellect, nor does an ethical, or aesthetic, or even religious examination of them make them shrink and vanish. On the contrary: the more you look, the more there they are. And the more you think, the more they mean.

On this level, science fiction deserves the title of a modern mythology.

Most science fiction doesn't, of course, and never will. There are never very many artists around. No doubt we'll continue most of the time to get rewarmed leftovers from Babylon and Northrop Frye served up by earnest snobs, and hordes of brawny Gerbilmen ground out by hacks. But there will be mythmakers, too. Even now—who knows?—the next Mary Shelley may be lying quietly in her tower-top room, just waiting for a thunderstorm.

NOTES

1. This schema is reproduced in Freudian psychology, where the myth or symbol is considered to be a disguise, and the raising into consciousness of unconscious contents leads to a progressive emptying or draining dry of the unconscious; in contrast to the schema followed by Jung and others, where the emphasis is on the irreducibility of symbol, and the compensatory, mutually creative relationship between the conscious and the unconscious.

2. Note that a manifestation is all we ever get; the archetype itself is beyond the reach of reason, art, or even madness. It is not a thing, an object, but is rather, Jung guessed, a psychic modality, a function comparable to a function/limitation such as the visual range of the human eye, which, by limiting our perception of electromagnetic vibrations to a certain range, enables us to see. The archetypes "do not in any sense represent things as they are in themselves, but rather the forms in which things can be perceived and conceived." They are "*a priori* structural forms of the stuff of consciousness" (Jung, *Memories, Dreams, Reflections*, 347).

FROM ELFLAND TO POUGHKEEPSIE

(1973)

Elfland is what Lord Dunsany called the place. It is also known as Middle Earth, and Prydain, and the Forest of Broceliande, and Once Upon a Time; and by many other names.

Let us consider Elfland as a great national park, a vast and beautiful place where a person goes alone on foot, to get in touch with reality in a special, private, profound fashion. But what happens when it is considered merely as a place to "get away to"?

Well, you know what has happened to Yosemite. Everybody comes, not with an ax and a box of matches, but in a trailer with a motorbike on the back and a motorboat on top and a butane stove, five aluminum folding chairs, and a transistor radio on the inside. They arrive totally encapsulated in a secondhand reality. And then they move on to Yellowstone, and it's just the same there, all trailers and transistors. They go from park to park, but they never really go anywhere; except when one of them who thinks that even the wildlife isn't real gets chewed up by a genuine, firsthand bear.

The same sort of thing seems to be happening in Elfland, lately. A great many people want to go there, without knowing what it is they're really looking for, driven by a vague hunger for something real. With the intention or under the pretense of obliging them, certain writers of fantasy are building six-lane highways and trailer parks with drive-in movies, so that the tourists can feel at home just as if they were back in Poughkeepsie.*

But the point about Elfland is that you are not at home there. It's not Poughkeepsie. It's different.

What is fantasy? On one level, of course, it is a game: a pure pretense with no ulterior motive whatever. It is one child saying to another child, "Let's be dragons," and then they're dragons for an hour or two. It is escapism of the most admirable kind—the game played for the game's sake.

On another level, it is still a game, but a game played for very high stakes. Seen thus, as art, not spontaneous play, its affinity is not with daydream, but with dream. It is a different approach to reality, an alternative technique for apprehending and coping with existence. It is not anti-rational, but para-rational; not realistic, but surrealistic, superrealistic, a heightening of reality. In Freud's terminology, it employs primary, not secondary process thinking. It employs archetypes, which, as Jung warned us, are dangerous things. Dragons are more dangerous, and a good deal commoner, than bears. Fantasy is nearer to poetry, to mysticism, and to insanity than naturalistic fiction is. It is a real wilderness, and those who go there should not feel too safe. And their guides, the writers of fantasy, should take their responsibilities seriously.

----

* Note for the British edition (1989). I don't know where "Poughkeepsie" is, in England. Reading, perhaps, or Surbiton?

After all these metaphors and generalities, let us get down to some examples; let us read a little fantasy.

This is much easier to do than it used to be, thanks very largely to one man, Lin Carter of Ballantine Books, whose Adult Fantasy Series of new publications and reprints of old ones has saved us all from a lifetime of pawing through the shelves of used bookstores somewhere behind several dusty cartons between "Occult" and "Children's" in hopes of finding, perhaps, the battered and half-mythical odd volume of Dunsany. In gratitude to Mr. Carter for the many splendid books, both new and old, in his series, I will read anything his firm sends me; and last year when they sent me a new one, I settled down with a pleasant sense of confidence to read it. Here is a little excerpt from what I read. The persons talking are a duke of the blood royal of a mythical Keltic kingdom, and a warrior-magician—great Lords of Elfland, both of them.

> "Whether or not they succeed in the end will depend largely on Kelson's personal ability to manipulate the voting."
>
> "Can he?" Morgan asked as the two clattered down a half flight of stairs and into the garden.
>
> "I don't know, Alaric," Nigel replied. "He's good—damned good—but I just don't know. Besides, you saw the key Council lords. With Ralson dead and Bran Coris practically making open accusations—well, it doesn't look good."
>
> "I could have told you that at Cardosa."[1]

At this point I was interrupted (perhaps by a person from Porlock, I don't remember), and the next time I sat down I happened to pick up a different kind of novel, a real Now novel, naturalistic, politically conscious, relevant, set in Washington, D.C. Here is a sample of a conversation from it, between a senator and a lobbyist for pollution control.

> "Whether or not they succeed in the end will depend largely on Kelson's personal ability to manipulate the voting."
>
> "Can he?" Morgan asked as the two clattered down a half flight of stairs and into the White House garden.
>
> "I don't know, Alaric," Nigel replied. "He's good—damned good—but I just don't know. Besides, you saw the key committee chairmen. With Ralson dead and Brian Corliss practically making open accusations—well, it doesn't look good."
>
> "I could have told you that at Poughkeepsie."

Now, I submit that something has gone wrong. The book from which I first quoted is not fantasy, for all its equipment of heroes and wizards. If it was fantasy, I couldn't have pulled that dirty trick on it by changing four words. You can't clip Pegasus's wings that easily—not if he has wings.

Before I go further I want to apologize to the author of the passage for making a horrible example of her. There are infinitely worse examples I could have used; I chose this one because in this book something good has gone wrong—something real has been falsified. There would be no use at all in talking about what is generally passed off as "heroic fantasy," all the endless Barbarians, with names like Barp and Klod, and the Tarnsmen and the Klansmen and all the rest of them—there would be nothing whatever to say. (Not in terms of art, that is; in terms of ethics, racism, sexism, and politics there would be a great deal to say.)*

---

* Note (1989). I don't find it as easy as I did in 1973 to separate "art" from "ethics, racism, sexism, and politics"—a dangerous, usually illusory, separation.

What is it, then, that I believe has gone wrong in the book and the passage quoted from it? I think it is the *style*. Presently I'll try to explain why I think so. It will be convenient, however, to have other examples at hand. The first passage was dialogue, and style in a novel is often particularly visible in dialogue; so here are some bits of conversations from other parts of Elfland. The books from which they were taken were all written in this century, and all the speakers are wizards, warriors, or Lords of Elfland, as in the first selection. The books were chosen carefully, of course, but the passages were picked at random; I just looked for a page where two or three suitably noble types were chatting.

> Now spake Spitfire saying, "Read forth to us, I pray thee, the book of Gro; for my soul is afire to set forth on this faring."
>
> "'Tis writ somewhat crabbedly," said Brandoch Daha, "and most damnably long. I spent half last night a-searching on't, and 'tis most apparent no other way lieth to these mountains save by the Moruna, and across the Moruna is (if Gro say true) but one way . . ."
>
> "If he say true?" said Spitfire. "He is a turncoat and a renegado. Wherefore not therefore a liar?"[2]

> "Detestable to me, truly, is loathsome hunger; abominable an insufficiency of food upon a journey. Mournful, I declare to you, is such a fate as this, to one of my lineage and nurture!"
>
> "Well, well," said Dienw'r Anffodion, with the bitter hunger awaking in him again, "common with me is knowledge of famine. Take you the whole of the food, if you will."
>
> "Yes," said Goreu. "That will be better."[3]

"Who can tell?" said Aragorn. "But we will put it to the test one day."

"May the day not be too delayed," said Boromir. "For though I do not ask for aid, we need it. It would comfort us to know that others fought also with all the means that they have."

"Then be comforted," said Elrond.[4]

Now, all those speakers speak English differently; but they all have the genuine Elfland accent. You could not pull the trick on them that I pulled on Morgan and Nigel—not unless you changed half the words in every sentence. You could not possibly mistake them for anyone on Capitol Hill.

In the first selection they are a little crazy, and in the second one they are not only crazy but Welsh—and yet they speak with power, with a wild dignity. All of them are heroic, eloquent, passionate. It may be the passion that is most important. Nothing is really going on in those first two passages: in one case they're reading a book, in the other they're dividing a cold leg of rabbit. But with what importance they invest these trivial acts, what emotion, what vitality!

In the third passage, the speakers are quieter, and use a less extraordinary English, or rather an English extraordinary for its simple timelessness. Such language is rare on Capitol Hill, but it has occurred there. It has sobriety, wit, and force. It is the language of men* of character.

Speech expresses character. It does so whether the speaker or

---

* Note (1989). All the heroes in the fantasies I quoted from, even the one written by a woman, are men.

the author knows it or not. (Presidential speechwriters know it very well.) When I hear a man say, "I could have told you that at Cardosa," or at Poughkeepsie, or wherever, I think I know something about that man. He is the kind who says, "I told you so."

Nobody who says "I told you so" has ever been, or will ever be, a hero.

The Lords of Elfland are true lords, the only true lords, the kind that do not exist on this Earth: their lordship is the outward sign or symbol of real inward greatness. And greatness of soul shows when man speaks. At least, it does in books. In life we expect lapses. In naturalistic fiction, too, we expect lapses, and laugh at an "overheroic" hero. But in fantasy, which, instead of imitating the perceived confusion and complexity of existence, tries to hint at an order and clarity underlying existence—in fantasy, we need not compromise. Every word spoken is meaningful, though the meaning may be subtle. For example, in the second passage, the fellow called Goreu is moaning and complaining and shamelessly conning poor Dienw'r out of the only thing he has to eat. And yet you feel that anybody who can talk like that isn't a mean-spirited man. He would never say, "I told you so." In fact, he's not a man at all, he is Gwydion son of Don in disguise, and he has a good reason for his tricks, a magnanimous reason. On the other hand, in the third quotation, the very slight whine in Boromir's tone is significant also. Boromir is a noble-hearted person, but there is a tragic flaw in his character and the flaw is envy.

I picked for comparison three master stylists: E. R. Eddison, Kenneth Morris, and J. R. R. Tolkien; which may seem unfair to any other authors mentioned. But I do not think it is unfair. In art, the best is the standard. When you hear a new violinist, you do not compare her to the kid next door; you compare her to Stern and

Heifetz. If she falls short, you will not blame her for it, but you will know what she falls short of. And if she is a real violinist, she knows it, too. In art, "good enough" is not good enough.

Another reason for picking those three is that they exemplify styles which are likely to be imitated by beginning writers of fantasy. There is a great deal of quite open influencing and imitating going on among the writers of fantasy. I incline to think that this is a very healthy situation. It is one in which most vigorous arts find themselves. Take for example music in the eighteenth century, when Handel and Haydn and Mozart and the rest of them were borrowing tunes and tricks and techniques from one another and building up the great edifice of music like a lot of masons at work on one cathedral; well, we may yet have a great edifice of fantasy. But you can't imitate what somebody does until you've learned how they do it.

The most imitated, and the most inimitable, writer of fantasy is probably Lord Dunsany. I did not include a passage of conversation from Dunsany because I could not find a suitable one. Genuine give-and-take conversations are quite rare in his intensely mannered, intensely poetic narratives, and when they occur they tend to be very brief, as they do in the Bible. The King James Bible is indubitably one of the profoundest formative influences on Dunsany's prose; another, I suspect, is Irish daily speech. Those two influences alone, not to mention his own gifts of a delicate ear for speech rhythms and a brilliantly exact imagination, remove him from the reach of any would-be imitator or emulator who is not an Irish peer brought up from the cradle on the grand sonorities of Genesis and Ecclesiastes. Dunsany mined a narrow vein, but it was all pure ore, and all his own. I have never seen any imitation Dunsany that consisted of anything beyond a lot of elaborate made-up names, some vague descriptions of gorgeous cities and unmentionable dooms, and a great many sentences beginning with "And."

Dunsany is indeed the First Terrible Fate that Awaiteth Unwary Beginners in Fantasy. But if they avoid him, there are others—many others. One of these is archaicizing, the archaic manner, which Dunsany and other master fantasists use so effortlessly. It is a trap into which almost all very young fantasy writers walk. I know; I did myself. They know instinctively that what is wanted in fantasy is a *distancing from the ordinary.* They see it done beautifully in old books, such as Malory's *Morte d'Arthur*, and in new books the style of which is grounded on the old books, and they think, "Aha! I will do it, too." But alas, it is one of those things, like bicycling and computer programming, that you have got to know how to do before you do it.

"Aha!" says our novice. "You have to use verbs with thee and thou." So she does. But she doesn't know how. There are very few Americans now alive who know how to use a verb in the second person singular. The general assumption is that you add *-est* and you're there. I remember Debbie Reynolds telling Eddie Fisher—do you remember Debbie Reynolds and Eddie Fisher?—"Whithersoever thou goest there also I goest." Fake feeling; fake grammar.

Then our novice tries to use the subjunctive. All the was's turn into were's, and leap out at the reader snarling. And the Quakers have got us all fouled up about which really is the nominative form of Thou. Is it Thee, or isn't it? And then there's the She-To-Whom Trap. "I shall give it to she to whom my love is given!"—"Him whom this sword smites shall surely die!"—Give it to she? Him shall die? It sounds like Tonto talking to the Lone Ranger. This is distancing with a vengeance. But we aren't through yet, no, we haven't had the fancy words. Eldritch. Tenebrous. Smaragds and chalcedony.

Mayhap. It can't be maybe, it can't be perhaps; it has to be mayhap, unless it's perchance. And then comes the final test, the infallible touchstone of the seventh-rate: Ichor. You know ichor. It oozes out of several tentacles, and beslimes tessellated pavements, and bespatters bejeweled courtiers, and bores the bejesus out of everybody.

The archaic manner is indeed a perfect distancer, but you have to do it perfectly. It's a high wire: one slip spoils all. The man who did it perfectly was, of course, Eddison. He really did write Elizabethan prose in the 1930s. His style is totally artificial, but it is never faked. If you love language for its own sake he is irresistible. Many, with reason, find him somewhat crabbed and most damnably long; but he is the real thing, and just to reaffirm that strange, remote reality, I am placing a longer quotation from him here. This is from *The Worm Ouroboros.* A dead king is being carried, in secrecy, at night, down to the beach.

> The lords of Witchland took their weapons and the men-at-arms bare the goods, and the King went in the midst on his bier of spear-shafts. So went they picking their way in the moonless night round the palace and down the winding path that led to the bed of the combe, and so by the stream westward toward the sea. Here they deemed it safe to light a torch to show them the way. Desolate and bleak showed the sides of the combe in the windblown flare; and the flare was thrown back from the jewels of the royal crown of Witchland, and from the armoured buskins on the King's feet showing stark with toes pointing upward from below his bearskin mantle, and from the armour and the weapons of them that bare him and walked beside him, and from the black cold surface of the little river hurrying for ever over its

bed of boulders to the sea. The path was rugged and stony,
and they fared slowly, lest they should stumble and drop the
King.[5]

That prose, in spite of or because of its archaisms, is good prose:
exact, clear, powerful. Visually it is precise and vivid; musically—
that is, in the sound of the words, the movement of the syntax, and
the rhythm of the sentences—it is subtle and very strong. Nothing
in it is faked or blurred; it is all seen, heard, felt. That style was his
true style, his own voice; that was how Eddison, an artist, spoke.

The second of our three "conversation pieces" is from *Book of
the Three Dragons*, by Kenneth Morris. This book one must still
seek on the dusty shelves behind the cartons, probably in the section marked "Children's"—at least that's where I found it—for Mr.
Carter has not yet reprinted more than a fragment of it, and if it
ever had a day of fame it was before our time. I use it here partly
in hopes of arousing interest in the book, for I think many people
would enjoy it. It is a singularly fine example of the re-creation of
a work magnificent in its own right (*The Mabinogion*)—a literary
event rather rare except in fantasy, where its frequency is perhaps
proof, if one were needed, of the ever-renewed vitality of myth. But
Morris is also useful to my purpose because he has a strong sense of
humor; and humor in fantasy is both a lure and a pitfall to imita-
tors. Dunsany is often ironic, but he does not mix simple humor
with the heroic tone. Eddison sometimes did, but I think Morris
and James Branch Cabell were the masters of the comic-heroic. One
does not smile wryly, reading them; one laughs. They achieve their
comedy essentially by their style—by an eloquence, a fertility and
felicity of invention that is simply overwhelming. They are outrageous, and they know exactly what they're doing.

Fritz Leiber and Roger Zelazny have both written in the comic-heroic vein, but their technique is different: they alternate the two styles. When humor is intended the characters talk colloquial American English, or even slang, and at earnest moments they revert to old formal usages. Readers indifferent to language do not mind this, but for others the strain is too great. I am one of these latter. I am jerked back and forth between Elfland and Poughkeepsie; the characters lose coherence in my mind, and I lose confidence in them. It is strange, because both Leiber and Zelazny are skillful and highly imaginative writers, and it is perfectly clear that Leiber, profoundly acquainted with Shakespeare and practiced in a very broad range of techniques, could maintain any tone with eloquence and grace. Sometimes I wonder if these two writers underestimate their own talents, if they lack confidence in themselves. Or it may be that, since fantasy is seldom taken seriously at this particular era in this country, they are afraid to take it seriously. They don't want to be caught believing in their own creations, getting all worked up about imaginary things; and so their humor becomes self-mocking, self-destructive. Their gods and heroes keep turning aside to look out of the book at you and whisper, "See, we're really just plain folks."

Now, Cabell never does that. He mocks everything: not only his own fantasy, but our reality. He doesn't believe in his dreamworld, but he doesn't believe in us, either. His tone is perfectly consistent: elegant, arrogant, ironic. Sometimes I enjoy it and sometimes it makes me want to scream, but it is admirable. Cabell knew what he wanted to do and he did it, and the marketplace be damned.

Evangeline Walton, whose books, like Kenneth Morris's, are reworkings of *The Mabinogion*, has achieved her own beautifully idiosyncratic blend of humor and heroism; there is no doubt that the Celtic mythos lends itself to such a purpose. And while we are on the subject of humor, Jack Vance must be mentioned, though his humor is so quiet you can miss it if you blink. Indeed the whole tone of his writing is so modest that sometimes I wonder whether, like Leiber and Zelazny, he fails to realize how very good a writer he is. If so, it is probably a result of the patronizing attitude American culture affects toward works of pure imagination. Vance, however, never compromises with the patronizing and ignorant. He never lets his creation down in order to make a joke and he never shows a tin ear for tone. The conversation of his characters is aloof and restrained, very like his own narrative prose; an unusual kind of English, but clear, graceful, and precisely suited to Vance's extraordinary imagination. It is an achieved style. And it contains no archaisms at all.

After all, archaisms are not essential. You don't have to know how to use the subjunctive in order to be a wizard. You don't have to talk like Henry the Fifth to be a hero.*

Caution, however, is needed. Great caution. Consider: Did Henry the Fifth of England really talk like Shakespeare's Henry? Did the real Achilles use hexameters? Would the real Beowulf please stand up and alliterate? We are not discussing history, but heroic fantasy. We are discussing a modern descendant of the epic.

Most epics are in straightforward language, whether prose or verse. They retain the directness of their oral forebears. Homer's metaphors may be extended, but they are neither static nor ornate. *The Song of Roland* has four thousand lines, containing one simile and no metaphors. *The Mabinogion* and the Norse sagas are as plain-spoken as they could well be. Clarity and simplicity are permanent

---

*   Note (1989). I'm more certain than ever of the second statement, but I think the preceding one is wrong. Wizards operate in the subjunctive mode.

virtues in a narrative. Nothing highfalutin is needed. A plain language is the noblest of all.

It is also the most difficult.

Tolkien writes a plain, clear English. Its outstanding virtue is its flexibility, its variety. It ranges easily from the commonplace to the stately, and can slide into metrical poetry, as in the Tom Bombadil episode, without the careless reader's even noticing. Tolkien's vocabulary is not striking; he has no ichor; everything is direct, concrete, and simple.

Now, the kind of writing I am attacking, the Poughkeepsie style of fantasy, is also written in a plain and apparently direct prose. Does that make it equal to Tolkien's? Alas, no. It is a fake plainness. It is not really simple, but flat. It is not really clear, but inexact. Its directness is specious. Its sensory cues—extremely important in imaginative writing—are vague and generalized; the rocks, the wind, the trees are not there, are not felt; the scenery is cardboard, or plastic. The tone as a whole is profoundly inappropriate to the subject.

To what then is it appropriate? To journalism. It is journalistic prose. In journalism, the suppression of the author's personality and sensibility is deliberate. The goal is an impression of objectivity. The whole thing is meant to be written fast and read faster. This technique is right, for a newspaper. It is wrong for a novel, and dead wrong for a fantasy. A language intended to express the immediate and the trivial is applied to the remote and the elemental. The result, of course, is a mess.

Why do we seem to be achieving just that result so often, these days? Well, undoubtedly avarice is one of the reasons. Fantasy is selling well, so let's all grind out a fantasy. The Old Baloney Factory. And sheer ineptness enters in. But in many cases neither greed nor lack of skill seems to be involved, and in such cases I suspect a failure to take the job seriously: a refusal to admit what you're in for when you set off with only an ax and a box of matches into Elfland.

A fantasy is a journey. It is a journey into the subconscious mind, just as psychoanalysis is. Like psychoanalysis, it can be dangerous; and *it will change you.*

The general assumption is that, if there are dragons or hippogriffs in a book, or if it takes place in a vaguely Keltic or Near Eastern medieval setting, or if magic is done in it, then it's a fantasy. This is a mistake.

A writer who doesn't know the West may deploy acres of sagebrush and rimrock without achieving a real Western. A writer may fumble about with spaceships and strains of mutant bacteria and never be anywhere near real science fiction. A writer may even write a five-hundred-page novel about Sigmund Freud which has absolutely nothing to do with Sigmund Freud; it has been done; it was done just a couple of years ago. And in the same way, a writer may use all the trappings of fantasy without ever actually imagining anything.

My argument is that this failure, this fakery, is visible instantly in the style.

Many readers, many critics, and most editors speak of style as if it were an ingredient of a book, like the sugar in a cake, or something added onto the book, like the frosting on the cake. The style, of course, *is* the book. If you remove the cake, all you have left is a recipe. If you remove the style, all you have left is a synopsis of the plot.

This is partly true of history; largely true of fiction; and absolutely true of fantasy.

In saying that the style is the book, I speak from the reader's point of view. From the writer's point of view, the style is the writer.

Style isn't just how you use English when you write. It isn't a mannerism or an affectation (though it may be mannered or affected). It isn't something you can do without, though that is what people assume when they announce that they intend to write something "like it is." You can't do without it. There is no "is," without it. Style is how you as a writer see and speak. It is how you see: your vision, your understanding of the world, your voice.

This is not to say that style cannot be learned and perfected, or that it cannot be borrowed and imitated. We learn to see and speak, as children, primarily by imitation. The artist is merely the one who goes on learning after growing up. A good learner will finally learn the hardest thing: how to see one's own world, how to speak one's own words.

Still, why is style of such fundamental significance in fantasy? Just because a writer gets the tone of a conversation a bit wrong, or describes things vaguely, or uses an anachronistic vocabulary or shoddy syntax, or begins going a bit heavy on the ichor before dinner—does that disqualify the book as a fantasy? Just because the style is weak and inappropriate—is that so important?

I think it is, because in fantasy there is nothing but the writer's vision of the world. There is no borrowed reality of history, or current events, or just plain folks at home in Peyton Place. There is no comfortable matrix of the commonplace to substitute for the imagination, to provide ready-made emotional response, and to disguise flaws and failures of creation. There is only a construct built in a void, with every joint and seam and nail exposed. To create what Tolkien calls "a secondary universe" is to make a new world. A world where no voice has ever spoken before; where the act of speech is the act of creation. The only voice that speaks there is the creator's voice. And every word counts.

This is an awful responsibility to undertake, when all the poor writer wants to do is play dragons, to entertain us all for a while. Nobody should be blamed for falling short of it. But all the same, if one undertakes a responsibility one should be aware of it. Elfland is not Poughkeepsie; the voice of the transistor is not heard in that land.

And lastly I believe that the reader has a responsibility; if we love the stuff we read, we have a duty toward it. That duty is to refuse to be fooled; to refuse to permit commercial exploitation of the holy ground of Myth; to reject shoddy work, and to save our praise for the real thing. Because when fantasy is the real thing, nothing, after all, is realer.

NOTES

1. Katherine Kurtz, *Deryni Rising* (New York: Ballantine Books, August 1970), 41.

2. E. R. Eddison, *The Worm Ouroboros* (New York: Ballantine Books, April 1967), 137.

3. Kenneth Morris, *Book of the Three Dragons*, Junior Literary Guild (New York: Longmans, Green and Company, 1930), 8. (This excerpt also contained in *Dragons, Elves and Heroes*, ed. Lin Carter [New York: Ballantine Books, October 1969], 59.)

4. J. R. R. Tolkien, *The Fellowship of the Ring* (New York: Ballantine Books, October 1965), 351.

5. Eddison, *The Worm Ouroboros*, 56–57.

AMERICAN SF AND
THE OTHER

(1975)

One of the great early socialists said that the status of women in a society is a pretty reliable index of the degree of civilization of that society. If this is true, then the very low status of women in SF should make us ponder about whether SF is civilized at all.

The women's movement has made most of us conscious of the fact that SF has either totally ignored women or presented them as squeaking dolls subject to instant rape by monsters—or old-maid scientists desexed by hypertrophy of the intellectual organs—or, at best, loyal little wives or mistresses of accomplished heroes. Male elitism has run rampant in SF. But is it only male elitism? Isn't the "subjection of women" in SF merely a symptom of a whole which is authoritarian, power-worshipping, and intensely parochial?

The question involved here is the question of The Other—the being who is different from yourself. This being can be different from you in its sex; or in its annual income; or in its way of speaking and dressing and doing things; or in the color of its skin, or the number of its legs and heads. In other words, there is the sexual Alien, and the social Alien, and the cultural Alien, and finally the racial Alien.

Well, how about the social Alien in SF? How about, in Marxist terms, "the proletariat"? Where are they in SF? Where are the poor, the people who work hard and go to bed hungry? Are they ever *persons*, in SF? No. They appear as vast anonymous masses fleeing from giant slime-globules from the Chicago sewers, or dying off by the billion from pollution or radiation, or as faceless armies being led to battle by generals and statesmen. In sword and sorcery they behave like the walk-on parts in a high school performance of *The Chocolate Prince*. Now and then there's a busty lass among them who is honored by the attentions of the Captain of the Supreme Terran Command, or in a spaceship crew there's a quaint old cook, with a Scots or Swedish accent, representing the Wisdom of the Common Folk.

The people, in SF, are not people. They are masses, existing for one purpose: to be led by their superiors.

From a social point of view most SF has been incredibly regressive and unimaginative. All those Galactic Empires, taken straight from the British Empire of 1880. All those planets—with 80 trillion miles between them!—conceived of as warring nation-states, or as colonies to be exploited, or to be nudged by the benevolent Imperium of Earth toward self-development—the White Man's Burden all over again. The Rotary Club on Alpha Centauri, that's the size of it.

What about the cultural and the racial Other? This is the Alien everybody recognizes as alien, supposed to be the special concern of SF. Well, in the old pulp SF, it's very simple. The only good alien is a dead alien—whether he is an Aldebaranian Mantis-Man or a German dentist. And this tradition still flourishes: witness Larry Niven's story "Inconstant Moon" (in *All the Myriad Ways*, 1971) which has a happy ending—consisting of the fact that America, including Los Angeles, was not hurt by a solar flare. Of course, a few million Europeans and Asians were fried, but that doesn't matter, it just makes the world a little safer for democracy, in fact. (It is interesting that the female character in the same story is quite brainless; her only function is to say Oh? and Ooooh! to the clever and resourceful hero.)

Then there's the other side of the same coin. If you hold a thing to be totally different from yourself, your fear of it may come out as hatred, or as awe—reverence. So we get all those wise and kindly beings who deign to rescue Earth from her sins and perils. The Alien ends up on a pedestal in a white nightgown and a virtuous smirk—exactly as the "good woman" did in the Victorian age.

In America, it seems to have been Stanley Weinbaum who invented the sympathetic alien, in "A Martian Odyssey." From then on, via people like Cyril Kornbluth, Ted Sturgeon, and Cordwainer Smith, SF began to inch its way out of simple racism. Robots—the alien intelligence—begin to behave nicely. With Smith, interestingly enough, the racial alien is combined with the social alien, in the "Underpeople," and they are allowed to have a revolution. As the aliens got more sympathetic, so did the heroes. They began to have emotions, as well as rayguns. Indeed they began to become almost human.

If you deny any affinity with another person or kind of person, if you declare it to be wholly different from yourself—as men have done to women, and class has done to class, and nation has done to nation—you may hate it or deify it; but in either case you have denied its spiritual equality and its human reality. You have made it into a thing, to which the only possible relationship is a power relationship. And thus you have fatally impoverished your own reality. You have, in fact, alienated yourself.

This tendency has been remarkably strong in American SF. The only social change presented by most SF has been toward authoritarianism, the domination of ignorant masses by a powerful elite—sometimes presented as a warning, but often quite complacently. Socialism is never considered as an alternative, and democracy is quite forgotten. Military virtues are taken as ethical ones. Wealth is assumed to be a righteous goal and a personal virtue. Competitive free-enterprise capitalism is the economic destiny of the entire Galaxy. In general, American SF has assumed a permanent hierarchy of superiors and inferiors, with rich, ambitious, aggressive males at the top, then a great gap, and then at the bottom the poor, the uneducated, the faceless masses, and all the women. The whole picture is, if I may say so, curiously, "un-American." It is a perfect baboon patriarchy, with the Alpha Male on top, being respectfully groomed, from time to time, by his inferiors.

Is this speculation? Is this imagination? Is this extrapolation? I call it brainless regressivism.

I think it's time SF writers—and their readers!—stopped daydreaming about a return to the age of Queen Victoria, and started thinking about the future. I would like to see the Baboon Ideal replaced by a little human idealism, and some serious consideration of such deeply radical, futuristic concepts as Liberty, Equality, and Fraternity. And remember that about 53 percent of the Brotherhood of Man is the Sisterhood of Woman.

SCIENCE FICTION AND
MRS. BROWN

(1975)

Just about fifty years ago, a woman named Virginia Woolf sat down in a carriage on the train going from Richmond to Waterloo, across from another woman, whose name we don't know. Mrs. Woolf didn't know either; she called her Mrs. Brown.

> She was one of those clean, threadbare old ladies whose extreme tidiness—everything buttoned, fastened, tied together, mended and brushed up—suggests more extreme poverty than rags and dirt. There was something pinched about her—a look of suffering, of apprehension, and, in addition, she was extremely small. Her feet, in their clean little boots, scarcely touched the floor. I felt that she had nobody to support her; that she had to make up her mind for herself; that, having been deserted, or left a widow, years ago, she had led an anxious, harried life, bringing up an only son, perhaps, who, as likely as not, was by this

time beginning to go to the bad. ("Mr. Bennett and Mrs. Brown")

Mrs. Woolf, who was an inveterate snooper, listened to the fragmentary conversation between the old lady and the man traveling with her—dull comments, snatches of incomprehensible business. Then all of a sudden Mrs. Brown said, "Can you tell me if an oak tree dies when the leaves have been eaten for two years in succession by caterpillars?" She spoke quite brightly, and rather precisely, in a cultivated, inquisitive voice. And while her companion was replying at length about plagues of insects at his brother's farm in Kent, Mrs. Brown took out a little white handkerchief and began to cry, very quietly, which annoyed the man. And then he got off at Clapham Junction; and then she got off at Waterloo. "I watched her disappear, carrying her bag, into the vast blazing station," says Mrs. Woolf. "She looked very small, very tenacious; at once very frail and very heroic. And I have never seen her again."

This Mrs. Brown, says Virginia Woolf, is the subject matter of the novel. She appears to the novelist, inside a railway carriage or inside the mind, and she says, Catch me if you can!

> I believe that all novels begin with an old lady in the corner opposite. I believe that all novels, that is to say, deal with character, and that it is to express character—not to preach doctrines, sing songs, or celebrate the glories of the British Empire, that the form of the novel, so clumsy, verbose, and undramatic, so rich, elastic, and alive, has been evolved . . . The great novelists have brought us to see whatever they wish us to see through some character. Otherwise they would not be novelists, but poets, historians, or pamphleteers. (Ibid.)

I accept this definition. I don't know if it is a critically fashionable one at the moment, and really don't care; it may seem banal to critics who love to talk about epiphanies, apocalypses, and other dim religious polysyllables, but to a novelist—this novelist, at any rate—it is simply, and profoundly, and in one syllable, true.

It was true in 1865, when Mrs. Brown was named Sarah Gamp; it was true in 1925, when Mrs. Brown was named Leopold Bloom; it is true in 1975. Mrs. Brown's name in England today is Rose, in Margaret Drabble's *The Needle's Eye*; Sylvia, in Angus Wilson's *Late Call*. She is Leni, in Heinrich Böll's *Group Portrait with Lady*. She has found her way to Australia, where her name is Voss, or Laura. She has never left Russia, where her name is of course Natasha or Anna or Raskolnikov, but also Yuri Zhivago, and Ivan Denisovich. Mrs. Brown turns up in India, in Africa, in South America, wherever novels are written. For as Mrs. Woolf said, "Mrs. Brown is eternal. Mrs. Brown is human nature. Mrs. Brown changes only on the surface; it is the novelists who get in and out. There she sits."

There she sits. And what I am curious about is this: Can the writer of science fiction sit down across from her? Is it possible? Have we any hope of catching Mrs. Brown, or are we trapped for good inside our great, gleaming spaceships hurtling out across the galaxy, antiseptic vehicles moving faster than the Richmond-Waterloo train, faster than the speed of light, ships capable of containing heroic captains in black and silver uniforms, and second officers with peculiar ears, and mad scientists with nubile daughters, ships capable of blasting other, inimical ships into smithereens with their apocalyptic, holocaustic rayguns, and of bringing loads of colonists from Earth to unknown worlds inhabited by incredibly sinister or beautiful forms of alien life, ships capable of anything, absolutely anything, except one thing: they cannot contain Mrs.

Brown. She simply doesn't fit. It's funny, the idea of Mrs. Brown in a spaceship. She's much too small to visit a Galactic empire or to orbit a neutron star. "Her feet, in their clean little boots, scarcely touched the floor." Or is that quite it? Could it be that Mrs. Brown is actually, in some way, too large for the spaceship? That she is, you might say, too *round* for it—so that when she steps into it, somehow it all shrinks to a shiny tin gadget, and the heroic captains turn to cardboard, and the sinister and beautiful aliens suddenly appear to be, most strangely, not alien at all, but mere elements of Mrs. Brown herself, lifelong and familiar, though startling, inhabitants of Mrs. Brown's unconscious mind?

So that's my first question: Can Mrs. Brown and science fiction ever sit down together in the same railway carriage, or spaceship? Or to put it plainly, Can a science fiction writer write a novel?

And then there will be a second question: Is it advisable, is it desirable, that this should come to pass? But I will come back to that later on.

I suspect that Virginia Woolf would have answered my first question with a characteristically subtle and apparently tentative but quietly decisive no. But in 1923 when she wrote the essay "Mr. Bennett and Mrs. Brown" she really could not have answered it, for there was very little science fiction available to her eye and judgment. H. G. Wells's scientific romances were a quarter-century old; he had put them behind him and was busy writing Utopias— Utopias of which Virginia Woolf said, very decisively indeed, "There are no Mrs. Browns in Utopia." And she was absolutely right.

But even as she said it, a book was being published in England, and another was being written in America; very strange books, written under strange circumstances, which prevented their receiving much critical notice or general attention. The one printed in

England was written by a Russian, Zamyatin, in Russian, though it was not, and has never been, published in Russia. It has existed for fifty years only in foreign editions and in translation—in exile. Its author died in exile. The pattern is not wholly unfamiliar now. As for the other book, it was not written for publication at all, and was published only after the death of the author, Austin Tappan Wright, in 1942.

A quite good simple test to detect the presence or absence of Mrs. Brown in a work of fiction is this: A month or so after reading the book, can you remember her name? It's silly, but it works pretty well. For instance, almost anybody who reads *Pride and Prejudice* will remember the names Elizabeth and Darcy, probably for very much longer than a month. But anyone who has read one of Mr. Norman Mailer's works of fiction need not apologize if he can't remember a single name from it—except one, of course: that of Norman Mailer. Because Mr. Mailer's books aren't about Mrs. Brown, they're about Mr. Mailer. He is a writer, but not a novelist. You see, it does work, roughly. But the first use I want to make of it on science fiction is an acid test, and I admit I failed it. I could remember only two of the three main characters' names. The women are O-90 and I-330; and there's that wonderful minor character named S-4711; but what's the name of the narrator, the central character? Oh, damn. I had to look at my copy of the book. D-503, of course, that's it. That's him. I will never forget him, poor soul; but I did forget his number. I plead the fact that I sometimes forget the telephone number we have had for sixteen years. I am very poor at mathematics. But I have sat facing D-503, not in a railway carriage to be sure, but in a great glass-walled, glass-floored, glass-roofed, super-Utopian building; have suffered with him; escaped with him; been recaptured and dragged back to Utopia, and lobotomized, with him; and I will not forget it. Nor the book's name, *We*, nor its author's name, Yevgeny Zamyatin, the author of the first science fiction novel.

We is a dystopia which contains a hidden or implied Utopia; a subtle, brilliant, and powerful book; emotionally stunning, and technically, in its use of the metaphorical range of science fiction, still far in advance of most books written since. Austin Tappan Wright's novel *Islandia* is quite another kettle of fish. It is old-fashioned. It does not look forward; neither does it look back. It looks sideways. It does not offer a Utopia, but merely an alternative. And the alternative seems, on the surface of it, an escapist one, a mere daydream. A lifelong daydream. A book written by a successful lawyer, secretly, for his private solace and delight; a child's imaginary country, maps and all, carried on for thirty years, a huge manuscript, whole volumes on the geology of the continent of Islandia, its history, its institutions . . . And also a story. A narrative, with characters. The author's daughter extracted the story, Knopf published it, and a few people found it. And since then there have always been a few people who find it, and who treasure it. It is not a great book perhaps, but a singularly durable one, and a durably singular one. There is nothing else in all literature like *Islandia*. It is a lifework; Wright put himself into it totally. It is a genuinely alternative society, worked out thoroughly, pragmatically, and humanely. And it is a novel. It is full of real people. There is plenty of room in Islandia for Mrs. Brown. That, in fact, is the point of it. I think that Wright saw a world, his America, his century, becoming psychotic, depersonalized, unlivable, and so he created a nonexistent continent, geology and weather and rivers and cities and houses and weaving looms and fireplaces and politicians and farmers and housewives and manners and misunderstandings and love affairs and all, for human beings to inhabit. And thus he rendered questionable Virginia Woolf's statement "There are no Mrs. Browns in Utopia." I think it possible she might have been quite pleased to know it.

But meanwhile, while Austin Tappan Wright is scribbling happily in his study, and Zamyatin is silent in exile in Paris, the 1930s are upon us, and science fiction is getting underway. The first rockets leave the launching pad. Decades of thrilling adventures ensue. Evil Venusians are thwarted. Scientists' nubile daughters are rescued, squeaking. Galactic empires rise and fall. Planets are bought and sold. Robots receive the Tablets of the Three Laws from Mount Sinai. Marvelous hardware is invented. Humanity grows old, destroys itself, redeems itself, replaces itself, transcends itself, reverts to bestiality, becomes God. The stars go out. The stars blink on again, like neon signs. Awful and wonderful tales are told—truly wonderful, some of them; some of them really awful. But in none of the spaceships, on none of the planets, in none of the delightful, frightening, imaginative, crazy, clever stories are there any people. There is Humanity, and After, as in Stapledon. There is Inhumanity, and After, as in Orwell and Huxley. There are captains and troopers, and aliens and maidens and scientists, and emperors and robots and monsters—all signs, all symbols, statements, effigies, allegories, everything between the Stereotype and the Archetype. But not Mrs. Brown. Name me a name. There are no names. The names don't matter. The names are mere labels—Gagarin, Glenn—symbols, heroic labels, names of astronauts. The humanity of the astronaut is a liability, a weakness, irrelevant to the mission. The astronaut is not a being but an act. It is the act that counts. We are in the age of Science, where nothing *is*. None of the scientists, none of the philosophers, can say what anything or anyone is. They can only say, accurately, beautifully, what it does. The age of Technology; of Behaviorism; the age of the Act.

And then?

Well, then, as the century nears its midpoint and the Act seems to be heading ever more inevitably toward a tragic dénouement, there comes along the most improbable Mrs. Brown we have yet seen, and coming from the most improbable direction. It must be some kind of sign and portent. If any field of literature has no, can have no Mrs. Browns in it, it is fantasy—straight fantasy, the modern descendant of folktale, fairy tale, and myth. These genres deal with archetypes, not with characters. The very essence of Elfland is that Mrs. Brown can't get there—not unless she is changed, changed utterly, into an old mad witch, or a fair young princess, or a loathly Worm.

But who is this character, then, who really looks very like Mrs. Brown, except that he has furry feet; a short, thin, tired-looking fellow, wearing a gold ring on a chain round his neck and heading rather disconsolately eastward, on foot? I think you know his name.

Actually, I will not argue hard in defense of Frodo Baggins as a genuine, fully developed, novelistic character; as I say, his importance to my theme here is rather as a sign and portent. If you put Frodo together into one piece with Sam, and with Gollum, and with Smeagol—and they fit together into one piece—you get, indeed, a complex and fascinating character. But, as traditional myths and folktales break the complex conscious daylight personality down into its archetypal unconscious dreamtime components, Mrs. Brown becoming a princess, a toad, a worm, a witch, a child—so Tolkien in his wisdom broke Frodo into four: Frodo, Sam, Smeagol, and Gollum; perhaps five, counting Bilbo. Gollum is probably the best character in the book because he got two of the components, Smeagol and Gollum, or as Sam calls them, Slinker and Stinker. Frodo himself is only a quarter or a fifth of himself. Yet even so he is something new to fantasy: a vulnerable, limited, rather unpredictable hero, who finally fails at his own quest—fails it at the very end of it, and has to have it accomplished for him by his mortal enemy, Gollum, who is, however, his kinsman, his brother, in fact himself . . . And who then goes home to the Shire, very much as Mrs. Brown would do if she only had the chance; but then he has to go on, leave home, make the voyage out, in fact die—something fantasy heroes never do, and allegories are incapable of doing.

I shall never cease to wonder at the critics who find Tolkien a "simple" writer. What marvelously simple minds they must have!

So now we have got a kind of primitive version of Mrs. Brown into fantasy, the ancient kingdom of which science fiction is a modern province. There she stands, quite steady on her furry feet. And we have met her twice in the borderlands of Utopia. But there haven't been any Utopias written for decades; the genre seems to have turned inside out, becoming purely satirical and admonitory. And what about science fiction proper? As we come into the sixties and seventies and a new kind of writer is writing science fiction, and science fiction is even being printed on a new kind of paper which doesn't get yellow and crumbly at the edges quite so fast, and as the real rockets really take off and land on the real moon and thus leave science fiction free to stop describing the future and to start imagining it—do we, now, find any more room in the spaceship for Mrs. Brown?

I am not sure.

I am going to have to talk about myself and my own work for a while here; but before I do so—and so that I don't seem to be setting myself up as a kind of stout Cortez, silent upon a peak in

Disneyland, sole discoverer of uncharted seas—let me mention a couple of names.

Mrs. Thea Cadence.

Mr. Nobusuke Tagomi.

Do those names mean anything to you? They do to me; a good deal. They are the names of two of the first Mrs. Browns I met in modern science fiction.

Mr. Tagomi turns up in Philip K. Dick's *Man in the High Castle*. Thea is the protagonist of D. G. Compton's *Synthajoy*.

They are not unique; they're rare birds, still, in science fiction, but not unique. I just picked those two because I like them. I like them as people. They are people. Characters. Round, solid, knobby. Human beings, with angles and protuberances to them, hard parts and soft parts, depths and heights.

They also stand for a great deal, of course. They are exemplars, teaching aids if you like; they express something the authors wanted urgently to say as clearly as possible. Something about human beings under stress, under peculiarly modern forms of moral pressure.

If the authors wanted to speak clearly why didn't they write an essay, a documentary, a philosophical or sociological or psychological study?

Because they are both novelists. Real novelists. They write science fiction, I imagine, because what they have to say is best said using the tools of science fiction, and the craftsman knows his tools. And still, they are novelists, because while using the great range of imagery available to science fiction, they say what is it they have to say through a character—not a mouthpiece, but a fully realized creation. The character is primary. And what used to be the entire object of science fiction—the invention of miraculous gadgets, the relation of alternate histories, and so on—is now used subjectively, as a metaphor, as a means for exploring and explaining what goes on inside Mrs. Brown, or Thea, or Tagomi. The writers' interest is no longer really in the gadget, or the size of the universe, or the laws of robotics, or the destiny of social classes, or anything describable in quantitative, or mechanical, or objective terms. They are not interested in what things do, but in how things are. Their subject is the subject, that which cannot be other than subject: ourselves. Human beings.

But these are human beings who live in the universe as seen by modern science, and in the world as transformed by modern technology. That is where science fiction still remains distinct from the rest of fiction. The presence of science and technology is essential, in both these books. It is the given. Only, as I say, the speculations and facts, the idea of relativity, the idea of a machine to reproduce emotions, are not used as ends in themselves, but as metaphors. Metaphors for what? For what is not given; an X; an X which the writers are pursuing. The elusive individual, upon whom all the givens act, but who simply is. The person, the human psyche, life, Mrs. Brown, "the spirit we live by." Catch me if you can! And I think they caught her. She's there. Thea, shrewd and tragic in her madhouse, Mr. Tagomi, shrewd and tragic in his business office, both of them trying, in a half-conscious, muddled agony, to reach freedom, both failing or succeeding depending on how you look at it, "very small, and very tenacious, at once very frail and very heroic . . ."

Welcome aboard the spaceship, Mrs. Brown.

Angus Wilson (whose book *The Old Men at the Zoo* is quite definable as science fiction, by the way, although I doubt he'd much like to have it *categorized* as science fiction) has described, in *The Wild Garden*, the way a novel first came to him.

In my original conception of *Hemlock and After* . . . I saw Mrs. Curry, obese, sweet, and menacing, certain in her hysteric sense of power that she can destroy a good man, Bernard Sands; and because my vision is primarily ironic, I saw Bernard painfully thin, bitter, inward-turning . . . A momentary powerful visual picture of a fat woman and a thin man. The whole of the rest of the novel, for good or bad, is simply an extension needed, as I thought, to communicate this very visual ironic picture to others . . .

The novels, in fact, *are* those moments of vision. No didactic, sociological, psychological, or technical elaboration can alter that significance for the novelist himself. Like any other artist's, the novelist's statement is a concentrated vision . . . but unlike the others he has chosen the most difficult of all forms, one that makes its own discipline as it goes along. We can never hope for perfection . . . that other arts can achieve. But any serious novelist who . . . does not announce this vision as his central impulse is either playing down to some imaginary "plain chap" audience or has forgotten his original true inspiration in the polemics of moral, social, or formal purpose. Everyone says as a commonplace that a novel is an extended metaphor, but too few, perhaps, insist that the metaphor is everything, the extension only the means of expression.

That is splendid, and splendidly continues the Virginia Woolf quotations with which I started. It moves me very much, because it states my experience very nearly. A book does not come to me as an idea, or a plot, or an event, or a society, or a message; it comes to me as a person. A person seen, seen at a certain distance, usually in a landscape. The place is there, the person is there. I didn't invent him, I didn't make her up: he or she is there. And my business is to get there, too.

Once, like Mr. Wilson, I saw two of them. As my vision is not ironic, but romantic, they were small figures, remote, in a tremendous waste landscape of ice and snow. They were pulling a sledge or something over the ice, hauling together. That is all I saw. I didn't know who they were. I didn't even know what sex they were (I must say I was surprised when I found out). But that is how my novel *The Left Hand of Darkness* began, and when I think of the book, it is still that vision I see. All the rest of it, with all its strange rearrangements of human gender and its imagery of betrayal, loneliness, and cold, is my effort to catch up, to get nearer, to get there, where I had seen those two figures on the snow, isolated and together.

The origin of my book *The Dispossessed* was equally clear, but it got very muddled before it ever came clear again. It too began with a person, seen much closer to, this time, and with intense vividness: a man, this time; a scientist, a physicist in fact; I saw the face more clearly than usual, a thin face, large clear eyes, and large ears—these, I think, may have come from a childhood memory of Robert Oppenheimer as a young man. But more vivid than any visual detail was the personality, which was most attractive—attractive, I mean, as a flame to a moth. There, there he is, I have got to get there this time . . .

My first effort to catch him was a short story. I should have known he was much too big for a short story. It's a writer's business to develop an infallible sense for the proper size and length of a work; the beauty of the novella and novel is essentially architectural, the beauty of proportion. It was a really terrible story, one of the worst I have written in thirty years of malpractice. This scientist was escaping from a sort of prison-camp planet, a stellar Gulag, and he gets to the rich comfortable spoiled sister planet, and finally can't stand it despite a love affair there, and so re-escapes and goes back to the Gulag, sadly but nobly. Nobly but feeble-mindedly. Oh, it was a stupid story. All the metaphors were mixed. I hadn't got anywhere near him. I'd missed him by so far, in fact, that I hadn't damaged him at all. There he stood, quite untouched. Catch me if you can!

All right. All right, what's your name. What is your name, by the way? Shevek, he told me promptly. All right. Shevek. So who are you? His answer was less certain this time. I think, he said, that I am a citizen of Utopia.

Very well. That sounded reasonable. There was something so decent about him, he was so intelligent and yet so disarmingly naïve, that he might well come from a better place than this. But where? The better place; no place. What did I know about Utopia? Scraps of More, fragments of Wells, Hudson, Morris. Nothing. It took me years of reading and pondering and muddling, and much assistance from Engels, Marx, Godwin, Goldman, Goodman, and above all Shelley and Kropotkin, before I could begin to see where he came from, and could see the landscape about him—and yes, in a way it was a prison camp, but what a difference!—and the other people, the people whom his eyes saw; and the place, the other place, to which he was going, and from which I now knew, as he had always known, *why* he must return.

Thus in the process of trying to find out who and what Shevek was, I found out a great deal else, and thought as hard as I was capable of thinking, about society, about my world, and about myself. I would not have found out or been able to communicate any of this if I had not been doggedly pursuing, through all byways and side roads, the elusive Mrs. Brown.

The book that resulted is a Utopia, of sorts; it is didactic, therefore satirical, and idealistic. It is a thematic novel, in Angus Wilson's definition, in that it does not entirely manage to "disseminate the moral proposition so completely in a mass of living experience that it is never directly sensed as you read but only apprehended at the end as a result of the life you have shared in the book. This," Mr. Wilson goes on, "is the real challenge and triumph of the novel" (*The Wild Garden*). I did not fully meet that challenge or achieve that triumph. The moral proposition of *The Dispossessed* is sometimes fully embodied, sometimes not. The sound of axes being ground is occasionally audible. Yet I do believe that it is, basically, a novel, because at the heart of it you will not find an idea, or an inspirational message, or even a stone ax, but something much frailer and obscurer and more complex: a person. I have been strengthened in this belief by noticing that almost every reviewer, however carried away in supporting or attacking or explaining the book's themes and ideas, somewhere in the discussion has mentioned its protagonist by name. There he is!—there, if only for a moment. If I had to invent two entire worlds to get to him, two worlds and all their woes, it was worth it. If I could give the readers one glimpse of what I saw: Shevek, Mrs. Brown, the Other, a soul, a human soul, "the spirit we live by . . ."

I suppose I have answered my second question before I got around to asking it. I was asking, if you remember, should a book of science fiction be a novel? If it is possible, all the same is it advisable or desirable that the science fiction writer be also a novelist of character?

I have already said yes. I have already admitted that this, to me, is the whole point. That no other form of prose, to me, is a patch on the novel. That if we can't catch Mrs. Brown, if only for a moment, then all the beautiful faster-than-light ships, all the irony and imagination and knowledge and invention are in vain; we might as well write tracts or comic books, for we will never be real artists.

So then let me play my own enemy for a little, and try to argue the other side: the antinovel, or postnovel, point of view, which says that science-fictioneers will never be novelists, and a good thing, too.

From this point of view, the novel, the novel of character, is dead—as dead as the heroic couplet, and for the same reason: the times have changed. Such writers as Wilson and Drabble are mere epigones, draining the last dregs of an emptied cask; such writers as Bhattacharya and García Márquez flourish only because their countries are marginal to the place of origin of the novel, which was late in arriving at the periphery and correspondingly late in dying there. The novel is dead; and the task, the hope, of a new form such as science fiction is not to continue the novel, or to revitalize it, but to replace it.

There is, really, no Mrs. Brown anymore. There are only classes, masses, statistics, body counts, subscription lists, insurance risks, consumers, randomly selected samples, and victims. Or, if somewhere beyond all the quantification some hint of quality remains, some wisp of Mrs. Brown, she is not to be reached any longer with any of the traditional tools of fiction. No one can catch her. She has been too profoundly changed by our life, and too rapidly changed. Mrs. Brown herself has attained the speed of light, and become invisible to our finest telescopes. What is "human nature" now, who dares talk about it seriously, in 1975? Has it any recognizable relation to what was called "human nature" in the novel a century ago, which we now see as one tiny, limited fragment of the vast range of human variety and potentiality? The subject matter of the novel was the conscious, articulate portion of the minds of certain Europeans and North Americans, mostly white, mostly Christian, mostly middle class, mostly quite unaffected by science and, though affected by technology, totally uninterested in it; a handful of natives intensely interesting to the ethnologist because of their elaborate developments of manners, and their extraordinary absorption in interpersonal relationships. They thought their nature was human nature; but we don't; we can't. They thought themselves a norm; we have no norm. Through technology, which lets us travel and converse, and through such sciences as anthropology and psychology, we have learned too much about the complexity and variety of human behavior and the even vaster complexity of the human mind, conscious and unconscious; we have learned, that is, that we really know almost nothing at all. Nothing solid is left, nothing to take hold of.

For an example of solidity, look at Mrs. Sarah Gamp. There she is. Everything about her is almost appallingly solid. She represents a definite, established social stratum, though I, an ignorant American, won't try to specify it exactly. She is English; she is white; she is Christian—at least, she would say she's Christian. She is a product of urbanization and the Industrial Revolution, but her traditions are much older than that, and you would find her ancestors hanging harpy-like about the bedsides of Ovid and Orestes. She is fixed in history, and in custom, and in her own self-opinion. She knows who she is and she knows what she wants. What she wants is a bottle to be placed handy on the mantelpiece, to which she "may place her lips from time to time when so dispoged."

Now, what is a modern, 1975 equivalent to Mrs. Gamp? Let me, to avoid odious comparisons, simply invent one. She would be younger than Mrs. Gamp, most likely. She might not bathe any oftener. If she was a Christian, she might be a Jesus freak, but more probably she would be on some kind of vague occultist trip, or into astrology. She would probably be better clothed, fed, and housed than Mrs. Gamp, and would take for granted some luxuries Mrs. Gamp had never heard of—automobiles, bottled shampoo, television in the sickroom, penicillin, and so forth. She would, however, have very much less certainty as to her place in society; she might be quite unable to say either who she is or what she wants. She would almost certainly not have a bottle handy. She would have a needle handy. Her addiction would not be funny, as Mrs. Gamp's, in its outrageous hypocrisy, is. It would be too visibly, drastically disastrous to be funny. She would be too far out of touch with daily reality, too incompetent, even to function as badly as Mrs. Gamp does as a night nurse. And her involvement with criminality would not be, like Mrs. Gamp's, a desperate grasping at respectability, or at least at the hope of unlimited gin. Her involvement with the criminal and the violent would be passive, helpless, pointless. Indeed, wherever Mrs. Gamp is most revoltingly indomitable, I see this modern version of her as most passive. It is very hard to loathe her, to laugh at her, or to love her—as we do Mrs. Gamp; or at least Dickens did, and I do. She doesn't amount to enough. She is a drifter, a pawn, a fragment, jagged bits of a person never annealed, never grown to a whole. Is there enough of her, indeed, to enter a novel as a real character, enough to paint a portrait of? Isn't she, aren't we all, too battered, too changed and changeable, too whirled about, future-shocked, relativized and inconstant, ever to sit still for a painted portrait, ever to stay still long enough that the slow, clumsy art of the novelist can catch up with us?

Click, the camera-eye—a moment, not a person, not a portrait, only a single moment implying nothing before or after, no continuity, click. And the whirr of the movie camera, catching the moment as it dissolves into the next, unrelated moment. These are our arts. The technological arts, dependent upon an incredible refinement of machinery and a vast expense of mechanical energy, expression of a technological age. There is poetry, still, but there is no more Mrs. Brown. There are snapshots of a woman at various moments. There are moving pictures of a woman in various places with various other persons. They do not add up to anything so solid, so fixed, so Victorian or medieval as a "character" or even a personality. They are moments; moods; the poetry of flux; fragments of the fragmented, of the changing of the changed.

Do we not see this foreshadowed in the art of Virginia Woolf herself?

And what is science fiction at its best but just such a "new tool" as Woolf avowedly sought for fifty years ago, a crazy, protean, left-handed monkey wrench, which can be put to any use the craftsman has in mind—satire, extrapolation, prediction, absurdity, exactitude, exaggeration, warning, message-carrying, tale-telling, whatever you like—an infinitely expandable metaphor exactly suited to our expanding universe, a broken mirror, broken into numberless fragments, any one of which is capable of reflecting, for a moment, the left eye and the nose of the reader, and also the farthest stars shining in the depths of the remotest galaxy?

If science fiction is this, or is capable of being this, a true metaphor to our strange times, then surely it is rather stupid and reactionary to try to enclose it in the old limits of an old art—like trying to turn a nuclear reactor into a steam engine. Why should anyone try to patch up this marvelously smashed mirror so that it can reflect poor old Mrs. Brown—who may not even be among us anymore? Do we care, in fact, if she's alive or dead?

Well, yes. Speaking strictly for myself—yes. I do care. If Mrs.

Brown is dead, you can take your galaxies and roll them up into a ball and throw them into the trash can, for all I care. What good are all the objects in the universe, if there is no subject? It isn't that mankind is all that important. I don't think that Man is the measure of all things, or even of very many things. I don't think Man is the end or culmination of anything, and certainly not the center of anything. What we are, who we are, and where we are going, I do not know, nor do I believe anybody who says he knows, except, possibly, Beethoven, in the last movement of the last symphony.* All I know is that we are here, and that we are aware of the fact, and that it behooves us to be aware—to pay heed. For we are not objects. That is essential. We are subjects, and whoever among us treats us as objects is acting inhumanly, wrongly, against nature. And with us, nature, the great Object, its tirelessly burning suns, its turning galaxies and planets, its rocks, seas, fish and ferns and fir trees and little furry animals, all have become, also, subjects. As we are part of them, so they are part of us. Bone of our bone, flesh of our flesh. We are their consciousness. If we stop looking, the world goes blind. If we cease to speak and listen, the world goes deaf and dumb. If we stop thinking, there is no thought. If we destroy ourselves, we destroy consciousness.

And all this, the seeing, hearing, speaking, thinking, feeling—all this we do one by one. The great mystics have gone deeper than community and sensed identity, the identity of all; but we ordinary souls cannot do that, or only for a moment, maybe one moment in a lifetime. One by one we live, soul by soul. The person, the single person. Community is the best we can hope for, and community

---

*   Note (1989). Or Schubert, in the Great Symphony, but he isn't saying at all what Beethoven said.

for most people means *touch*: the touch of your hand against the other's hand, the job done together, the sledge hauled together, the dance danced together, the child conceived together. We have only one body apiece, and two hands. We can form a circle, but we cannot *be* a circle. The circle, the true society, is formed of single bodies and single souls. If not, it is not formed at all. Only a mechanical, insensate imitation of true society, true community, is made up out of objectified, quantified, persons—a social class, a nation-state, an army, a corporation, a power bloc. There is no more hope in that direction. We have followed it to the end. I really see no hope anywhere except in Mrs. Brown.

Most of us these days could do with a little hope; and I incline to think that you as readers have a right to ask—not to demand, never to demand, but to ask—for some hope from our arts. We really cannot ask for it from science. Science isn't the hope business and never was. When it offers us something affirmative, it's a mere spin-off, a secondary application; meanwhile science proceeds on its true course, which is toward an ever closer imitation of nature, an ever completer objectivity. The freer science is to proceed thus toward the inevitable, the freer it leaves art in its own domain of subjectivity, where it can play, in its own way, and if it has the courage, with nature, and with science itself, our surrogate nature.

In Stanislaw Lem's *The Invincible*, the protagonist Rohan and others of the crew of starship *Invincible* face a hostile and enigmatic world. They gradually develop an elegant explanation of the nature of that world, a literally mechanical explanation; but the explanation isn't the point of the book. It's not a mystery story. The book's theme is moral, and its climax is an extremely difficult ethical choice made by an individual. Neither reward nor punishment ensues. All that we and Rohan have learned is something about himself, and something about what is and what is not invincible. In Lem's *Solaris*, the protagonist takes on a world which cannot be understood objectively at all. A large part of the book is Lem's delighted, Borgesian send-up of the efforts of scientists to explain the planet Solaris, which resists and confounds them all, and yet which participates in the very deepest psychic motivations and troubles of the protagonist Kelvin, so that in the end, if he has not understood Solaris, yet Solaris seems in a way to have understood him. The dazzlingly rich, inventive, and complex metaphors of these novels serve to express, or symbolize, or illuminate the mind and emotions of late-twentieth-century man* as exactly and as powerfully as the slums of London, the Court of Chancery, the Circumlocution Office, and Mrs. Gamp's bottle served Dickens to illuminate the characters and destinies of his contemporaries.

In the essay with which I began, Virginia Woolf was criticizing the school of Arnold Bennett because, as she saw it, such writers had substituted the external, the objective—houses, occupations, rents, income, possessions, mannerisms, etc.—for the subject, in whom they were really no longer interested. They had deserted novel-writing for sociology. The modern "psychological novel" is a similar case, usually being not a portrait of a person, but a case study. "Socialist Realism" is another example of the same flight from subjectivity. And most science fiction has shown the same tendency. It may rise from a yearning for the seemingly godlike detachment of the scientist, but what it results in is an evasion of the artist's obligation to reproduce—indirectly, for it cannot be reproduced directly—a vision. Science fiction has mostly settled for a pseudo-objective

---

*   Note (1989). I let "man" continue here to stand for "humanity," since Lem, in fact, writes only about men. The women in *Solaris* are mental constructs of the male characters, and many Lem novels contain no women at all.

listing of marvels and wonders and horrors which illuminate nothing beyond themselves and are without real moral resonance: day-
dreams, wishful thinking, and nightmares. The invention is superb,
but self-enclosed and sterile. And the more eccentric and childish
side of science fiction fandom, the defensive, fanatic in-groups, both
feed upon and nourish this kind of triviality, which is harmless in
itself, but which degrades taste, by keeping publishers' standards,
and readers' and critics' expectations, very low. It's as if they wanted
us all to play poker without betting. But the real game is played for
real stakes. It's a pity that this trivial image is perpetuated, when the
work of people from Zamyatin to Lem has shown that when science
fiction uses its limitless range of symbol and metaphor novelistically,
with the subject at the center, it can show us who we are, and where
we are, and what choices face us, with unsurpassed clarity, and with
a great and troubling beauty.

The beauty of fiction is always troubling, I suppose. It cannot
offer transcendence, the peace that passes understanding, as poetry
and music can: nor can it offer pure tragedy. It's too muddled. Its essence is muddled. Yet the novel, fiction concerned with individuals,
in its stubborn assertion of human personality and human morality,
does seem even now to affirm the existence of hope. Despite the
best efforts of talented antinovelists, it continues to avoid the clean
and gleaming sterility of despair. It is muddled, elastic, inventive,
adaptable.

It needs to be adaptable. These are bad times, and what is art to
do in a bad time? Art never fed anyone—often not even the artist.
Half the world is hungry, and art feeds only the spirit, on an imma-
terial food. Words, words, words. I may well live to eat my words.

But till then, here is what I think: I think art remains centrally
important in any age, the best or the worst, because it doesn't lie.

The hope it offers is not a false hope. And I think the novel is an important art, because it talks about what we live by, other than bread. And I think science fiction is—well, no, not important, yet still worth talking about, because it is a promise of continued life for the imagination, a good tool, an enlargement of consciousness, a possible glimpse, against a vast dark background, of the very frail, very heroic figure of Mrs. Brown.

DO-IT-YOURSELF COSMOLOGY

(1977)

It would seem that the writer who composes a universe, invents a planet, or even populates a drawing room, is playing God. The creation of people, of worlds, of galaxies—since it all comes out of one's head, surely it must also go to one's head?

Some years ago, in the *Bulletin* of the Science Fiction Writers Association, Poul Anderson published an article called (if I remember rightly) "How to Create a World." Taking it for granted that any reader of the publication would understand the pleasures of auto-cosmology, he warned gently of the dangers of carelessness, and then got down to the groundwork. Which kind of star is likely to have planets? What size of planet is likely to have life aboard it? At what distance from what size sun? Is the moon's role functional or decorative? And so on, and on.

People ignorant of science or science fiction are usually convinced that "sci-fi writers just make all that up," but of course any halfway serious science fiction writer has to have studied such topics, and to keep reference books handy. Imagination is the essence; but it is controlled, exactly as the profuse strains of unpremeditated Art are controlled by the requirements of fixed or free rhythm and rhyme. As soon as you, the writer, have said, "The green sun had already set, but the red one was hanging like a bloated salami above the mountains," you had better have a pretty fair idea in your head concerning the type and size of green suns and red suns—especially green ones, which are not the commonest sort—and the arguments concerning the existence of planets in a binary system, and the probable effects of a double primary on orbit, tides, seasons, and biological rhythms; and then of course the mass of your planet and the nature of its atmosphere will tell you a good deal about the height and shape of those mountains; and so on, and on. You may even feel impelled to make a cursory study of the effect of senility upon salamis. None of this background work may actually get into the story. But if you are ignorant of these multiple implications of your pretty red and green suns, you'll make ugly errors, which every fourteen-year-old reading your story will wince at; and if you're bored by the labor of figuring them out, then surely you shouldn't be writing science fiction. A great part of the pleasure of the genre, for both writer and reader, lies in the solidity and precision, the logical elegance, of fantasy stimulated by and extrapolated from scientific fact.

Wasting no time on apologies, Mr. Anderson provided a good batch of the sort of facts the universe-maker wants, including several mathematical equations useful in various situations. His essay was exemplary. It has received grateful response ever since—except for one letter in the next issue, which went like this:

Dear Mr. Anderson:
> *That is not the way I do it.*
>> *Yours truly,*
>>> *GOD*

Undeterred, Mr. Anderson has gone on to enlarge and reprint his useful article. On this particular subject, science fiction writers can only ignore the opinion of God. They have to do it their own way.

Some quite practical values of their method are beginning to be appreciated. The Russians have used science fiction in the classroom for many years, and there are now American textbooks in sociology, political science, anthropology, and psychology presenting science fiction stories as problems or statements of ideas; but, more specifically, a course was offered at an Oregon university last year, taught by a physicist with assistance from astronomers, geologists, etc., which the catalogue cautiously called Planetology, but which the joyful students more accurately called Planet-Building. It was highly successful. The more one thinks about it the more one sees the usefulness of Do-It-Yourself cosmology as a device for teaching the general principles, mechanics, and history of the cosmos, of the solar system and the planet Earth.

A notable feature of this type of world-making—the sober science-fictional and the classroom-heuristical—is its modesty. God, as you can see by his letter, is not offended by it; no thunderbolt is called for; he merely points out that it's not the way *he* goes about the job. He's perfectly aware that these writers and students are not pretending to be, or trying to be, or mistaking themselves for, himself. If they were, he would warn them against what the Greeks called hubris and the Christians pride and the Jungians inflation. But that arrogant identification of the Ego with the Creator Spirit is quite absent here. This kind of world-making is a thought experiment, performed with the caution and in the controlled, receptive spirit of experiment. Scientist and science-fictioneer invent worlds in order to reflect, and so to clarify, perhaps to glorify, the "real world," the objective Creation. The more closely their work resembles and so illuminates the solidity, complexity, amazingness, and coherence of the original, the happier they are.

If we turn from science fiction to fantasy, and the making of new heavens and earths by fantasists, I'm not sure we'll find such devout and genuine modesty at work. Modesty is a rational virtue, and this turn is away from the rational. With the shift from the outside to the inside, from the object to the subject, things begin to slip and change. We fall down rabbit holes where the laws of gravity do not apply at all, and no equations can save us. The science-fictioneer imitates the Creation; the fantasist emulates the Creator. But now God himself has changed. We are no longer dealing with rational, masculine, jealous types such as Zeus or Jehovah. Here Shiva dances and, dancing, becomes Kali with her tongue hanging out a yard between her pointed teeth. The Creator is the Destroyer; the Mother devours. Personality and opinion are quite meaningless illusions. The ego simply vanishes; but the self becomes all. Literally, precisely all. The dream is the dreamer; the dancer is the dance.

The original and instinctive movement of fantasy is, of course, inward. Fantasy is so introverted by nature that often some objective "hook" is necessary to bring it out into the open and turn it into literature. Classically, satire provided this hook, as in Ariosto or Swift. Or the reforming impulse shaped the dreamworld into a rational Utopia. Or identification with nature enabled the Romantic fantasist to speak, at least briefly, out of the silence of the moors. Nowadays it is science that often gives fantasy a hand up from the interior depths, and we have science fiction, a modern, intellectualized, extraverted form of fantasy. Its limitations and strengths are those of extraversion: the power and the intractability of the *object*.

The strength of fantasy is the strength of the Self; but its limitation or danger is that of extreme introversion: left to itself, the vision may go clear out of sight, remaining entirely private to the fantasist's consciousness, or even remaining unconscious, exactly like a dream. The purer the fantasy, the more subjective the creation, the likelier this is to happen. It is a miracle, and pretty much a modern one, that we have *any* great non-satirical fantasies in print. Perhaps it is because our culture is at long last turning toward introversion in an effort to restore balance, that, within the last hundred years, some of these private worlds have been saved and, like marvelous and fragile national parks, even opened to the public.

People who are threatened by the imagination usually dismiss works of fantasy as "childish." Though the dismissal is a confession of impotence, the description is exact. In the creation and preservation of fantasy worlds, the role of the child seems central.

The politician, the profiteer, and the sensualist have no patience with the otherworldly. The other world . . . Jesus referred to it in its religious aspect when he remarked that access to it was limited to those willing to become little children. The kingdom of God is within you; the burning-ground where the goddess dances is the heart.

Sometimes the fantasy world was created for the sake of a child—a particular, beloved child, or just children, any child. Carroll, Grahame, Nesbit, Saint-Exupéry, Tolkien—I am just rattling off the first who come to mind. Or the world may be saved by a child: there is *Islandia*, which Austin Tappan Wright worked on happily all his life long and never tried to publish; after his death his daughter lovingly abridged, arranged, and published it. That is not a book *for* children at all. Neither is the *Gormenghast* trilogy, which is the story of a child leaving home, the child who is the author, Mervyn Peake, dying of a terrible disease in his forties, the child who is the Self.

Fantasists are childish, childlike. They play games. They dance on the burning-ground. Neither arrogance nor modesty is a very useful term, in this context. Even when they are making entire universes, they are only playing. But they are not playing God. It looks as if they were, to the rational mind; but the rational mind notoriously cannot see what's happening in fantasy, or why it happens. How can you play God, after all, when you have understood what the intellect cannot understand—that God is only playing God?

III
THE BOOK IS WHAT IS REAL

As a child I paid very little attention to authors' names; they were irrelevant; I did not believe in authors. To be perfectly candid, this is still true. I do not believe in authors. A book exists, it's there. The author isn't there—some grown-up you never met— may even be dead. The book is what is real. You read it, you and it form a relationship, perhaps a trivial one, perhaps a deep and lasting one. As you read it word by word and page by page, you participate in its creation, just as a cellist playing a Bach suite participates, note by note, in the creation, the coming-to-be, the existence, of the music. And, as you read and reread, the book of course participates in the creation of you, your thoughts and feelings, the size and temper of your soul. Where, in all this, does the author come in? Like the God of the eighteenth-century deists, only at the beginning. Long ago, before you and the book met each other. The author's work is done, complete; the ongoing work, the present act of creation, is a collaboration by the words that stand on the page and the eyes that read them.

from "Books Remembered," Children's Book Council
Calendar xxxvi, no. 2 (November 1977)

I have found, somewhat to my displeasure, that I am an extremely moral writer. I am always grinding axes and making points. I wish I wasn't so moralistic, because my interest is aesthetic. What I want to do is make something beautiful like a good pot or a good piece of music, and the ideas and moralism keep getting in the way. There's a definite battle on.

from "An Interview with Ursula Le Guin:
Creating Realistic Utopias," by Win McCormack
and Ann Mendel, *Seven Days* (April 11, 1977)

INTRODUCTION

Le Guin in the preceding essays has deplored biographical criticism and inquiry, saying in "Dreams Must Explain Themselves" that the answer to "Who are you?" is "It's all there, in the book. All that matters." In the essays that follow, Le Guin talks, not about herself, but about her work, with the object of finding out what this genre called "science fiction" *is* and how, given specific examples, it can be made better. Her specific concerns include the differences and similarities between SF and fantasy; the creation of characters, and experiments with gender and role; the dangers of relevance and of "inextricably confusing ideas with opinions"; and the strengths and limitations both of the genre and of the English language, as they affect her attempts to express a true vision. Her general concern is, as always, the responsibilities of freedom; as she says again in the introduction to *The Word for World Is Forest*, "The pursuit of art . . . is the pursuit of liberty."

Rocannon's World appeared in 1966 from Ace Books; this introduction was written for the 1977 hardcover edition published by Harper & Row, and is noteworthy particularly for Le Guin's comments on the differences between SF and fantasy. *Planet of Exile* appeared in 1966 from Ace; this introduction was for the 1978 Harper & Row hardcover edition. Le Guin's retrospective comments on feminism and her use of male protagonists are particularly interesting. Her views that in her work "the sex itself is seen as a *relationship rather than an act*" and that "both sex and gender seem to be used mainly to define the meaning of 'person' or of 'self'" have a particular relevance to *The Left Hand of Darkness*. In *Science-Fiction Studies* 6 (July 1975), Le Guin defined the two ruling myths of *The Left Hand of Darkness* as "the myth of winter" and "the archetypal figure of the Androgyne," which, she feels,

> is one of the archetypes/potentialities of the human psyche which is of real importance now, which is alive now and full of creative-destructive energy; and so it is urgent that it be brought into consciousness.

In her own work, she continues to create characters through which to explore ideas about gender, sex, self, and archetype. As she says in the 1978 introduction to *Planet of Exile*: "I keep on digging. I use the tools of feminism, and try to figure out what makes me work and how I work, so that I will no longer work in ignorance or irresponsibly."

City of Illusions appeared in 1967 from Ace; this introduction was also written for the 1978 Harper & Row hardcover edition. It is interesting because it indicates the ideas out of which the complete novel grew; because it raises the perennial problem of the distance between the vision and the final artifact; and because it touches on the problem of preaching, with which Le Guin deals in her introduction to *The Word for World Is Forest*. This novella was written in 1968, published in Harlan Ellison's anthology *Again, Dangerous Visions* (New York: Doubleday, 1972), and won the 1973 Hugo Award for Best Novella. This introduction was written for the 1977 single-volume reprint by Gollancz of London; the 1975 single-volume American edition from Berkley did not contain an introduction. Here, Le Guin gives a candid account of how easily "a pure pursuit of freedom and the dream" can be misdirected by "the lure of the pulpit," as powerful a limitation as the lures of fame and money.

The artist needs freedom to seek and express the truth; and the nature of truth is the theme of Le Guin's introduction to the 1976 Ace paperback reprinting of *The Left Hand of Darkness*. This novel, first published by Ace in 1969, won both the Nebula Award of the Science Fiction Writers of America and the Hugo Award of the 28th World Science Fiction Convention as best science fiction novel of its year. It may well be Le Guin's best-known work; certainly it is controversial. Le Guin deals with some of the issues raised by the ambisexual nature of her imagined people, the Gethenians, in the essay "Is Gender Necessary?" This essay, first delivered to a class in women's studies at the University of Washington, taught by Susan Anderson, was published in *Aurora: Beyond Equality*, edited by Anderson and Vonda N. McIntyre (Greenwich, CT: Fawcett, 1976), an anthology of stories attempting to depict nonsexist societies. (Le Guin also stresses that *Left Hand* is not "about" sexuality so much as "about betrayal and fidelity"; and that it does what SF is uniquely suited to do, that is, set up a human experiment and observe the results as they are demonstrated through individuals.) The criticism "that the Gethenians seem like *men*, instead of menwomen" was raised most notably by the Polish critic Stanislaw Lem, in an essay published in the German journal *Quarber Merkur* and translated, revised, and published in the Australian fanzine *SF Commentary* 24 (November 1971). In her reply published in *SF Commentary* 26 (April 1972), Le Guin commented: "Is it possible we tend to insist that Estraven and the other Gethenians are men, because most of us are unwilling or unable to imagine women as scheming prime ministers, haulers of sledges across icy wastes, etc.?" This, with the later self-criticism that she did not show Gethenians acting in "female" roles, shows Le Guin pushing again at the "limits" imposed on SF, and the SF writer, the experimenter, by the assumptions of contemporary society.

The Left Hand of Darkness opens with the protagonist, envoy Genly Ai, writing: "I'll make my report as if I told a story, for I was taught on my homeworld that Truth is a matter of the imagination." Le Guin's introduction discusses the paradoxical nature of Truth, a paradox borne out by the "real" story she discusses in her introduction to *Star Songs of an Old Primate*, a collection of short stories by James Tiptree Jr. (New York: Ballantine, 1978). This essay complements Le Guin's own speculations about truth, reality, gender, social role, and the unimportance of the author's biography. It also, like the tributes to Tolkien and Dick, shows Le Guin's own values in action, as she discusses work that she respects. The Tolkien essay was a posthumous tribute published in *Vector* 67/68 (Spring 1974), the journal of the British Science Fiction Association, then edited by Malcolm Edwards. The essay on Philip K. Dick appeared in the *New Republic* 175 (October 30, 1976) under the heading "Science Fiction as Prophecy: Philip K. Dick." I have restored Le Guin's original title, "The Modest One." Like Le Guin's praise of Lem and the Strugatskys, this essay repeats her central idea that the highest task of the SF writer, of any writer, is to act as poet and prophet, expressing a clear moral vision in the most artistically satisfying way possible. If this can be accomplished, then indeed "all that matters" will be "there, in the book" for each reader.

INTRODUCTION TO
ROCANNON'S WORLD

(1977)

When I set out to write my first science fiction novel, in the century's mid-sixties and my own mid-thirties, I had written several novels, but I had never before invented a planet. It is a mysterious business, creating worlds out of words. I hope I can say without irreverence that anyone who has done it knows why Jehovah took Sunday off. Looking back on this first effort of mine, I can see the timidity, and the rashness, and the beginner's luck, of the apprentice demiurge.

When asked to "define the difference between fantasy and science fiction," I mouth and mumble and always end up talking about the spectrum, that very useful spectrum, along which one thing shades into another. Definitions are for grammar, not literature, I say, and boxes are for bones. But of course fantasy and science fiction *are* different, just as red and blue are different; they have different frequencies; if you mix them (on paper—I work on paper) you get purple, something else again. *Rocannon's World* is definitely purple.

I knew very little about science fiction when I wrote it. I had read a good deal of science fiction, in the early forties and in the early sixties, and that was absolutely all I knew about it: the stories and novels I had read. Not many knew very much more about it, in 1964. Many had read more; and there was Fandom; but very few besides James Blish and Damon Knight had *thought* much about science fiction. It was reviewed, in fanzines, as I soon discovered, and in a very few—mainly *SFR* and *ASFR*—criticized; outside the science fiction magazines it was seldom reviewed and never criticized. It was not studied. It was not taught. There were no schools—in any sense. There were no theories; only the opinions of editors. There was no aesthetic. All that—the New Wave, the academic discovery, Clarion, theses, counter-theses, journals of criticism, books of theory, the big words, the exciting experiments—was just, as it were, poised to descend upon us, but it hadn't yet, or at least it hadn't reached my backwater. All I knew was that there was a kind of magazine and book labeled SF by the publishers, a category into which I had fallen, impelled by a mixture of synchronicity and desperation.

So there I was, getting published at last, and I was supposed to be writing science fiction. How?

I think there may have already existed a book or two on How to Write SF, but I have always avoided all such manuals since being exposed to a course in Creative Writing at Harvard and realizing that I was allergic to Creative Writing. How do you write science fiction? Who knows? cried the cheerful demiurge, and started right in to do it.

Demi has learned a few things since then. We all have. One thing he learned (if Muses are female, I guess demiurges are male) was that red is red and blue is blue and if you want either red or blue, don't mix them. There is a lot of promiscuous mixing going on in *Rocannon's World*. We have NAFAL and FTL spaceships, we also have Brisingamen's necklace, windsteeds, and some imbecilic angels. We have an extremely useful garment called an impermasuit, resistant to "foreign elements, extreme temperatures, radioactivity, shocks and blows of moderate velocity and weight such as sword-strokes or bullets," and inside which the wearer would die of suffocation within five minutes. The impermasuit is a good example of where fantasy and science fiction *don't* shade gracefully into one another. A symbol from collective fantasy—the Cloak of Protection (invisibility, etc.)—is decked out with some pseudoscientific verbiage and a bit of vivid description, and passed off as a marvel of Future Technology. This can be done triumphantly if the symbol goes deep enough (Wells's *Time Machine*), but if it's merely decorative or convenient, it's cheating. It degrades both symbol and science; it confuses possibility with probability, and ends up with neither. The impermasuit is a lost item of engineering, which you won't find in any of my books written after *Rocannon's World*. Maybe it got taken up by the people who ride in the Chariots of the Gods.

This sort of thing is beginner's rashness, the glorious freedom of ignorance. It's my world, I can do anything! Only, of course, you can't. Exactly as each word of a sentence limits the choice of subsequent words, so that by the end of the sentence you have little or no choice at all, so (you see what I mean? having said "exactly as," I must now say "so") each word, sentence, paragraph, chapter, character, description, speech, invention, and event in a novel determines and limits the rest of the novel—but no, I am not going to end this sentence as I expected to, because my parallel is *not* exact: the spoken sentence works only in time, while the novel, which is not conceived or said all at once, works both ways, forward and back. The beginning is implied in the end, as much as the end is in the beginning. (This is not circularity. Fascinating circular novels exist—*Finnegans Wake*, *Gravity's Rainbow*, *Dhalgren*—but if all novels achieved or even attempted circularity, novel readers would rightly rebel; the normal run-of-the-mill novel begins in one "place" and ends somewhere else, following a pattern—line, zigzag, spiral, hopscotch, trajectory—which has what the circle in its perfection does not have: direction.) Each part shapes every other part. So, even in science fiction, all that wonderful freedom to invent worlds and creatures and sexes and devices has, by about page 12 of the manuscript, become strangely limited. You have to be sure all the things you invented, even if you haven't mentioned them or even thought of them yet, hang together; or they will all hang separately. As freedom increases, so, alas, does responsibility.

As for the timidity I mentioned, the overcaution in exploring my brave new world: though I sent my protagonist Rocannon un-protected (he does finally lose his impermasuit) into the unknown, I was inclined to take refuge myself in the very-well-known-indeed. My use of fragments of the Norse mythology, for instance: I lacked the courage of experience, which says, Go on, make up your own damn myth, it'll turn out to be one of the Old Ones anyhow. In-stead of drawing on my own unconscious, I borrowed from legend. It didn't make very much difference in this case, because I had heard Norse myths before I could read, and read *The Children of Odin* and later the Eddas many, many times, so that that mythos was a shaping influence on both my conscious and unconscious mind (which is why I hate Wagner). I'm not really sorry I borrowed from the Norse; it certainly did them no harm; but still, Odin in an im-permasuit—it's a bit silly. The borrowing interfered, too, with the tentative exploration of my own personal mythology, which this book inaugurated. That is why Rocannon was so much braver than I was. He knew jolly well he wasn't Odin, but simply a piece of me, and that my job was to go toward the shared, collective ground of myth, the root, the source—by nobody's road but my own. It's the only way anybody gets there.

Timidity, again, in the peopling of my world. Elves and dwarves. Heroes and servants. Male-dominated feudalism. The never-never-Bronze Age of sword and sorcery. A League of Worlds. I didn't know yet that the science in my fiction was mostly going to be social science, psychology, anthropology, history, etc., and that I had to figure out how to use all that, and work hard at it, too, because nobody else had yet done much along those lines. I just took what came to hand, the FTL drive and the Bronze Age, and used them without much thinking about it, saving the courage of real invention for pure fantasies—the Winged Ones, the windsteeds, the Kiemhrir. A lesser courage, but a delight; one I have pretty much lost. You can't take everything with you as you go on.

I hope this doesn't read as if I were knocking the book, or worse, trying to defuse criticism by anticipating it, a very slimy trick in the art of Literary Self-Defense. I like this book. Like Bilbo, I like rather more than half of it nearly twice as much as it deserves. I certainly couldn't write it now, but I can read it; and the thirteen-year distance lets me see, peacefully, what isn't very good in it, and what is—the Kiemhrir, for instance, and Semley, and some of the things Kyo says, and that gorge where they camp near a waterfall. And it has a good shape.

May I record my heartfelt joy at the final disappearance in this edition of the typographical errors which, plentiful in the first edition, have been multiplying like gerbils ever since. One of them—Clayfish for Clayfolk—even got translated into French. The

Clayfolk, euphoniously, become Argiliens, but the misprint, "the burrowing Clayfish," became "*ces poissons d' argilière qui fouissaient le sol*," which I consider one of the great triumphs of French Reason in the service of pure madness. There may be some typos in this edition, but I positively look forward to them. At least, with any luck at all, they'll be new ones.

INTRODUCTION TO
PLANET OF EXILE

(1978)

All science fiction writers are asked, with wonderful regularity, "Where do you get your ideas from?" None of us knows what to answer, except Harlan Ellison, who replies crisply, "Schenectady!"

The question has become a joke, even a *New Yorker* cartoon; and yet it is usually asked with sincerity, even with yearning; it isn't meant to be a stupid question. The trouble with it, the reason why the only possible answer to it is "Schenectady" is that it isn't the right question; and there are no right answers to wrong questions—as witness the works of those who attempted to discover the properties of Phlogiston. Sometimes the trouble is merely a matter of vague phrasing; what the asker really wants to know is "Do you get the science in your science fiction from knowing or reading science?" (Ans.: Yes.) Or, "Do SF writers ever steal ideas from each other?" (Ans.: Constantly.) Or, "Do you get the action in your books from having lived all the experiences the characters live?" (Ans.: God forbid!) But sometimes the questioners can't specify;

they just shift and say well, like, y'know . . . and then I suspect that what they're really trying to get at is a complex, difficult and important thing: they are trying to understand the imagination, how it works, how an artist uses it or is used by it. We know so little about the imagination that we can't even ask the right questions about it, let alone give the right answers. The springs of creation remain unsounded by the wisest psychology; and an artist is often the last person to say anything comprehensible about the process of creation. Though nobody else has said very much that makes sense. I guess the best place to start is in Schenectady, reading Keats.

Of recent years I (only I, in this case) am always asked a second question. It is "Why do you write so much about men?"

This is never a stupid question. Nor is it a wrong question, not at all, though sometimes there is a bias in it that makes it hard to answer directly. There are women in my books and stories, and often they are the protagonists or the central viewpoint characters; and so if people ask, "Why do you always write about men?" I reply, "I don't," and I say it rather crossly, because the question so phrased is both accusatory and inaccurate. I can swallow some accusation, or some inaccuracy, but the combination is poison.

But again and still, however the question is phrased, what it brings up is a real and urgent concern. A flip answer is detestable; a brief answer is impossible.

Planet of Exile was written in 1963–64, before the reawakening of feminism from its thirty-year paralysis. The book exhibits my early, "natural" (i.e., happily acculturated), unawakened, unconsciousness-raised way of handling male and female characters. At that time, I could say with a perfectly clear conscience, indeed with self-congratulation, that I simply didn't care whether my characters were male or female, so long as they were human. Why on earth should a woman have to write only about women? I was un-selfconscious, without sense of obligation: therefore self-confident, unexperimental, contentedly conventional.

The story starts with Rolery, but presently the point of view shifts off to Jakob and to Wold, and then back to Rolery, and off again: it's an alternating-viewpoints story. The men are more overtly active, and far more articulate. Rolery, a young and inexperienced woman of a rigidly traditional, male-supremacist culture, does not fight, or initiate sexual encounters, or become a leader of society, or assume any other role which, in her culture or ours of 1964, would be labeled "male." She is, however, a rebel, both socially and sexually. Although her behavior is not aggressive, her desire for freedom drives her to break right out of her culture-mold: she changes herself entirely by allying herself with an alien self. She chooses the Other. This small personal rebellion, coming at a crucial time, initiates events which lead to the complete changing and remaking of two cultures and societies.

Jakob is the hero, active, articulate, rushing about fighting bravely and governing busily; but the central mover of the events of the book, the *one who chooses*, is, in fact, Rolery. Taoism got to me earlier than modern feminism did. Where some see only a dominant Hero and a passive Little Woman, I saw, and still see, the essential wastefulness and futility of aggression and the profound effectiveness of *wu wei*, "action through stillness."

All very well; the fact remains that in this book, as in most of my other novels, the men do most of the acting, in both senses of the word, and thus tend to occupy the center of the stage. I "didn't care" whether my protagonist was male or female; well, that care-freeness is culpably careless. The men take over.

Why does one let them? Well, it's ever so much easier to write about men doing things, because most books about people doing things are about men, and that is one's literary tradition . . . and because, as a woman, one probably has not done awfully much in the way of fighting, raping, governing, etc., but has observed that men do these things . . . and because, as Virginia Woolf pointed out, English prose is unsuited to the description of feminine being and doing, unless one to some extent remakes it from scratch. It is hard to break from tradition; hard to invent; hard to remake one's mother tongue. One drifts along and takes the easy way. Nothing can rouse one to go against the stream, to choose the hard way, but a profoundly stirred, and probably an angry, conscience.

But the conscience must *be* angry. If it tries to reason itself into anger it produces only guilt, which chokes the springs of creation at their source.

I am often very angry, as a woman. My feminist anger is an element in, a part of, the rage and fear that possess me when I face what we are all doing to each other, to the earth, and to the hope of liberty and life. I still "don't care" whether people are male or female, when they are all of us and all of our children. One soul unjustly imprisoned, am I to ask which sex it is? A child starving, am I to ask which sex it is?

The answer of some radical feminists is yes. Granted the premise that the root of *all* injustice, exploitation, and blind aggression is sexual injustice, this position is sound. I cannot accept the premise; therefore I cannot act upon it. If I forced myself to—and my form of action is writing—I would write dishonestly and badly. Am I to sacrifice the ideal of truth and beauty in order to make an ideological point?

Again, the radical feminist's answer may be yes. Though that answer is sometimes identical with the voice of the Censor, speaking merely for fanatic or authoritarian bigotry, it may not be: it may speak in the service of the ideal itself. To build, one must tear down the old. The generation that has to do the tearing down has all the pain of destruction and little of the joy of creation. The courage that accepts that task and all the ingratitude and obloquy that go with it is beyond praise.

But it can't be forced or faked. If it is forced it leads to mere spitefulness and self-destructiveness; if it is faked it leads to Feminist Chic, the successor to Radical Chic. It's one thing to sacrifice fulfillment in the service of an ideal; it's another to suppress clear thinking and honest feeling in the service of an ideology. An ideology is valuable only insofar as it is used to *intensify* clarity and honesty of thought and feeling.

Feminist ideology has been immensely valuable to me in this respect. It has forced me and every thinking woman of this generation to know ourselves better: to separate, often very painfully, what we really think and believe from all the easy "truths" and "facts" we were (subliminally) taught about being male, being female, sex roles, female physiology and psychology, sexual responsibility, etc., etc. All too often we have found that we had *no* opinion or belief of our own, but had simply incorporated the dogmas of our society; and so we must discover, invent, make our own truths, our values, ourselves.

This remaking of the womanself is a release and relief to those who want and need group support, or whose womanhood has been systematically reviled, degraded, exploited in childhood, marriage, and work. To others like myself, to whom the peer group is no home and who have not been alienated from their own being-as-woman, this job of self-examination and self-birth does not come easy. "I like women; I like myself; why mess it all up?"—"I don't *care* if they're men or women"—"Why on earth should a woman have to write about only women?" All the questions are valid; none has an easy answer; but they must, now, be *asked* and *answered.* A political activist can take her answers from the current ideology of her movement, but an artist has got to dig those answers out of herself, and keep on digging until she knows she has got as close as she can possibly get to the truth.

I keep digging. I use the tools of feminism, and try to figure out what makes me work and how I work, so that I will no longer work in ignorance or irresponsibly. It's not a brief or easy business; one is groping down in the dark of the mind and body, a long, long way from Schenectady. How little we really know about ourselves, woman or man!

One thing I seem to have dug up is this: the "person" I tend to write about is often not exactly, or not totally, either a man or a woman. On the superficial level, this means there is little sexual stereotyping—the men aren't lustful and the women aren't gorgeous—and the sex itself is seen as a *relationship rather than an act.* Sex serves mainly to define gender, and the gender of the person is not exhausted, or even very nearly approached, by the label "man" or "woman." Indeed both sex and gender seem to be used mainly to define the meaning of "person," or of "self." Once, as I began to be awakened, I closed the relationship into one person, an androgyne. But more often it appears conventionally and overtly, as a couple. Both in one: or two making a whole. Yin does not occur without yang, nor yang without yin. Once I was asked what I thought the central, constant theme of my work was, and I said spontaneously, "Marriage."

I haven't yet written a book worthy of that tremendous (and staggeringly unfashionable) theme. I haven't even figured out yet what I meant. But rereading this early, easygoing adventure story, I think the theme is there—not clear, not strong, but being striven toward. "I learn by going where I have to go."

INTRODUCTION TO
CITY OF ILLUSIONS

(1978)

Once upon a time I set out to write a story about a man with two different minds in his head, to be called *The Two-Minded Man*. It didn't quite work out that way.

Always the book one imagines and the book one writes are different things. The one exists objectively, a scribbled manuscript or so many thousand printed copies. The other exists subjectively. It is the other's first cause and final cause. Toward it the written book, during its writing, continually strives, like the image in a mirror approaching the person moving toward it. But they do not merge. Only in poetry, which breaks all barriers, do the two ever meet, each becoming the other.

When I reread a work of my own I have always before my mind's eye the book I imagined before I wrote this one. And that book is the better one. All the strengths and beauties of this one are only shadows and reflections of the power, the splendor, I saw and could not keep.

When the discrepancy is particularly huge, it is comforting to think Platonically that that subjective or visionary book is itself a mere shadow of the ideal Book, which nobody can ever get to.

But meanwhile, the first publisher went and called it *City of Illusions*, a title which I sometimes fail to recognize at all, though I don't think I've yet got to the point where I ask who wrote it.

This book has villain trouble. It's not the only one, in SF or out of it.

The modern literary cliché is: bad people are interesting, good people are dull. This isn't true even if you accept the sentimental definition of evil upon which it's based; good people, like good cooking, good music, good carpentry, etc., whether judged ethically or aesthetically, tend to be more interesting, varied, complex, and surprising than bad people, bad cooking, etc. The lovable rogue, the romantic criminal, the revolutionary Satan are essentially literary creations, not met with in daily life. They are embodiments of desire, types of the soul; thus their vitality is immense and lasting; but they are better suited to poetry and drama than to the novel. People in novels, like those in daily life, tend to be all more or less stupid, meddling, incompetent, and greedy, doing evil without exactly intending to; among them the full-blown Villain seems improbable (just as he does in daily life). It takes a very great novelist to write a character that is both truly and convincingly evil, such as Dickens's Uriah Heep, or, more subtly, Steerforth. Real villains are rare; and they never, I believe, occur in flocks. Herds of Bad Guys are the death of a novel. Whether they're labeled politically, racially, sexually, by creed, species, or whatever, they just don't work. The Shing are the least convincing lot of people I ever wrote. It came of trying to obey my elder daughter's orders. Elisabeth at eight came and said, "I thought of some people named Shing, you ought to write a story about them." "What are they like?" I asked, and she said, with a divine smile and shining eyes, "They're *bad*."—Well, I fluffed it. A troop of little Hitlers from Outer Space; the guys in the black hats. I should have made Elisabeth tell me how to do it. She could have, too. Eight-year-olds know what bad is. Grown-ups get confused.

Every novel gives you a chance to do certain things you could not do without it; this is true for the writer as for the reader. Gratitude seems the only fit response. Some things I am grateful to this book for:

The chance to invent the patterning frame (I wish I had one).

The chance to use my own "translation" (collation-ripoff) of the *Tao Te Ching*.

The chance to imagine my country, America, without cities, almost without towns, as sparsely populated by our species as it was five hundred years ago; the vastness of this land, the empty beauty of it; here and there (random, the pattern broken) a little settlement of human beings; a buried supermarket or a ruined freeway made mysterious and pathetic as all things are by age. The sense of time, but more than that the sense of space, extent, the wideness of the continent. The wideness, the wilderness. Prairie, forest; undergrowth, bushes, grass, weeds; the wilderness. We talk patronizingly now of "saving the wilderness" for "recreational purposes," but the wilderness has no purpose and can neither be destroyed nor saved. Where we tame the prairie, the used-car lots and the slums arise, terrible, crowded, empty. The wilderness is disorder. The wilderness is the earth itself, and the dust between the stars, from which new earths are made.

The chance to play with forests. The forest of the mind. Forests one within another.

The chance to speak of civilization not as a negative force—

restraint, constraint, repression, authority—but as an opportunity lost, an ideal of truth. The City as goal and dream. The interdependence of order and honesty. No word or moment or way of being is more or less "real" than any other, and all is "natural"; what varies is vividness and accuracy of perception, clarity, and honesty of speech. The measure of a civilization may be the individual's ability to speak the truth.

Thus, the chance to remark that programmed pigs may talk ethics but not truth.

The chance to take another journey. Most of my stories are excuses for a journey. (We shall henceforth respectfully refer to this as the Quest Theme.) I never did care much about plots, all I want is to go from A to B—or, more often, from A to A—by the most difficult and circuitous route.

The chance to give the country between Wichita and Pueblo a ruler worthy of it.

The chance to build a city across the Black Canyon of the Gunnison.

The chance to argue inconclusively with the slogan "reverence for life," which by leaving out too much lets the lie get in and eat the apple rotten.

The chance to give Rolery and Jakob Agat a descendant.

The chance to begin and end a book with darkness, like a dream.

INTRODUCTION TO
THE WORD FOR WORLD
IS FOREST

(1977)

ON WHAT THE ROAD TO HELL IS PAVED WITH

There is nothing in all Freud's writing that I like better than his assertion that artists' work is motivated by the desire "to achieve honour, power, riches, fame, and the love of women." It is such a comforting, such a complete statement; it explains everything about the artist. There have been artists who agreed with it; Ernest Hemingway, for instance; at least, he said he wrote for money, and since he was an honored, powerful, rich, famous artist beloved by women, he ought to know.

There is another statement about the artist's desire that is, to me, less obscure; the first two stanzas of it read,

Riches I hold in light esteem
And Love I laugh to scorn
And lust of Fame was but a dream
That vanished with the morn—

And if I pray, the only prayer
That moves my lips for me
Is—"Leave the heart that now I bear
And give me liberty."

Emily Brontë wrote those lines when she was twenty-two. She was a young and inexperienced woman, not honored, not rich, not powerful, not famous, and you see that she was positively rude about love ("of women" or otherwise). I believe, however, that she was rather better qualified than Freud to talk about what motivates the artist. He had a theory. But she had authority.

It may well be useless, if not pernicious, to seek a single motive for a pursuit so complex, long-pursued, and various as art; I imagine that Brontë got as close to it as anyone needs to get, with her word "liberty."

The pursuit of art, then, by artist or audience, is the pursuit of liberty. If you accept that, you see at once why truly serious people reject and mistrust the arts, labeling them as "escapism." The captured soldier tunneling out of prison, the runaway slave, and Solzhenitsyn in exile are escapists. Aren't they? The definition also helps explain why all healthy children can sing, dance, paint, and play with words; why art is an increasingly important element in psychotherapy; why

Winston Churchill painted, why mothers sing cradle-songs, and what is wrong with Plato's *Republic*. It really is a much more useful statement than Freud's, though nowhere near as funny.

I am not sure what Freud meant by "power," in this context. Perhaps significantly, Brontë does not mention power. Shelley does, indirectly: "Poets are the unacknowledged legislators of the world." This is perhaps not too far from what Freud had in mind, for I doubt he was thinking of artists' immediate and joyous power over their material—the shaping hand, the dancer's leap, the novelist's power of life and death over characters; it is more probable that he meant the power of the idea to influence other people.

The desire for power, in the sense of power over others, is what pulls most people off the path of the pursuit of liberty. The reason Brontë does not mention it is probably that it was never even a temptation to her, as it was to her sister Charlotte. Emily did not give a damn about other people's morals. But many artists, particularly artists of the word, whose ideas must actually be spoken in their work, succumb to the temptation. They begin to see that they can do good to other people. They forget about liberty, then, and instead of legislating in divine arrogance, like God or Shelley, they begin to preach.

In this tale, *The Word for World Is Forest*, which began as a pure pursuit of freedom and the dream, I succumbed, in part, to the lure of the pulpit. It is a very strong lure to a science fiction writer, who deals more directly than most novelists with ideas, whose metaphors are shaped by or embody ideas, and who therefore is always in danger of inextricably confusing ideas with opinions.

I wrote *The Little Green Men* (its first editor, Harlan Ellison, retitled it, with my rather morose permission) in the winter of 1968, during a year's stay in London. All through the sixties, in my home city in the States, I had been helping organize and participating in nonviolent demonstrations, first against atomic bomb testing, then against the pursuance of the war in Vietnam. I don't know how many times I walked down Alder Street in the rain, feeling useless, foolish, and obstinate, along with ten or twenty or a hundred other foolish and obstinate souls. There was always somebody taking pictures of us—not the press—odd-looking people with cheap cameras: John Birchers? FBI? CIA? Crackpots? No telling. I used to grin at them, or stick out my tongue. One of my fiercer friends brought a camera once and took pictures of the picture-takers. Anyhow, there was a peace movement, and I was in it, and so had a channel of action and expression for my ethical and political opinions totally separate from my writing.

In England that year, a guest and a foreigner, I had no such outlet. And 1968 was a bitter year for those who opposed the war. The lies and hypocrisies redoubled; so did the killing. Moreover, it was becoming clear that the ethic which approved the defoliation of forests and grainlands and the murder of noncombatants in the name of "peace" was only a corollary of the ethic which permits the despoliation of natural resources for private profit or the GNP, and the murder of the creatures of the Earth in the name of "man." The victory of the ethic of exploitation, in all societies, seemed as inevitable as it was disastrous.

It was from such pressures, internalized, that this story resulted: forced out, in a sense, against my conscious resistance. I have said elsewhere that I never wrote a story more easily, fluently, surely— and with less pleasure.

I knew, because of the compulsive quality of the composition, that it was likely to become a preachment, and I struggled against this. Say not the struggle naught availeth. Neither Lyubov nor Selver is mere Virtue Triumphant; moral and psychological complexity was salvaged, at least, in those characters. But Davidson is, though not uncomplex, pure; he is purely evil—and I don't, consciously, believe purely evil people exist. But my unconscious has other opinions. It looked into itself and produced, from itself, Captain Davidson. I do not disclaim him.

American involvement in Vietnam is now past; the immediately intolerable pressures have shifted to other areas; and so the moralizing aspects of the story are now plainly visible. These I regret, but I do not disclaim them, either. The work must stand or fall on whatever elements it preserved of the yearning that underlies all specific outrage and protest, whatever tentative outreaching it made, amidst anger and despair, toward justice, or wit, or grace, or liberty.

SYNCHRONICITY CAN HAPPEN AT ALMOST ANY TIME

A few years ago, a few years after the first publication in America of *The Word for World Is Forest*, I had the great pleasure of meeting Dr. Charles Tart, a psychologist well known for his researches into and his book on *Altered States of Consciousness*. He asked me if I had modeled the Athsheans of the story upon the Senoi people of Malaysia. The who? said I, so he told me about them. The Senoi are, or were, a people whose culture includes and is indeed substantially based upon a deliberate training in and use of the dream. Dr. Tart's book includes a brief article on them by Kilton Stewart.[1]

> Breakfast in the Senoi is like a dream clinic, with the father
> and older brothers listening to and analysing the dreams of
> all the children . . .

> When the Senoi child reports a falling dream, the adult
> answers with enthusiasm, "That is a wonderful dream, one
> of the best dreams a man can have. Where did you fall to,
> and what did you discover?"

The Senoi dream is meaningful, active, and creative. Adults deliberately go into their dreams to solve problems of interpersonal and intercultural conflict. They come out of their dreams with a new song, tool, dance, idea. The waking and the dreaming states are equally valid, each acting upon the other in complementary fashion.

The article implies, by omission rather than by direct statement, that the men are the "great dreamers" among the Senoi; whether this means that the women are socially inferior or that their role (as among the Athsheans) is equal and compensatory is not clear. Nor is there any mention of the Senoi conception of divinity, the numinous, etc.; it is merely stated that they do not practice magic, though they are perfectly willing to let neighboring peoples think they do, as this discourages invasion.

> They have built a system of inter-personal relations which,
> in the field of psychology, is perhaps on a level with
> our attainments in such areas as television and nuclear
> physics.

It appears that the Senoi have not had a war, or a murder, for several hundred years.

There they are, twelve thousand of them, farming, hunting, fishing, and dreaming, in the rainforests of the mountains of Malaysia. Or there they were, in 1935—perhaps. Kilton Stewart's report on them has had no professional sequels that I know of.* Were they ever there, and if so, are they still there? In the waking time, I mean, in what we so fantastically call "the real world." In the dreamtime, of course, they are there, and here. I thought I was inventing my own lot of imaginary aliens, and I was only describing the Senoi. It is not only the Captain Davidsons who can be found in the unconscious, if one looks. The quiet people who do not kill each other are there, too. It seems that a great deal is there, the things we most fear (and therefore deny), the things we most need (and therefore deny). I wonder, couldn't we start listening to our dreams, and our children's dreams?

"Where did you fall to, and what did you discover?"

NOTE

1. "Dream Theory in Malaya," by Kilton Stewart, in *Altered States of Consciousness*, ed. Charles T. Tart (New York: Wiley & Sons, 1969; New York: Anchor/Doubleday, 1972). The quotations are on pages 164 and 163 of the Anchor second edition.

---

* Note (1989). It has since been pretty conclusively shown that his work was closer to fiction than to fieldwork—if not totally invented, almost unsubstantiated.

INTRODUCTION TO *THE LEFT HAND OF DARKNESS*

(1976)

Science fiction is often described, and even defined, as extrapolative. The science fiction writer is supposed to take a trend or phenomenon of the here and now, purify and intensify it for dramatic effect, and extend it into the future. "If this goes on, this is what will happen." A prediction is made. Method and results much resemble those of a scientist who feeds large doses of a purified and concentrated food additive to mice, in order to predict what may happen to people who eat it in small quantities for a long time. The outcome seems almost inevitably to be cancer. So does the outcome of extrapolation. Strictly extrapolative works of science fiction generally arrive about where the Club of Rome arrives: somewhere between the gradual extinction of human liberty and the total extinction of terrestrial life.

This may explain why many people who do not read science fiction describe it as "escapist," but when questioned further, admit they do not read it because "it's so depressing."

Almost anything carried to its logical extreme becomes depressing, if not carcinogenic.

Fortunately, though extrapolation is an element in science fiction, it isn't the name of the game by any means. It is far too rationalist and simplistic to satisfy the imaginative mind, whether the writer's or the reader's. Variables are the spice of life.

This book is not extrapolative. If you like you can read it, and a lot of other science fiction, as a thought experiment. Let's say (says Mary Shelley) that a young doctor creates a human being in his laboratory; let's say (says Philip K. Dick) that the Allies lost the Second World War; let's say this or that is such and so, and see what happens . . . In a story so conceived, the moral complexity proper to the modern novel need not be sacrificed, nor is there any built-in dead end; thought and intuition can move freely within bounds set only by the terms of the experiment, which may be very large indeed.

The purpose of a thought experiment, as the term was used by Schrödinger and other physicists, is not to predict the future—indeed Schrödinger's most famous thought experiment goes to show that the "future," on the quantum level, *cannot* be predicted—but to describe reality, the present world.

Science fiction is not predictive; it is descriptive.

Predictions are uttered by prophets (free of charge); by clairvoyants (who usually charge a fee, and are therefore more honored in their day than prophets); and by futurologists (salaried). Prediction is the business of prophets, clairvoyants, and futurologists. It is not the business of novelists. A novelist's business is lying.

The weather bureau will tell you what next Tuesday will be like, and the Rand Corporation will tell you what the twenty-first century will be like. I don't recommend that you turn to the writers of fiction for such information. It's none of their business. All they're trying to do is tell you what they're like, and what you're like— what's going on—what the weather is now, today, this moment, the rain, the sunlight, look! Open your eyes; listen, listen. That is what the novelists say. But they don't tell you what you will see and hear. All they can tell you is what they have seen and heard, in their time in this world, a third of it spent in sleep and dreaming, another third of it spent in telling lies.

"The truth against the world!"—Yes. Certainly. Fiction writers, at least in their braver moments, do desire the truth; to know it, speak it, serve it. But they go about it in a peculiar and devious way, which consists in inventing persons, places, and events which never did and never will exist or occur, and telling about these fictions in detail and at length and with a great deal of emotion, and then when they are done writing down this pack of lies, they say, There! That's the truth!

They may use all kinds of facts to support their tissue of lies. They may describe the Marshalsea Prison, which was a real place, or the Battle of Borodino, which really was fought, or the process of cloning, which really takes place in laboratories, or the deterioration of a personality, which is described in real textbooks of psychology; and so on. This weight of verifiable place-event-phenomenon-behavior makes readers forget that they are reading a pure invention, a history that never took place anywhere but in that unlocalizable region, the author's mind. In fact, while we read a novel, we are insane—bonkers. We believe in the existence of people who aren't there, we hear their voices, we watch the Battle of Borodino with them, we may even become Napoleon. Sanity returns (in most cases) when the book is closed.

Is it any wonder that no truly respectable society has ever trusted its artists?

But our society, being troubled and bewildered, seeking guidance, sometimes puts an entirely mistaken trust in its artists, using them as prophets and futurologists.

I do not say that artists cannot be seers, inspired: that the *awen* cannot come upon them, and the god speak through them. Who would be an artist if they did not believe that that happens? If they did not *know* it happens, because they have felt the god within them use their tongue, their hands? Maybe only once, once in their lives. But once is enough.

Nor would I say that the artist alone is so burdened and so privileged. The scientist is another who prepares, who makes ready, working day and night, sleeping and awake, for inspiration. As Pythagoras knew, the god may speak in the forms of geometry as well as in the shapes of dreams; in the harmony of pure thought as well as in the harmony of sounds; in numbers as well as in words.

But it is words that make the trouble and confusion. We are asked now to consider words as useful in only one way: as signs. Our philosophers, some of them, would have us agree that a word (sentence, statement) has value only insofar as it has one single meaning, points to one fact which is comprehensible to the rational intellect, logically sound, and—ideally—quantifiable.

Apollo, the god of light, of reason, of proportion, harmony, number—Apollo blinds those who press too close in worship. Don't look straight at the sun. Go into a dark bar for a bit and have a beer with Dionysios every now and then.

I talk about the gods, I am an atheist. But I am an artist, too, and therefore a liar. Distrust everything I say. I am telling the truth.

The only truth I can understand or express is, logically defined, a lie. Psychologically defined, a symbol. Aesthetically defined, a metaphor.

Oh, it's lovely to be invited to participate in Futurological Congresses where Systems Science displays its grand apocalyptic graphs, to be asked to tell the newspapers what America will be like in 2001, and all that, but it's a terrible mistake. I write science fiction, and science fiction isn't about the future. I don't know any more about the future than you do, and very likely less.

This book is not about the future. Yes, it begins by announcing that it's set in the "Ekumenical Year 1490–97," but surely you don't *believe* that?

Yes, indeed the people in it are androgynous, but that doesn't mean that I'm predicting that in a millennium or so we will all be androgynous, or announcing that I think we damned well ought to be androgynous. I'm merely observing, in the peculiar, devious, and thought-experimental manner proper to science fiction, that if you look at us at certain odd times of day in certain weathers, we already are. I am not predicting, or prescribing. I am describing. I am describing certain aspects of psychological reality in the novelist's way, which is by inventing elaborately circumstantial lies.

In reading a novel, any novel, we have to know perfectly well that the whole thing is nonsense, and then, while reading, believe every word of it. Finally, when we're done with it, we may find—if it's a good novel—that we're a bit different from what we were before we read it, that we have been changed a little, as if by having met a new face, crossed a street we never crossed before. But it's very hard to *say* just what we learned, how we were changed.

The artist deals with what cannot be said in words.

The artist whose medium is fiction does this *in words*. The novelist says in words what cannot be said in words.

Words can be used thus paradoxically because they have, along with a semiotic usage, a symbolic or metaphoric usage. (They also have a sound—a fact the linguistic positivists take no interest in. A sentence or paragraph is like a chord or harmonic sequence in music: its meaning may be more clearly understood by the attentive ear, even though it is read in silence, than by the attentive intellect.)

All fiction is metaphor. Science fiction is metaphor. What sets it apart from older forms of fiction seems to be its use of new metaphors, drawn from certain great dominants of our contemporary life—science, all the sciences, and technology, and the relativistic and the historical outlook among them. Space travel is one of these metaphors; so is an alternative society, an alternative biology; the future is another. The future, in fiction, is a metaphor.

A metaphor for what?

If I could have said it nonmetaphorically, I would not have written all these words, this novel; and Genly Ai would never have sat down at my desk and used up my ink and typewriter ribbon in informing me, and you, rather solemnly, that the truth is a matter of the imagination.

IS GENDER NECESSARY?

(1976)

REDUX

(1988)

In the mid-1960s the women's movement was just beginning to move again, after a fifty-year halt. There was a groundswell gathering. I felt it, but I didn't know it was a groundswell; I just thought it was something wrong with me. I considered myself a feminist: I didn't see how you could be a thinking woman and not be a feminist; but I had never taken a step beyond the ground gained for us by Emmeline Pankhurst and Virginia Woolf.[1]

Along about 1967, I began to feel a certain unease, a need to step on a little farther, perhaps,

[1] *Feminism has enlarged its ground and strengthened its theory and practice immensely, and enduringly, in these past twenty years; but has anyone actually taken a step "beyond" Virginia Woolf? The image, implying an ideal of "progress," is not one I would use now.*

on my own. I began to want to define and understand the meaning of sexuality and the meaning of gender, in my life and in our society. Much had gathered in the unconscious—both personal and collective—which must either be brought up into consciousness or else turn destructive. It was that same need, I think, that had led de Beauvoir to write *The Second Sex*, and Friedan to write *The Feminine Mystique*, and that was, at the same time, leading Kate Millett and others to write their books, and to create the new feminism. But I was not a theoretician, a political thinker or activist, or a sociologist. I was and am a fiction writer. The way I did my thinking was to write a novel. That novel, *The Left Hand of Darkness*, is the record of my consciousness, the process of my thinking.

Perhaps, now that we have all[2] moved on to a plane of heightened consciousness about these matters, it might be of some interest to look back on

[2] *Well, quite a lot of us, anyhow.*

the book, to see what it did, what it tried to do, and what it might have done, insofar as it is a "feminist"[3] book. (Let me repeat the last qualification, once. The fact is that the real subject of the book is not feminism or sex or gender or anything of the sort; as far as I can see, it is a book about betrayal and fidelity. That is why one of its two dominant sets of symbols is an extended metaphor of winter, of ice, snow, cold: the winter journey. The rest of this discussion will concern only half, the lesser half, of the book.)[4]

It takes place on a planet called Gethen, whose human inhabitants differ from us in their sexual physiology. Instead of our continuous sexuality, the Gethenians have an oestrous period, called *kemmer*. When they are not in kemmer, they are sexually inactive and impotent; they are also androgynous. An observer in the book describes the cycle:

[3] *Strike the quotation marks from the word "feminist," please.*

[4] *This parenthesis is overstated; I was feeling defensive, and resentful that critics of the book insisted upon talking only about its "gender problems," as if it were an essay, not a novel. "The fact is that the real subject of the book is . . ." This is bluster. I had opened a can of worms and was trying hard to shut it. "The fact is," however, that there are other aspects to the book, which are involved with its sex/gender aspects quite inextricably.*

In the first phase of kemmer [the individual] remains completely androgynous. Gender, and potency, are not attained in isolation . . . Yet the sexual impulse is tremendously strong in this phase, controlling the entire personality . . . When the individual finds a partner in kemmer, hormonal secretion is further stimulated (most importantly by touch—secretion? scent?) until in one partner either a male or female hormonal dominance is established. The genitals engorge or shrink accordingly, foreplay intensifies, and the partner, triggered by the change, takes on the other sexual role (apparently without exception) . . . Normal individuals have no predisposition to either sexual role in kemmer; they do not know whether they will be the male or the female, and have no choice in the matter . . . The culminant phase of kemmer lasts from two to five days, during which sexual drive and capacity are at maximum. It ends fairly abruptly, and if conception has not taken place, the individual returns to the latent phase and the cycle begins anew. If the individual was in the female role and was impregnated, hormonal activity of course continues, and for the gestation and lactation periods this individual remains female . . . With the cessation of lactation the female becomes once more a perfect androgyne. No physiological habit is established, and the mother of several children may be the father of several more.

Why did I invent these peculiar people? Not just so that the book could contain, halfway through it, the sentence "The king was pregnant"—though I admit that

I am fond of that sentence. Not, certainly not, to propose Gethen as a model for humanity. I am not in favor of genetic alteration of the human organism—not at our present level of understanding. I was not recommending the Gethenian sexual setup: I was using it. It was a heuristic device, a thought experiment. Physicists often do thought experiments. Einstein shoots a light ray through a moving elevator; Schrödinger puts a cat in a box. There is no elevator, no cat, no box. The experiment is performed, the question is asked, in the mind. Einstein's elevator, Schrödinger's cat, my Gethenians are simply a way of thinking. They are questions, not answers; process, not stasis. One of the essential functions of science fiction, I think, is precisely this kind of question-asking: reversals of a habitual way of thinking, metaphors for what our language has no words for as yet, experiments in imagination.

The subject of my experiment, then, was something like this: because of our lifelong social conditioning, it is hard for us to see clearly what, besides purely physiological form and function, truly differentiates men and women. Are there real differences in temperament, capacity, talent, psychic process, etc.? If so, what are they? Only comparative ethnology offers, so far, any solid evidence on the matter, and the evidence is incomplete and often contradictory. The only going social experiments that are truly relevant are the kibbutzim and the Chinese communes, and they, too, are inconclusive—and hard to get unbiased information about. How to find out? Well, one can always put a cat in a box. One can send an imaginary, but conventional, indeed rather stuffy, young man from Earth into an imaginary culture which is totally free of sex roles because there is no, absolutely no, physiological sex distinction. I eliminated gender to find out what was left. Whatever was left would be, presumably, simply human. It would define the area that is shared by men and women alike.

I still think that this was a

rather neat idea. But as an experiment, it was messy. All results were uncertain; a repetition of the experiment by someone else, or by myself seven years later, would probably[5] give quite different results. Scientifically, this is most disreputable. That's all right; I am not a scientist. I play the game where the rules keep changing.

Among these dubious and uncertain results, achieved as I thought, and wrote, and wrote, and thought, about my imaginary people, three appear rather interesting to me.

First: the absence of war. In the thirteen thousand years of recorded history on Gethen, there has not been a war. The people seem to be as quarrelsome, competitive, and aggressive as we are; they have fights, murders, assassinations, feuds, forays, and so on. But there have been no great invasions by peoples on the move, like the Mongols in Asia or the Whites in the New World: partly because Gethenian populations seem to remain stable in size, they do not move in large masses, or rapidly.

[5] *Strike the word "probably" and replace it with "certainly."*

Their migrations have been slow, no one generation going very far. They have no nomadic peoples, and no societies that live by expansion and aggression against other societies. Nor have they formed large, hierarchically governed nation-states, the mobilizable entity that is the essential factor in modern war. The basic unit all over the planet is a group of two hundred to eight hundred people, called a hearth, a structure founded less on economic convenience than on sexual necessity (there must be others in kemmer at the same time), and therefore more tribal than urban in nature, though overlaid and interwoven with a later urban pattern. The hearth tends to be communal, independent, and somewhat introverted. Rivalries between hearths, as between individuals, are channeled into a socially approved form of aggression called *shifgrethor*, a conflict without physical violence, involving one-upmanship, the saving and losing of face—conflict ritualized, stylized, controlled. When shifgrethor breaks down there may be physical violence, but it does not become mass violence, remaining limited, personal. The active group remains small. The dispersive trend is as strong as the cohesive. Historically, when hearths gathered into a nation for economic reasons, the cellular pattern still dominated the centralized one. There might be a king and a parliament, but authority was not enforced so much by might as by the use of shifgrethor and intrigue, and was accepted as custom, without appeal to patriarchal ideals of divine right, patriotic duty, etc. Ritual and parade were far more effective agents of order than armies or police. Class structure was flexible and open; the value of the social hierarchy was less economic than aesthetic, and there was no great gap between rich and poor. There was no slavery or servitude. Nobody owned anybody. There were no chattels. Economic organization was rather communistic or syndicalistic than capitalistic, and was seldom highly centralized.

During the time span of the novel, however, all this is changing. One of the two large nations of the planet is becoming a genuine nation-state, complete with patriotism and bureaucracy. It has achieved state capitalism and the centralization of power, authoritarian government, and a secret police; and it is on the verge of achieving the world's first war.

Why did I present the first picture, and show it in the process of changing to a different one? I am not sure. I think it is because I was trying to show a balance—and the delicacy of a balance. To me the "female principle" is, or at least historically has been, basically anarchic. It values order without constraint, rule by custom not by force. It has been the male who enforces order, who constructs power structures, who makes, enforces, and breaks laws. On Gethen, these two principles are in balance: the decentralizing against the centralizing, the flexible against the rigid, the circular against the linear. But balance is a precarious state, and at the moment of the novel the balance, which had leaned toward the "feminine," is tipping the other way.[6]

Second: the absence of exploitation. The Gethenians do not rape their world. They have developed a high technology, heavy industry, automobiles, radios, explosives, etc., but they have done so very slowly, absorbing their technology rather than letting it overwhelm them. They have no myth of Progress at all. Their calendar calls the current year always the Year One, and they count backward and forward from that.

In this, it seems that what I was after again was a balance: the driving linearity of the "male," the pushing forward to the limit, the logicality that admits no boundary—and the circularity of the "female," the valuing of patience, ripeness, practicality, livableness. A model for this balance, of course, exists on Earth: Chinese civilization over the past six millennia. (I did not know when I wrote the book that the parallel extends even to the calendar; the

6 *At the very inception of the whole book, I was interested in writing a novel about people in a society that had never had a war. That came first. The androgyny came second. (Cause and effect? Effect and cause?)*

I would now write this paragraph this way: . . . The "female principle" has historically been anarchic; that is, anarchy has historically been identified as female. The domain allotted to women— "the family," for example—is the area of order without coercion, rule by custom not by force. Men have reserved the structures of social power to themselves (and those few women whom they admit to it on male terms, such as queens, prime ministers); men make the wars and peaces, men make, enforce, and break the laws. On Gethen, the two polarities we perceive through our cultural conditioning as male and female are neither, and are in balance: consensus with authority, decentralizing with centralizing, flexible with rigid, circular with linear, hierarchy with network. But it is not a motionless balance, there being no such thing in life, and at the moment of the novel, it is wobbling perilously.

Chinese historically never had a linear dating system such as the one that starts with the birth of Christ.)[7]

Third: the absence of sexuality as a continuous social factor. For four-fifths of the month, a Gethenian's sexuality plays no part at all in his social life (unless he's pregnant); for the other one-fifth, it dominates him absolutely. In kemmer, one must have a partner, it is imperative. (Have you ever lived in a small apartment with a tabby-cat in heat?) Gethenian society fully accepts this imperative. When a Gethenian has to make love, he does make love, and everybody expects him to, and approves of it.[8]

But still, human beings are human beings, not cats. Despite our continuous sexuality and our intense self-domestication (domesticated animals tend to be promiscuous, wild animals pair-bonding, familial, or tribal in their mating), we are very seldom truly promiscuous. We do have rape, to be sure—no other animal has equaled us there. We have mass rape, when an army

[7] *A better model might be some of the pre-Conquest cultures of the Americas, though not those hierarchical and imperialistic ones approvingly termed, by our hierarchical and imperialistic standards, "high." The trouble with the Chinese model is that their civilization instituted and practiced male domination as thoroughly as the other "high" civilizations. I was thinking of a Taoist ideal, not of such practices as bride-selling and foot-binding, which we are trained to consider unimportant, nor of the deep misogyny of Chinese culture, which we are trained to consider normal.*

[8] *I would now write this paragraph this way: . . . For four-fifths of the month, sexuality plays no part at all in a Gethenian's social behavior; for the other one-fifth, it controls behavior absolutely. In kemmer, one must have a partner, it is imperative. (Have you ever lived in a small apartment with a tabby-cat in heat?) Gethenian society fully accepts this imperative. When Gethenians have to make love, they do make love, and everybody else expects it and approves of it.*

(male, of course) invades; we have prostitution, promiscuity controlled by economics; and sometimes ritual abreactive promiscuity controlled by religion; but in general we seem to avoid genuine license. At most we award it as a prize to the Alpha Male, in certain situations; it is scarcely ever permitted to the female without social penalty. It would seem, perhaps, that the mature human being, male or female, is not satisfied by sexual gratification without psychic involvement, and in fact may be *afraid of it*, to judge by the tremendous variety of social, legal, and religious controls and sanctions exerted over it in all human societies. Sex is a great mana, and therefore the immature society, or psyche, sets great taboos about it. The mature culture, or psyche, can integrate these taboos or laws into an internal ethical code, which, while allowing great freedom, does not permit the treatment of another person as an object. But, however irrational or rational, there is always a code.

Because the Gethenians cannot have sexual intercourse unless both partners are willing, because they cannot rape or be raped, I figured that they would have less fear and guilt about sex than we tend to have; but still it is a problem for them, in some ways more than for us, because of the extreme, explosive, imperative quality of the oestrous phase. Their society would have to control it, though it might move more easily than we from the taboo stage to the ethical stage. So the basic arrangement, I found, in every Gethenian community, is that of the kemmerhouse, which is open to anyone, in kemmer, native or stranger, so that he can find a partner.[9] Then there are various customary (not legal) institutions, such as the kemmering group, a group who choose to come together during kemmer as a regular thing; this is like the primate tribe, or group marriage. Or there is the possibility of vowing kemmering, which is marriage, pair-bonding for life, a personal commitment without legal sanction. Such commitments have intense moral and psychic significance, but they are not controlled by Church or State.

[9] *Read: . . . so that they can find sexual partners.*

Finally, there are two forbidden acts, which might be taboo or illegal or simply considered contemptible, depending on which of the regions of Gethen you are in: first, you don't pair off with a relative of a different generation (one who might be your own parent or child); second, you may mate, but not vow kemmering, with your own sibling. These are the old incest prohibitions. They are so general among us—and with good cause, I think, not so much genetic as psychological—that they seemed likely to be equally valid on Gethen.

These three "results," then, of my experiment, I feel were fairly clearly and successfully worked out, though there is nothing definitive about them.

In other areas where I might have pressed for at least such plausible results, I see now a failure to think things through, or to express them clearly. For example, I think I took the easy way in using such familiar governmental structures as a feudal monarchy and a modern-style bureaucracy for the two Gethenian countries that are the scene of the novel. I doubt that Gethenian governments, rising out of the cellular hearth, would resemble any of our own so closely. They might be better, they might be worse, but they would certainly be different.

I regret even more certain timidities or ineptnesses I showed in following up the psychic implications of Gethenian physiology. Just for example, I wish I had known Jung's work when I wrote the book: so that I could have decided whether a Gethenian had *no* animus or anima, or *both*, or an animum[10] . . . But the central failure in this area comes up in the frequent criticism I receive, that the Gethenians seem like *men*, instead of menwomen.

This rises in part from the choice of pronoun. I call Gethenians "he" because I utterly refuse to mangle English by inventing a pronoun for "he/she."[11]

"He" is the generic pronoun, damn it, in English. (I envy the Japanese, who, I am told, do have

[10] *For another example (and Jung wouldn't have helped with this, more likely hindered) I quite unnecessarily locked the Gethenians into heterosexuality. It is a naively pragmatic view of sex that insists that sexual partners must be of opposite sex! In any kemmerhouse homosexual practice would, of course, be possible and acceptable and welcomed—but I never thought to explore this option; and the omission, alas, implies that sexuality is heterosexuality. I regret this very much.*

[11] *This "utter refusal" of 1968 restated in 1976 collapsed, utterly, within a couple of years more. I still dislike invented pronouns, but now dislike them less than the so-called generic pronoun he/him/his, which does in fact exclude women from discourse; and which was an invention of male grammarians, for until the sixteenth century the English generic singular pronoun was they/them/their, as it still is in English and American colloquial speech. It should be restored to the written language, and let the pedants and pundits squeak and gibber in the streets.*

In a screenplay of The Left

a he/she pronoun.) But I do not consider this really very important.[12]

The pronouns wouldn't matter at all if I had been cleverer at *showing* the "female" component of the Gethenian characters in *action*.[13]

Unfortunately, the plot and structure that arose as I worked the book out cast the Gethenian protagonist, Estraven, almost exclusively into roles that we are culturally conditioned to perceive as "male"—a prime minister (it takes more than even Golda Meir and Indira Gandhi to break a stereotype), a political schemer, a fugitive, a prison-breaker, a sledge-hauler . . . I think I did this because I was privately delighted at watching, not a man, but a manwoman, do all these things, and do them with considerable skill and flair. But, for the reader, I left out too much. One does not see Estraven as a mother, with his children,[14] in any role that we automatically perceive as "female": and therefore, we tend to see him as a man.[15] This is a real flaw in

Hand of Darkness *written in 1985, I referred to Gethenians not pregnant or in kemmer by the invented pronouns a/un/a's, modeled on a British dialect. These would drive the reader mad in print, I suppose; but I have read parts of the book aloud using them, and the audience was perfectly happy, except that they pointed out that the subject pronoun, "a" pronounced "uh" [a], sounds too much like "I" said with a Southern accent.*

[12] *I now consider it very important.*

[13] *If I had realized how the pronouns I used shaped, directed, controlled my own thinking, I might have been "cleverer."*

[14] *Strike "his."*

[15] *Place "him" in quotation marks, please.*

the book, and I can only be very grateful to those readers, men and women, whose willingness to participate in the experiment led them to fill in that omission with the work of their own imagination, and to see Estraven as I saw him,[16] as man and woman, familiar and different, alien and utterly human.

It seems to be men, more often than women, who thus complete my work for me: I think because men are often more willing to identify as they read with poor, confused, defensive Genly, the Earthman, and therefore to participate in his painful and gradual discovery of love.[17]

Finally, the question arises, Is the book a Utopia? It seems to me that it is quite clearly not; it poses no *practicable* alternative to contemporary society, since it is based on an imaginary, radical change in human anatomy. All it tries to do is open up an alternative viewpoint, to widen the imagination, without making any very definite suggestions as to what might be

[16] *Read: . . . as I did.*

[17] *I now see it thus: Men were inclined to be satisfied with the book, which allowed them a safe trip into androgyny and back, from a conventionally male viewpoint. But many women wanted it to go further, to dare more, to explore androgyny from a woman's point of view as well as a man's. In fact, it does so, in that it was written by a woman. But this is admitted directly only in the chapter "The Question of Sex," the only voice of a woman in the book. I think women were justified in asking more courage of me and a more rigorous thinking through of implications.*

seen from that new viewpoint. The most it says is, I think, something like this: If we were socially ambisexual, if men and women were completely and genuinely equal in their social roles, equal legally and economically, equal in freedom, in responsibility, and in self-esteem, then society would be a very different thing. What our problems might be, God knows; I only know we would have them. But it seems likely that our central problem would not be the one it is now: the problem of exploitation—exploitation of the woman, of the weak, of the earth. Our curse is alienation, the separation of yang from yin.[18] Instead of a search for balance and integration, there is a struggle for dominance. Divisions are insisted upon, interdependence is denied. The dualism of value that destroys us, the dualism of superior/inferior, ruler/ruled, owner/owned, user/used might give way to what seems to me, from here, a much healthier, sounder, more promising modality of integration and integrity.

[18] *—and the moralization of yang as good, of yin as bad.*

THE STARING EYE

(1974)

They were displayed on the new acquisitions rack of the university library: three handsome books, in the Houghton Mifflin edition, with beige and black dust jackets, each centered with a staring black and red Eye.

Sometimes one, or two, or all three of them were out; sometimes all three were there together. I was aware of them every time I was in the library, which was often. I was uneasily aware of them. They stared at me.

The *Saturday Review* had run a special notice upon the publication of the last volume, praising the work with uncharacteristic vigor and conviction. I had thought then, I must have a look at this. But when it appeared in the library, I shied away from it. I was afraid of it. It looks dull, I thought—like the *Saturday Review.* It's probably affected. It's probably allegorical. Once I went so far as to pick up Volume II, when it alone was on the rack, and look at the first page. "The Two Towers." People were rushing around on a hill, looking for one another. The language looked a bit stilted. I put it back. The Eye stared through me.

I was (for reasons now obscure to me) reading all of Gissing. I think I had gone to the library to return *Born in Exile*, when I stopped to circle warily about the new acquisitions rack, and there they were again, all three volumes, staring. I had had about enough of the Grub Street Blues. Oh well, why not? I checked out Volume I and went home with it.

Next morning I was there at nine, and checked out the others. I read the three volumes in three days. Three weeks later I was still, at times, inhabiting Middle Earth: walking, like the Elves, in dreams waking, seeing both worlds at once, the perishing and the imperishable.

Tonight, eighteen years later, just before sitting down to write this, I was reading aloud to our nine-year-old. We have just arrived at the ruined gates of Isengard, and found Merry and Pippin sitting amongst the ruins having a snack and a smoke. The nine-year-old likes Merry, but doesn't much like Pippin. I never could tell them apart to that extent.

This is the third time I have read the book aloud—the nine-year-old has elder sisters, who read it now for themselves. We seem to have acquired three editions of it. I have no idea how many times I have read it myself. I reread a great deal, but have lost count only with Dickens, Tolstoy, and Tolkien.

Yet I believe that my hesitation, my instinctive distrust of those three volumes in the university library, was well founded. To put it in the book's own terms: something of great inherent power, even if wholly good in itself, may work destruction if used in ignorance, or at the wrong time. One must be ready; one must be strong enough.

I envy those who, born later than I, read Tolkien as children— my own children among them. I certainly have had no scruples about exposing them to it at a tender age, when their resistance is minimal. To have known, at age ten or thirteen, of the existence of Ents, and of Lothlórien—what luck!

But very few children (fortunately) are going to grow up to write fantastic novels; and despite my envy, I count it lucky that I, personally, did not and could not have read Tolkien before I was twenty-five. Because I really wonder if I could have handled it.

From the age of nine, I was writing fantasy, and I never wrote anything else. It wasn't in the least like anybody else's fantasy. I read whatever imaginative fiction I could get hold of then—*Astounding Stories*, and this and that: Dunsany was the master, the man with the keys to the gates of horn and ivory, so far as I knew. But I read everything else, too, and by twenty-five, if I had any admitted masters or models in the art of fiction, in the craft of writing, they were Tolstoy and Dickens. But my immodesty was equaled by my evasiveness, for I had kept my imagination quite to myself. I had no models there. I never tried to write like Dunsany, nor even like *Astounding*, once I was older than twelve. I had somewhere to go and, as I saw it, I had to get there by myself.

If I had known that one was there before me, one very much greater than myself, I wonder if I would have had the witless courage to go on.

By the time I read Tolkien, however, though I had not yet written anything of merit, I was old enough, and had worked long and hard enough at my craft, to be set in my ways: to know my own way. Even the sweep and force of that incredible imagination could not dislodge me from my own little rut and carry me, like Gollum, scuttling and whimpering along behind. So far as *writing* is concerned, I mean. When it comes to *reading*, there's a different matter. I open the book, the great wind blows, the Quest begins, I follow . . .

It is no matter of wonder that so many people are bored by, or detest, *The Lord of the Rings*. For one thing, there was the faddism of a few years ago—Go Go Gandalf—enough to turn anybody against it. Judged by any of the Seven Types of Ambiguity that haunt the groves of Academe, it is totally inadequate. For those who seek allegory, it must be maddening. (It must be an allegory! Of course Frodo is Christ!—Or is Gollum Christ?) For those whose grasp on reality is so tenuous that they crave ever-increasing doses of "realism" in their reading, it offers nothing—unless, perhaps, a shortcut to the loony bin. And there are many subtler reasons for disliking it; for instance the peculiar rhythm of the book, its continual alternation of distress and relief, threat and reassurance, tension and relaxation: this rocking horse gait (which is precisely what makes the huge book readable to a child of nine or ten) may well not suit a jet-age adult. And there's Aragorn, who is a stuffed shirt; and Sam, who keeps saying "sir" to Frodo until one begins to have mad visions of founding a Hobbit Socialist Party; and there isn't any sex. And there is the Problem of Evil, which some people think Tolkien muffs completely. Their arguments are superficially very good. They are the same arguments which Tolkien completely exploded, thereby freeing *Beowulf* forever from the dead hands of the pedants, in his brilliant 1934 article "The Monster and the Critics"—an article which anyone who sees Tolkien as a Sweet Old Dear, by the way, would do well to read.

Those who fault Tolkien on the Problem of Evil are usually those who have an *answer* to the Problem of Evil—which he did not. What kind of answer, after all, is it to drop a magic ring into an imaginary volcano? No ideologues, not even religious ones, are going to be happy with Tolkien, unless they manage it by misreading him. For like all great artists he escapes ideology by being too quick for its nets, too complex for its grand simplicities, too fantastic for its rationality, too real for its generalizations. They will no more keep Tolkien labeled and pickled in a bottle than they will *Beowulf,* or the *Elder Edda,* or the *Odyssey.*

It does not seem right to grieve at the end of so fulfilled a life. Only, when we get to the end of the book, I know I will have to put on a stiff frown so that little Ted will not notice that I am in tears when I read the last lines:

> He went on, and there was yellow light, and fire within; and the evening meal was ready, and he was expected. And Rose drew him in, and set him in his chair, and put little Elanor upon his lap.
>
> He drew a deep breath. "Well, I'm back," he said.

THE MODEST ONE

(1976)

A certain fanfare—the flair for self-announcement, the solemn posture assumed at the right moment, the keynote struck loudly to attract reviewers' attention—can win a genuinely original artist the readership his work deserves. Philip K. Dick comes on without fanfare. His novels are published as science fiction, which limits their "packaging" to purple-monster jackets, ensures but restricts their sales, and, above all, prevents their being noticed by most serious critics or reviewers. His prose is austere, sometimes hasty, always straightforward, with no Nabokovian fiddle-faddle. His characters are ordinary—extraordinarily ordinary—the inept small businessman, the ambitious organization girl, the minor craftsman or repairman, etc. That some of them have odd talents such as precognition is common; they're just ordinary neurotic precognitive slobs. His humor is dry and zany. You can't quote funny bits from Dick, because you have to have read the whole book up to that point to know why it's so funny when the taxicab gravely assures Barney, "I think you're doing the right thing." Taxicabs often talk in Dick's novels; they are usually earnest, but mistaken. Finally, his inventive, intricate plots move on so easily and entertainingly that the reader, guided without effort through the maze, may put the book down believing it to be a clever SF-thriller and nothing more. The fact that what Dick is entertaining us about is reality and madness, time and death, sin and salvation—this has escaped most readers and critics. Nobody notices; nobody notices that we have our own homegrown Borges, and have had him for thirty years.

I think I'm the first to bring up Borges, but Dick has once or twice been compared with Kafka. One cannot take that very far, for Dick is not an absurdist. His moral vocabulary is Christian, though never explicitly so. The last word is not despair. Well as he knows the world of the schizophrenic, the paranoid, even the autistic, his work is not (as Kafka's was) autistic, because there are other people in it; and other people are not (as they are to Sartre) hell, but salvation.

> Always, in his middle level of the human, a man risked the sinking. And yet the possibility of ascent lay before him; any aspect or sequence of reality *could become either*, at any instant. Hell and heaven, not after death but now! Depression, all mental illness, was the sinking. And the other . . . how was it achieved?
>
> Through empathy. Grasping another, not from outside, but from the inner. (*The Three Stigmata of Palmer Eldritch*)

So Mr. Tagomi, the shrewd capitalist-Taoist businessman in Japanese-occupied San Francisco (in *The Man in the High Castle*), when put to the test, sacrifices himself by refusing an act that would harm another man, though not himself. He sees evil and, nervously and unhappily, he says no to it. His gesture is modest, its results are uncertain, and his personal reward for virtue is a heart attack. There are no heroics in Dick's books, but there are heroes. One is

reminded of Dickens: what counts is the honesty, constancy, kind-
ness, and patience of ordinary people. The flashier qualities such
as courage are merely contributory to that dull, solid goodness in
which—alone—lies the hope of deliverance from evil.

Dickens addicts all know that one forgets which novel the
unforgettable character turns up in. Sarah Gamp, now, is she in
Copperfield? *Rudge*? For all their strong plots and distinct moods,
the books coalesce in memory into one huge Dickens Novel, or
Dickens Universe. The same is true of Dick's books; because he,
like Dickens, keeps a direct line open to the unconscious, it is the
powerful personal psychic imprint that dominates in retrospect.
Further, his novels are linked by obsessively recurring motifs and
details, each of which is itself a key or cue to the nature of reality
in the Dick Universe. A disk jockey circling a planet in a satellite,
bringing reassurance to distressed folk on the surface; the android,
the person who is (or is schizophrenically perceived to be) a maze of
circuitry; the wonder drug or process which alters reality, usually toward a shift or overlap of time-planes; precognition; entropy, decay,
the tombworld; the subworld (often a Barbie doll–type toy): all
these themes, and others, interconnect, one or another dominating
each book, each implying the others. In the earlier and some recent
books, the compulsiveness of the themes is evident, threatening the
artist's control. The earlier books, of which *A Maze of Death* and
Time Out of Joint are good examples, suffer somewhat from the tension of overcontrol; and from *Ubik* through *Flow My Tears* a gap has
been growing between the expression of rational opinion or belief
and the intractable, overwhelming witness of the irrational psyche.
When in full control of his dangerous material, Dick has written at
least five books which walk the high wire with grace from end to
end: *The Man in the High Castle, Dr. Bloodmoney, Martian Time-*

Slip, Clans of the Alphane Moon, and the extremely funny *Galactic Pot-Healer.*

The task of a writer who writes about madness from within is an appalling one. The risk Virginia Woolf took in writing Septimus in *Mrs. Dalloway* is the risk Philip Dick took in writing Manfred in *Martian Time-Slip.* The price paid is a price no artist, nobody, can be expected to pay; the prize won is invaluable. These are genuine reports from the other side, controlled by the intelligence and skill of an experienced novelist, and illuminated by compassion.

> It is the stopping of time. The end of experience, of anything new. Once the person becomes psychotic, nothing ever happens to him again. (*Martian Time-Slip*)

So the schizoid Jack Bohlen understands the schizophrenic boy Manfred; so we, experiencing the terrifying imagery of the book, also come to understand. And therefore Dick can compress all the shock and splendor of salvation into a few characteristically offhand sentences, and three plain words:

> One of the Bleekman females shyly offered him a cigarette from those she carried. Thanking her, he accepted it. They continued on.
>
> And as they moved along, Manfred Steiner felt something strange happening inside him. He was changing.

The shy offer of a cigarette is a thoroughly Dickian gesture of salvation. Nobody ever saves the Galactic Empire from the Tentacled Andromedans. Something has indeed been saved, but only a human soul. We are about as far from the panoply of space operas as we can get. And yet Dick is a science fiction writer—not borrowing the trappings to deck out old nonsense with shiny chromium fittings, but using the new metaphors *because he needs them*; using them with power and beauty, because they are the language appropriate to what he wants to say, to us, about ourselves. Dick is no escapist, and no "futurist." He is a prophet, yes, but in the *I Ching* sense, in the sense in which poets are prophets: not because he plays foretelling games with Rand, extrapolates the next technological gimmick, but because his moral vision is desperately clear, and because his art is adequate to express that vision.

But you know what prophets don't get in their own country.

INTRODUCTION TO
STAR SONGS OF
AN OLD PRIMATE

*Abominations, that's what they are; afterwords, introductions,
all the dribble around the story.*

James Tiptree Jr., 1971

When the author of this book requested me to write an introduction for it, I was honored, delighted, and appalled. Omitting the civilities and apologies customary between old primates, and which went on for about a week, the request appeared in these terms, and I quote: "Write a two-line introduction saying, Here are some stories."

I have been trying to obey these instructions ever since. Various versions have been tested; for example:

1) Here

Are some stories.

2) Here are

Some stories.

3) Here are some

Stories.

Since none of these efforts seemed entirely satisfactory, I took the liberty of expanding upon the basic instructions, at the risk of offending the profound and authentic modesty of the author, and arrived at this:

> 4) Here are some superbly strong sad funny and very beautiful
> Stories.

That seems a little more like it. I may return to this problem later, with renewed vigor. There must be some way to do it.

I have known James Tiptree Jr. for several years now; known him well, and with ever-increasing trust and pleasure, and to the profit of my soul. He is a rather slight, fragile man of about sixty, shy in manner, courteous; wears a straw hat; has lived in, and still vacations in, some of the more exotic parts of the world; has been through the army, the government, and the university; an introvert, but active; a warm friend, a man of candor, wit, and style. He always types with a blue typewriter ribbon, and the only question I have asked him which he has always evaded is "Where do you get so many blue typewriter ribbons?" When he himself is blue, he has told me so, and I've tried to cheer him up, and when I have been blue I've been turned right round into the sunlight simply by getting one of Tiptree's preposterous, magnificent letters. Tiptree has introduced me to the Clerihew; Tiptree has pulled me from the slough of despond by means of a single squid drawn (in blue ink) on a postcard. The only thing better than Tiptree's letters is his stories. He is a man whose friendship is an honor and a joy.

The most wonderful thing about him is that he is also Alice Sheldon.

Recently I've been hearing from people who have friends who

say, "I knew all along that Tiptree was a woman. I could tell it from the prose style," or "from the male characters," or "from the female characters," or "from the Vibrations." I don't know any of these people who knew all along; they didn't say much about it; never even happened to mention that they knew, for some reason, until all the rest of us knew. We (the rest of us) knew rather suddenly and utterly unexpectedly. I don't think I have ever been so completely surprised in my life—or so happily. All I can say is I'm glad I didn't know all along, because I would have missed that joyous shock of revelation, recognition—that beautiful Jill-in-the-box.

Quite a lot of us did, however, suspect the short story writer Raccoona Sheldon of being either an invention of Tiptree's or his natural daughter, and we were quite right; only what is right? What does it mean to say that "Tiptree is Sheldon," or that "James Tiptree Jr. is a woman"? I am not sure at all, except that it's a fine example of the pitfalls built into the English verb *to be*. You turn it around and say, "A woman is James Tiptree Jr.," and you see you have said something quite different.

As for *why* Alice is James and James is Alice, that is still another matter, and one where speculation very soon becomes prying and invasion of privacy. But there are fascinating precedents. Mary Ann Evans was a Victorian woman living with a Victorian man to whom she wasn't married; she took a pen name to protect her work from censure. But why a male pen name? She could, after all, have called herself Sara Jane Williams. It appears that she needed to be George Eliot, or George Eliot needed to be her, for a while. She and he together got past creative and spiritual dead ends and morasses that the woman Mary Ann alone was in danger of getting stuck in. As soon as she felt herself free, she admitted and announced the George Eliot/Mary Ann Evans identity. George's name continued to appear on the title pages of the great novels; as a practical matter, of course—the name was a bestseller—but also, I should guess, in gratitude, and in sheer, and characteristic, integrity.

Dr. Alice Sheldon isn't a Victorian, nor are we, and her reasons for using pen names may be assumed to be personal rather than social; and that's really all we have any right to assume about the matter. But since she did use a male persona, and kept it up publicly with perfect success for years, there are some assumptions that we ought to be examining, gazing at with fascinated horror, revising with loud cries and dramatic gestures of contrition and dismay; and these are our assumptions—all of us, readers, writers, critics, feminists, masculinists, sexists, nonsexists, straights, gays—concerning "the way men write" and "the way women write." The kind of psychic bias that led one of the keenest, subtlest minds in science fiction to state, "It has been suggested that Tiptree is a female, a theory that I find absurd, for there is to me something ineluctably masculine about Tiptree's writing. I don't think the novels of Jane Austen could have been written by a man nor the stories of Ernest Hemingway by a woman." The error was completely honest, and we all made it: but the justification and the generalization—even with such supposedly extreme examples as Austen and Hemingway—that bears some thinking about. We ought to think about it. And about all our arguments concerning Women in Fiction, and why we have them; and all the panels on Women in Science Fiction (omitting, of course, James Tiptree Jr.).* And all the stuff that has been written about "feminine style," about its inferiority or superiority to "masculine style," about the necessary, obligatory difference of the two. All the closed-shop attitudes of radical feminism, which invited Tiptree out of certain inner sanctums because, although

---

*   Note (1989). I believe a science fiction convention finally had a panel on Men in Science Fiction, but I don't know what they said.

his stories were so very good and so extraordinary in their understanding of women, still, he was a man. All the ineffable patronization and put-down Sheldon is going to receive now from various male reviewers because, although her stories are so very good and so extraordinary in their understanding of men, still, she is a woman. All that. All that kipple, gubbish, garble, and abomination which Alice James Raccoona Tiptree Sheldon Jr. showed for what it is when she appeared, smiling a little uncertainly, from her postbox in McLean, Virginia. She fooled us. She fooled us good and proper. And we can only thank her for it.

For though she stood us all on our heads, isn't it true that she played her game without actually lying—without deceit?

The army, the government, the university, the jungles, all that is true. Mr. Tiptree's biography is Dr. Sheldon's.

The beautiful story "The Women Men Don't See" (oh—now that we know—what a gorgeously ironic title!) got a flood of nominations for the Nebula Award in 1974. So much of the praise of the story concerned the evidence it gave that a man could write with full sympathy about women, that Tiptree felt a prize for it would involve deceit, false pretenses. She withdrew the story from the competition, muttering about not wanting to cut younger writers out of all the prizes. I don't think this cover-up was false, either: the truth, if not the whole truth. She had had a Nebula in 1973 for "Love Is the Plan the Plan Is Death," and a Hugo in the same year for "The Girl Who Was Plugged In." These prizes sneaked up on her and caught her by surprise, I think. Her 1976 Nebula for the powerful "Houston, Houston, Do You Read?," in this volume, came so soon after the disclosure of her name that she didn't have time to think up a good excuse for withdrawing it; so she went off and hid in a jungle instead. She practices that "low profile" which Carlos Castaneda, standing in high profile on the rooftops, preaches. The cult of personality, prevalent in art as in politics, is simply not her game.

Yet she did fool us; and the fact is important, because it makes a point which no amount of argument could have made. Not only does it imperil all theories concerning the woman as writer and the writer as woman, but it might make us question some of our assumptions concerning the existence of the writer per se. It's idiotic to say, "There is no such person as James Tiptree Jr." There is. The proof that there is, which will incidentally outlast us all, is these stories. But, because James wrote them, is Alice now to be besieged by people asking impertinent questions about her family life, where she gets her ideas from, and what she eats for breakfast—which is what we do to writers? Can anyone explain to her, or to me, what all that has to do with the stories, and which is more real: the old primate or the star songs?

Again, there are lovely precedents; this time the one I'd choose is Woolf's novel *Orlando*. Alice Sheldon has quite a lot in common with Orlando, and like Orlando, is an unanswerable criticism of the rational and moral fallacies of sexism, simply by being what and who she is. She also provides an exhilarating criticism of what real life, or reality, is, by being a fictional character who writes real stories; here she surpasses Orlando. On the edge of the impenetrable jungles of Yucatán, on the beach, the straw-hatted figure stands, dapper, fragile, smiling; just before vanishing into the shadows of the trees he murmurs, "Are you real?" and Alice, in a house in far Virginia, replacing the blue ribbon in her typewriter, smiles also and replies, "Oh, yes, certainly." And I, who have never met either of them, agree. They are real. Both of them. But not so real, perhaps, as their stories. This book you hold now in your hand, this is the genuine article. No fooling.

5) Here are
Some real stories.

IV
TELLING THE TRUTH

I have never found anywhere, in the domain of art, that you don't have to walk to. (There is quite an array of jets, buses and hacks which you can ride to Success; but that is a different destination.) It is a pretty wild country. There are, of course, roads. Great artists make the roads; good teachers and good companions can point them out. But there ain't no free rides, baby. No hitchhiking. And if you want to strike out in any new direction—you go alone. With a machete in your hand and the fear of God in your heart.

from "Fifteen Vultures, the Strop, and the Old Lady,"
in *Clarion II*, ed. Robin Scott Wilson
(New York: NAL Signet, 1972)

INTRODUCTION

*E*ncore Magazine of the Arts, April–May 1977, carried this poem by Ursula Le Guin:

EVEREST

How long to climb the mountain?

Forty years. The native guides
are dark, small, brave, evasive.
They cannot be bribed.

Would you advise
the North Face?

All the faces
frown; so choose. The travelers describe
their traveling, not yours.
Footholds don't last in ice.
Read rocks. Their word endures.

And at the top?

You stop.

They say that you can see
the Town.

I don't know.
You look down. It's strange
not to be looking up; hard to be sure
just what it is you're seeing.
Some say the Town; others perceive
a farther Range. The guides turn back.
Shoulder your pack, put on your coat.
From here on down no track,
no goal, no way, no ways.
In the immense downward of the evening
there may be far within the golden haze
a motion or a glittering: waves,
towers, heights? remote, remote.
The language of the rocks has changed.
I knew once what it meant.

How long is the descent?

Fiction writer, poet, critic and teacher, guide: Le Guin is all these. Though writing is a solitary exploration, as critic and teacher she offers maps, suggestions about equipment, and descriptions of her own traveling. The excerpt from her introduction to *The Altered I* (Melbourne: Norstrilia Press, 1976; New York: Berkley, 1978) outlines some of her experiences as the leader of the workshop on the writing of science fiction. (The book itself contains the best stories and exercises from the 1975 Australian writers' workshop, including a Le Guin story and the workshop comments on it. The exercises, and the participants' essays on their experiences, are a useful source of inspiration for would-be writers. "Where do you get your ideas?" "Oh, this story started with the Le Guin One-Change Bit, and that story came from the Avram Davidson Word Game, and . . .")

The second essay, which I have titled "Talking about Writing," is a previously unpublished talk given at Southern Oregon College, Ashland, in February 1977, a revision of a talk given in Reading, England, in January 1976.

Both essays emphasize the recurrent theme of the writer's need for self-exploration, self-knowledge, and self-criticism. Like "A Citizen of Mondath," they repeat the musical metaphor important to Le Guin and to her characters, like Shevek of *The Dispossessed* and Owen Griffiths of *Very Far Away from Anywhere Else*, who discovers that "thinking is another kind of music" as he watches Natalie Field play Bach on the viola. "Natalie was trying to confirm what Bach had reported to some church congregation in Germany two hundred and fifty years ago. If she did it absolutely right, it might turn out to be true. To be the truth."

In her essay "Escape Routes," published in the science fiction magazine *Galaxy* (December 1974) and reprinted here with her own introduction, Le Guin emphasizes the idea that the reading of a science fiction story is as serious and important as the playing of a Bach suite. Le Guin repeats and summarizes her major critical values: her view of science fiction as a literature with both "the capacity to face an open universe" and the aesthetic and moral *necessity* to face that universe honestly.

INTRODUCTION TO *THE ALTERED I* (EXCERPT)

(1976)

The usual scenario for a writer's conference or workshop, I am told by those who have been there, is something like this: The Writer sits on a dais facing a group of Postulant Writers. He criticizes the works which they have submitted to him, and lectures on the art of writing. In the evening, he reads to them from his works.

The kind of workshop I seem to get involved in is not like that at all; it is incredibly messy. There are all these people, about twenty of them, sitting, or lying, or lounging, or assuming the lotus position, or whatever, in a sort of circle. Somewhere nearby are stacks of the manuscripts submitted for tomorrow; they have all already read the manuscripts submitted for today. They start in on the first story, and one by one, round the circle, they voice their criticisms and reactions: anything relevant, from grammar and structure through factual probability to the implicit Outlook on Life. The author of the story is not allowed to reply until they are all done; then he/she can reply passionately and at length. The professional writer, often

called the "resident"—President without the capital *P*, perhaps—
can either criticize in turn, or try to sum up at the end; she/he has
no special authority, except to say, "Come on, Susan already said
all that," when people begin repeating one another, and to open
general discussion, and to prevent fistfights. This round-robin of
discussion usually goes on from nine till noon, and again in the
afternoon if there's a backlog of stories to work on. The rest of the
day and night, everybody writes—perhaps on a theme or exercise
proposed by the resident, perhaps on their own hook—and reads
what everybody else has written, and talks, and writes, and writes,
and talks, and eats meals with the others, and occasionally, for brief
periods in the small hours, even sleeps a little. This goes on, twenty
hours a day, five or six days a week, for six weeks. Residents last only
a week apiece, and are taken away to rest homes; fresh victims are
supplied regularly.

This system of mutual criticism sessions was worked out at a
conference of professional science fiction writers at Milford, Pennsylvania (and Milford Conferences still take place annually both in
the United States and England). A survivor of a "Milford," Professor
Robin Scott Wilson, applied its egalitarian method to a workshop
for aspiring SF writers at Clarion, Pennsylvania. The experiment
was notably successful, and "Clarions" have been held annually at
one or more places in the States each summer since then.

I have been a resident three times at the six-week Clarion West
workshops organized by Vonda McIntyre at the University of
Washington, and have also applied the system, so far as is possible,
to once-a-week courses in the writing of SF and fantasy, twice with
Professor Anthony Wolk in Oregon, and once at the University of
Reading in England. When I needed to earn my way to Australia to
attend the World Science Fiction Convention in Melbourne in Au-

gust of 1975, the Australian Literature Board generously provided the opportunity for a one-week "Clarion of the Antipodes." I leapt at the chance with delight, having found workshop residence as exciting as it is exhausting.

The excitement is twofold. Part of it is that, under these rather extreme conditions—twenty people living, eating, talking, and working together, in a situation of extreme ego-exposure, and with obsessive concentration on a single goal—a group forms: the kind of group, I take it, that encounter therapy sets out deliberately to form. Participation in a real group is always exciting for a writer, whose work is done in solitude (usually outer, always inner): a rare and invigorating experience. The other element of the excitement is the functioning of the system itself. The participants write; and they tend to write better as they go along. Stories written in the workshop, under pressure, often in a half day or a night, are often very much better than the lovingly worked-on stories submitted ahead of time as evidence of qualification. This improvement must rise from the fact that the participants are getting practice in criticism and therefore in self-criticism—and a taste of the self-confidence that comes with self-criticism; and also I think they write better because they are caught up in and carried by the momentum and energy of the group. When the system works, as it usually does, it is not a competitive situation; just the reverse. It provides mutual inspiration.

This is the most commonplace thing in the world to a performing musician, whose art is a group performance, and who depends upon that mutual release of energy through skill. To a writer, it can be a revelation. "The competition," to a young fiction writer, usually consists of famous or successful authors, none of whom he knows personally, and most of whom are dead: a remote untouchable

crowd of luminaries. To meet, live with, work with a group of ambitious, serious, nonfamous, not-yet-successful writers like one's self,
to find that you aren't the only nut on the walnut tree, to discuss the
craft, to argue ideas, to expose your work to others as they expose it
to you, no-holds-barred, is to experience what the musician experiences and relies upon in every performance: cooperation on the job,
skill reinforcing skill, not competition but emulation. And music is
made. Stories are written.

The American Clarions have produced a remarkable percentage
of participants who go on to become professional writers. This is
something to be proud of. But it's not the real point. I think. The
real point is to make music together.

TALKING ABOUT WRITING

Tonight we are supposed to be talking about writing. I think probably the last person who ought to be asked to talk about writing is a writer. Everybody else knows so much more about it than a writer does.

I'm not just being snide; it's only common sense. If you want to know all about the sea, you go and ask a sailor, or an oceanographer, or a marine biologist, and they can tell you a lot about the sea. But if you go and ask the sea itself, what does it say? Grumble grumble swish swish. It is too busy being itself to know anything about itself.

Anyway, meeting writers is always so disappointing. I got over wanting to meet live writers quite a long time ago. There is this terrific book that has changed your life, and then you meet the author, and he has shifty eyes and funny shoes and he won't talk about anything except the injustice of the United States income tax structure toward people with fluctuating income, or how to breed Black Angus cows, or something.

Well, anyhow, I am supposed to talk about writing, and the part I really like will come soon, when *you* get to talk to *me* about writing, but I will try to clear the floor for that by dealing with some of the most basic questions.

People come up to you if you're a writer, and they say, I want to be a writer. How do I become a writer?

I have a two-stage answer to that. Very often the first stage doesn't get off the ground, and we end up standing around the ruins on the launching pad, arguing.

The first-stage answer to the question, how do I become a writer, is this: you learn to type.*

The only alternative to learning to type is to have an inherited income and hire a full-time stenographer. If this seems unlikely, don't worry. Touch-typing is easy to learn. My mother became a writer in her sixties, and realizing that editors will not read mss. written left-handed in illegible squiggles, taught herself touch-typing in a few weeks; and she is not only a very good writer but one of the most original, creative typists I have ever read.

Well, the person who asked, How do I become a writer, is a bit cross now, and mumbles, But that isn't what I meant. (And I say, I know it wasn't.) I want to write short stories, what are the rules for writing short stories? I want to write a novel, what are the rules for writing novels?

Now I say, Ah! and get really enthusiastic. You can find all the rules of writing in the book called *Fowler's Handbook of English Usage*, and a good dictionary—I recommended the *Shorter Oxford*, *Webster's* is too wishy-washy.† There are only a very few rules of writing not covered in those two volumes, and I can summarize them thus: your story may begin in longhand on the backs of old shopping lists, but when it goes to an editor, it should be typed, double-spaced, on one side of the paper only, with generous margins—especially the left-hand one—and not too many really grotty corrections per page.

---

*   Note (1989). Or, these days, to word-process.

†   Note (1989). See the Note on page 43.

Your name and its name and the page number should be on the top of every single page; and when you mail it to the editor it should have enclosed with it a stamped, self-addressed envelope. And those are the Basic Rules of Writing.

I'm not being funny. Those are the basic requirements for a readable, therefore publishable, manuscript. And, beyond grammar and spelling, they are the only rules of writing I know.

All right, that is stage one of my answer. If the person listens to all that without hitting me, and still says, All right all right, but how *do* you become a writer, then we've got off the ground, and I can deliver stage two. How do you become a writer? Answer: you write.

It's amazing how much resentment and disgust and evasion this answer can arouse. Even among writers, believe me. It is one of those Horrible Truths one would rather not face.

The most frequent evasive tactic is for the would-be writer to say, But before I have anything to say, I must get *experience*.

Well, yes; if you want to be a journalist. But I don't know anything about journalism, I'm talking about fiction. And of course fiction is made out of experience, your whole life from infancy on, everything you've thought and done and seen and read and dreamed. But experience isn't something you go and *get*—it's a gift, and the only prerequisite for receiving it is that you be open to it. A closed soul can have the most immense adventures, go through a civil war or a trip to the moon, and have nothing to show for all that "experience"; whereas the open soul can do wonders with nothing. I invite you to meditate on a pair of sisters. Emily and Charlotte. Their life experience was an isolated vicarage in a small, dreary English village, a couple of bad years at a girls' school, another year or two in Brussels, which is surely the dullest city in all Europe, and a lot of housework. Out of that seething mass of raw, vital, brutal, gutsy Experience they made two of the greatest novels ever written: *Jane Eyre* and *Wuthering Heights*.

Now, of course they were writing from experience; writing about what they knew, which is what people always tell you to do; but what was their experience? What was it they knew? Very little about "life." They knew their own souls, they knew their own minds and hearts; and it was not a knowledge lightly or easily gained. From the time they were seven or eight years old, they wrote, and thought, and learned the landscape of their own being, and how to describe it. They wrote with the imagination, which is the tool of the farmer, the plow you plow your own soul with. They wrote from inside, from as deep inside as they could get by using all their strength and courage and intelligence. And that is where books come from. The novelist writes from inside.

I'm rather sensitive on this point, because I write science fiction, or fantasy, or about imaginary countries, mostly—stuff that, by definition, involves times, places, events that I could not possibly experience in my own life. So when I was young and would submit one of these things about space voyages to Orion or dragons or something, I was told, at extremely regular intervals, "You should try to write about things you know about." And I would say, But I do; I know about Orion, and dragons, and imaginary countries. Who do you think knows about my own imaginary countries, if I don't?

But they didn't listen, because they don't understand, they have it all backward. They think an artist is like a roll of photographic film, you expose it and develop it and there is a reproduction of Reality in two dimensions. But that's all wrong, and if any artist tells you, "I am a camera," or "I am a mirror," distrust them instantly, they're fooling you, pulling a fast one. Artists are people who are not at all interested in the facts—only in the truth. You get the facts from outside. The truth you get from inside.

OK, how do you go about getting at that truth? You want to tell the truth. You want to be a writer. So what do you do?

You write.

Honestly, why do people ask that question? Does anybody ever come up to a musician and say, Tell me, tell me—how should I become a tuba player? No! It's too obvious. If you want to be a tuba player you get a tuba, and some tuba music. And you ask the neighbors to move away or put cotton in their ears. And probably you get a tuba teacher, because there are quite a lot of objective rules and techniques both to written music and to tuba performance. And then you sit down and you play the tuba, every day, every week, every month, year after year, until you are good at playing the tuba; until you can—if you desire—play the truth on the tuba.

It is exactly the same with writing. You sit down and you do it, and you do it, and you do it, until you have learned how to do it.

Of course, there are differences. Writing makes no noise, except groans, and it can be done anywhere, and it is done alone.

It is the experience or premonition of that loneliness, perhaps, that drives a lot of young writers into this search for rules. I envy musicians very much, myself. They get to play together, their art is largely communal; and there are rules to it, an accepted body of axioms and techniques, which can be put into words or at least demonstrated, and so taught. Writing cannot be shared, nor can it be taught as a technique, except on the most superficial level. All a writer's real learning is done alone, thinking, reading other people's books, or writing—practicing. A really good writing class or workshop can give us some shadow of what musicians have all the time—the excitement of a group working together, so that each member outdoes himself—but what comes out of that is not a collaboration, a joint accomplishment, like a string quartet or a symphony performance, but a lot of totally separate, isolated works, expressions of individual souls. And therefore there are no rules, except those each individual makes up.

I know. There are lots of rules. You find them in the books about The Craft of Fiction and The Art of the Short Story and so on. I know some of them. One of them says: Never begin a story with dialogue! People won't read it; here is somebody talking and they don't know who and so they don't care, so—Never begin a story with dialogue.

Well, there is a story I know, it begins like this:

"*Eh bien, mon prince!* so Genoa and Lucca are now no more than private estates of the Bonaparte family!"

It's not only a dialogue opening, the first four words are in *French*, and it's not even a French novel. What a horrible way to begin a book! The title of the book is *War and Peace*.

There's another Rule I know: introduce all the main characters early in the book. That sounds perfectly sensible, mostly I suppose it is sensible, but it's not a rule, or if it is somebody forgot to tell it to Charles Dickens. He didn't get Sam Weller into *The Pickwick Papers* for ten chapters—that's five months, since the book was coming out as a serial in installments.

Now, you can say, All right, so Tolstoy can break the rules, so Dickens can break the rules, but they're geniuses; rules are made for geniuses to break, but for ordinary, talented, not-yet-professional writers to follow, as guidelines.

And I would accept this, but very very grudgingly, and with so many reservations that it amounts in the end to nonacceptance. Put it this way: if you feel you need rules and want rules, and you find a rule that appeals to you, or that works for you, then follow it. Use it. But if it doesn't appeal to you or doesn't work for you, then ignore it; in fact, if you want to and are able to, kick it in the teeth, break it, fold staple mutilate and destroy it.

See, the thing is, as a writer you are free. You are about the freest person that ever was. Your freedom is what you have bought with your solitude, your loneliness. You are in the country where *you* make up the rules, the laws. You are both dictator and obedient populace. It is a country nobody has ever explored before. It is up to you to make the maps, to build the cities. Nobody else in the world can do it, or ever could do it, or ever will be able to do it again.

Absolute freedom is absolute responsibility. The writer's job, as I see it, is to tell the truth. The writer's truth—nobody else's. It is not an easy job. One of the biggest implied lies going around at present is the one that hides in phrases like "self-expression" or "telling it like it is"—as if that were easy, anybody could do it if they just let the words pour out and didn't get fancy. The "I am a camera" business again. Well, it just doesn't work that way. You know how hard it is to say to somebody, just somebody you know, how you *really* feel, what you *really* think—with complete honesty? You have to trust them, and you have to *know yourself*, before you can say anything anywhere near the truth. And it's hard. It takes a lot out of you.

You multiply that by thousands; you replace the listener, the live flesh-and-blood friend you trust, with a faceless unknown audience of people who may possibly not even exist; and you try to write the truth to them, you try to draw them a map of your inmost mind and feelings, hiding nothing and trying to keep all the distances straight and the altitudes right and the emotions honest . . . And you never succeed. The map is never complete, or even accurate. You read it over and it may be beautiful, but you realize that you have fudged here, and smeared there, and left this out, and put in some stuff that isn't really there at all, and so on—and there is nothing to do then but say, OK; that's done; now I come back and start a new map, and try to do it better, more truthfully. And all of this, every time, you do alone—absolutely alone. The only questions that really matter are the ones you ask yourself.

You may have gathered from all this that I am not encouraging people to try to be writers. Well, I can't. You hate to see a nice young person run up to the edge of a cliff and jump off, you know. On the other hand, it is awfully nice to know that some other people are just as nutty and just as determined to jump off the cliff as you are. You just hope they realize what they're in for.

ESCAPE ROUTES

(1974–75)

This paper is an amalgamation and summation of several talks I have given during the past year to various groups of teachers of SF, in Oregon, at the California Association of Teachers of English, and in Milwaukee. Parts of the talks were directed toward specific problems and techniques of teaching SF, and I have omitted these. But, if I have been creeping around behind science fiction's back talking about it to academics, science fiction has a right to know what I've been saying. So I tried to put the drift and gist of it into this paper.

At the 1974 meeting of the Science Fiction Research Association, an annual event which I like to call The Bride of Frankenstein in the Grove of Academe, Alexei and Cory Panshin held forth eloquently against the teaching of science fiction in schools and colleges. It seemed a bit quixotic, since their audience consisted of teachers of science fiction, people so interested in and committed to the subject that they had come from all over the country to talk about it and learn how to do it better; since thousands of high schools give science fiction courses now, and the stuffiest college

English departments are stooping to conquer. I don't think there's really much question now of keeping the professors off Aldebaran. They're there. And that face looking out of the fifth-story window of the Ivory Tower, that's the Little Green Man. For myself, I accept this miscegenation happily, and am simply interested in what the offspring may be.

For undoubtedly the recent great increase in the teaching of SF is going to affect the writing of SF. Our audience has widened immensely; and for the first time, we in the SF ghetto are beginning to get criticism—not brush-offs from literary snobs, and not blasts of praise and condemnation from jealous, loyal, in-group devotees, but real criticism, by trained, intelligent people who have read widely both inside and outside the field. This could be the best thing that ever happened to SF, the confirmation of it, both to its readers and to its writers, as a powerful and responsible art form.

A ghetto can be a comfortable, reassuring place to live, but what makes it a ghetto, after all, is that you are *forced* to live there. Now that the walls are breaking down, I think it behooves us to step across the rubble and face the city outside. We need not lose our solidarity in doing so. Solidarity, loyalty, is not a prison, where you can't choose: it is a choice freely made. But equally we shouldn't expect to be welcomed with songs of praise by all the strangers out there. Why should we be? We're strangers to them, too. If we have weaknesses we must learn to take criticism of them; if we have strengths we must prove them.

One way we can show our strength is by helping the serious critics of SF to set up a critical apparatus, a set of standards, suited to the study and teaching of SF. Some of the criteria by which the conventional novel is discussed and judged apply to SF, and some don't. Teachers can't switch from *A Tale of Two Cities* to *The Man in the High Castle* without changing gears; if they do, one book or the other is going to be misinterpreted, mistreated. Fortunately, in two areas at least, SF has established its own standards, and has been applying them with increasing severity, in writing, in teaching writing, and in teaching SF as literature.

The first of these is the criterion of intellectual coherence and scientific plausibility.

The basic canon of fantasy, of course, is: you get to make up the rules, but then you've got to follow them. Science fiction refines upon this: you get to make up the rules, but within limits. A science fiction story must not flout the evidence of science, must not, as Chip Delany puts it, deny what is known to be known. Or if it does, the writer must know it, and defend the liberty taken, either with a genuine hypothesis or with a sound, convincing fake. If I give my spaceships FTL speed, I must be aware that I'm contradicting Albert Einstein, and accept the consequences—all the consequences. In this, precisely, lies the unique aesthetic delight of SF, in the intense, coherent following-through of the implications of an idea, whether it's a bit of far-out technology, or a theory in quantum mechanics, or a satirical projection of current social trends, or a whole world created by extrapolating from biology and ethnology. When such an idea is consistently worked out in material, intellectual, social, psychological, and moral terms, something solid has been done, something real: a thing which can be read, taught, and judged squarely on its own terms. The "sense of wonder" isn't a feeble perfume, it's built right into a good story, and the closer you look the stronger the sense of wonder.

A second criterion is that of stylistic competence.

You know what SF was like in the Golden Age of Science Fiction. You know. It was like this. "Oh, Professor Higgins," cooed the slender, vivacious Laura, "but do tell me how does the anti-pastomatter denudifier work?" Then Professor Higgins, with a kindly, absent-minded smile, explains how it works for about six pages, garble garble garble. Then the Starship Captain steps in, with a tight, twisted smile on his lean, bronzed face. His steely gray eyes glint. He lights a cigarette and inhales deeply. "Oh, Captain Tommy," Laura inquires with a vivacious toss of her head, "is there anything wrong?" "Don't worry your pretty little head about it," the Captain replies, inhaling deeply. "A fleet of nine thousand Gloobian Slime Monsters off the port side, that's all." And so on. You know, American SF used to be a pulp medium, popcult, all that. Now it isn't—not all of it, anyhow. It has rejoined the SF of England and Europe, which was sparse, but which never was schlock except when it imitated us, and which was always part of the major tradition of fiction. And therefore it is to be judged, not as schlock, not as junk, but as fiction.

What I'm saying is neither self-evident nor popular. Within the SF ghetto, many people don't want their books, or their favorite writers' books, judged as literature. They want junk, and they bit-terly resent aesthetic judgment of it. And outside the ghetto, there are critics who like to stand above SF, looking down upon it, and therefore want it to be junky, popcult, contemptible. There was a strong vein of this in Gerald Jonas's otherwise perceptive *New Yorker* article, and it's one of the many games Leslie Fiedler plays. Fortu-nately it's a game that our best SF critic, Darko Suvin, never plays. I consider it a real cop-out, an arrogance toward both the books and their readers.

There is an area where SF has most often failed to judge itself, and where it has been most harshly judged by its nonpartisans. It is an area where we badly need intelligent criticism and discussion. The oldest argument against SF is both the shallowest and the profoundest: the assertion that SF, like all fantasy, is escapist.

This statement is shallow when made by the shallow. When an insurance broker tells you that SF doesn't deal with the Real World, when a chemistry freshman informs you that Science has disproved Myth, when a censor suppresses a book because it doesn't fit an ideological canon and so forth, that's not criticism; it's bigotry. If it's worth answering, the best answer was given by Tolkien, author, critic, and scholar. Yes, he said, fantasy is escapist, and that is its glory. If a soldier is imprisoned by the enemy, don't we consider it his duty to escape? The moneylenders, the know-nothings, the authoritarians have us all in prison; if we value the freedom of the mind and soul, if we're partisans of liberty, then it's our plain duty to escape, and to take as many people with us as we can.

But people who are not fools or bigots, people who love both art and liberty, critics as responsible as Edmund Wilson, reject science fiction flatly as a genre not worth discussing. Why? What makes them so sure?

The question, after all, must be asked: From what is one escaping, and to what?

Evidently, if we're escaping a world that consists of *Newsweek*, *Pravda*, and the Stock Market Report, and asserting the existence of a primary, vivid world, an intenser reality where joy, tragedy, and morality exist, then we're doing a good thing, and Tolkien is right. But what if we're doing just the opposite? What if we're escaping from a complex, uncertain, frightening world of death and taxes into a nice simple cozy place where heroes don't have to pay taxes, where death happens only to villains, where Science, plus Free Enterprise, plus the Galactic Fleet in black and silver uniforms, can solve all problems, where human suffering is something that can be *cured*—like scurvy? This is no escape from the phony. This is an escape into the phony. This doesn't take us in the direction of the great myths and legends, which is always toward an intensification of the mystery of the real. This takes us the other way, toward a rejection of reality, in fact toward madness: infantile regression, or paranoid delusion, or schizoid insulation. The movement is retrograde, autistic. We have escaped by locking ourselves in jail.

And inside the padded cell the people sit and say, Gee wow have you read the latest Belch the Barbarian story? It's the greatest.

They don't care if anybody outside is listening. They don't want to know that there is an outside.

Because the most famous works of SF are socially and ethically speculative, the field has got a reputation for being inherently "relevant." Accused of escapism, it defends itself by pointing to Wells, Orwell, Huxley, Čapek, Stapledon, Zamyatin. But that won't wash: not for us. Not one of those writers was an American. My feeling is that American SF, while riding on the reputation of great European works, still clings to the pulp tradition of escapism.

That's overstated and perhaps unfair. Recent American SF has been full of stories tackling totalitarianism, nationalism, overpopulation, pollution, prejudice, racism, sexism, militarism, and so on: all the "relevant" problems. *Again, Dangerous Visions* was a regular textbook in Problems (and my story was one of the chapters). But what worries me is that so many of these stories and books have been written in a savagely self-righteous tone, a tone that implies that there's an answer, a simple answer, and why can't all you damn fools out there see it? Well, I call this escapism: a sensationalist raising of a real question, followed by a quick evasion of the weight and pain and complexity involved in really, experientially, trying to understand and cope with that question. And by the way, I'm not talking only about the reactionary, easy-answer schools of SF, the technocrats, scientologists, "libertarians," and so on, but also about the chic nihilism affected by many talented American and English writers of my generation. Annihilation is the easiest answer of all. You just close all the doors.

If science fiction has a major gift to offer literature, I think it is just this: the capacity to face an open universe. Physically open, psychically open. No doors shut.

What science, from physics and astronomy to history and psychology, has given us is the open universe: a cosmos that is not a simple, fixed hierarchy but an immensely complex process in time. All the doors stand open, from the prehuman past through the incredible present to the terrible and hopeful future. All connections are possible. All alternatives are thinkable. It is not a comfortable, reassuring place. It's a very large house, a very drafty house. But it's the house we live in.

And science fiction seems to be the modern literary art which is capable of living in that huge and drafty house, and feeling at home there, and playing games up and down the stairs, from basement to attic.

I think that's why kids like SF, and demand to be taught it, to study it, to take it seriously. They feel this potential it has for playing games with and making sense and beauty out of our fearfully enlarged world of knowledge and perception. And that's why it gripes me when I see SF failing to do so, falling back on silly, simplistic reassurances, or whining Woe, woe, repent, or taking refuge in mere wishful thinking.

So I welcome the study and teaching of SF—so long as the

teachers will criticize us, demandingly, responsibly, and make the students read us demandingly, responsibly. If SF is treated, not as junk, not as escapism, but as an intellectually, aesthetically, and ethically responsible art, a great form, it will become so: it will fulfill its promise. The door to the future will be open.

V
PUSHING AT THE LIMITS

SF operates effectively only in an open system.
The open system is not, cannot be, merely the writer's society;
essentially it exists in the writer's mind.

from "Surveying the Battlefield,"
Science-Fiction Studies 2 (Fall 1973)

The only valid reason for excluding science fiction from the
literary canon has been its predominant lack of passion—
human and intellectual—and therefore of beauty.

from "Out of the Ice Age," *Times Literary Supplement*
(July 30, 1976)

INTRODUCTION

The July 30, 1976, issue of the *Times Literary Supplement* contained Le Guin's review of four new British and American SF novels. It began:

> Science fiction, submitting to literary snobbery, has regarded itself as a craft rather than an art, and hence has regarded its authors not as artists but as craftsmen, distinguished from the large amateur element, the fans, only by professionalism. The necessity of professionalism as a means, and the insufficiency of professionalism as an end, is variously shown in these four novels.

Le Guin's view of SF as a serious art like any other demanding artistic responsibility is best expressed in "The Stalin in the Soul." This essay began as a talk given at the Clarion West Writers' Workshop at the University of Washington in July 1973, and was revised for publication in *The Future Now: Saving Tomorrow*, edited by Robert Hoskins (Greenwich, CT: Fawcett, 1977). This collection, said Hoskins in his introduction, presents stories in which authors attempt to "face the problems of tomorrow in terms of their relevance to the problems of today." Le Guin, facing the immediate problem of the "censorship of the market" accepted by Western SF writers, deals with the larger issues which underlie all her work, fiction and nonfiction: the "moral, intellectual, and social content" of art, and the necessity for intellectual freedom and responsibility.

Finally, Le Guin's central concerns as a writer are summed up in "The Stone Ax and the Muskoxen," her guest of honor speech delivered in Melbourne at the 33rd World Science Fiction Convention, in August of 1975. The speech has been published in the British journal *Vector* 71 (December 1975), then edited by Christopher Fowler, apparently from Le Guin's uncorrected notes; and in the *SunCon Convention Journal* 1 (Winter 1976), edited by JoeD Siclari, in a slightly different version taken from Le Guin's hand-corrected manuscript. The latter version has been used here.

As Peter Nicholls observed of Le Guin's London speech, the slight figure in the elegant black velvet suit and the propeller beanie, rather nervously reading the prepared speech, quickly turned into a companion speaking directly to each of the six hundred people in the ballroom of the Southern Cross Hotel. That directness survives onto the printed page: "The walls are down, we're free at last," she tells us. "Now that we're free, where are we going?"

These essays, like Le Guin's fiction, sketch out some maps.

THE STALIN IN THE SOUL

(1973–77)

SKETCH FOR A SCIENCE FICTION NOVEL

Our hero, Y., a naval engineer, is in a foreign country when at last the Revolution breaks out at home. Having always been a radical, to the extent of undergoing several arrests, interrogations, jail sentences, and house arrests, he hurries home to greet the dawn of the new day.

A talented writer, he joins a group of young authors who, free of the old censorship, are experimenting with a lively and iconoclastic art. He soon wins a high reputation as a writer. But the period of freedom lasts only a very few years. As the Revolution consolidates its hard-won victory and solidifies into an effective government, Y. does not solidify with it; he remains a heretic. His stance is independent, ironic, and critical. He accepts no value and no reward without question. Therefore the new government sees him as unpatriotic, destructive, dangerous—just as the old one did. Y. doesn't much mind; he enjoys danger. He goes on writing. At the height of his creative powers, he writes a novel. It is a science fiction novel, a negative Utopia. It is a brilliant testimony against the growing rigidity and authoritarianism of his nation, and a passionate affirmation of liberty. It is a romantic, imaginative, intelligent, powerful, and beautiful book—perhaps the finest science fiction novel ever written. The manuscript must be submitted for governmental approval before publication. It is not approved.

Three years later, a smuggled copy of the manuscript is printed abroad; translations are made and the book appears in many languages—but not in his own language in his own land.

Ten years later, worn out by the ceaseless campaign waged against him by bureaucrats and by fellow writers currying favor with the government, he requests that the chief of state grant him permission to leave the country. "I beg to be permitted to go abroad," he writes, "with the right to return as soon as it becomes possible in our country to serve great ideas in literature without cringing before little men." Scarcely a humble letter, but his request is granted. He goes to Paris. Those of his friends who stayed home are, one by one, silenced by censorship, or by trial and imprisonment, or execution. Y.'s escape is only apparent; he is as silent now as his friends in the prison camps or the common graves. He tries to make a living writing movie scripts, but writes nothing of any importance. After seven years of exile, he dies.

Thirty-six years later, fifty-two years after it was written, now in 1973, his great novel has still not been published in his own country.

This is, of course, a sketch for a true novel—a biography. Y. is Yevgeny Ivanovich Zamyatin; his novel, which I do consider the best single work of science fiction yet written, is called *We*, in English. In Russia it has, in a sense, no name. It does not exist. It was censored.

ON CENSORSHIP BY THE MARKET

Zamyatin's life was a tragedy; it was also a triumph, because he never used power against his enemies; he never used violence; he was not even vindictive. He spoke up, loud and clear, with wit and courage, as long as he could speak without betraying what he loved; when as an exile he could do so no longer, he fell silent.

He is worth keeping in mind, because in America when we talk about censorship we tend to whine. Radicals whine at the Establishment; the White House whines at the Press—you're not fair, you're biased, you suppress the truth—you just wait, I'm gonna get you yet.

The only way to defeat suppression, oppression, and censorship—and where there is institutionalized power, there is censorship—is to refuse it. Not to reply to it in kind—if you try to silence me I'll try to silence you—but to refuse both its means and its ends. To bypass it entirely. To be larger than it is. That is precisely what Zamyatin was. He was larger in spirit than his enemies, and he consciously refused to let their smallness infect him and decrease his stature. He would not play the dirty little games. He would not admit Stalin into his soul.

To achieve anything like that conscious refusal, one must consider the whole question of censorship urgently and earnestly. The suppression of material called pornographic is only one aspect of the issue and, in my opinion, not a central one; though the recent regressive decision by the Supreme Court has reopened the whole battle on that flank. Again, direct political censorship is, in the United States, only one aspect of the issue. Urgent as it is, when the Government can call anything it likes "Classified" and bury it, when the police and the IRS are used to harass avowed or suspected Marxist writers, again it is not—yet—the central issue. It affects only some of us. What affects every writer, every book published in the United States, is censorship by the market.

We are not a totalitarian state; we continue to be a democracy in more than name—but a capitalist, corporate democracy. Our form of censorship rises from the nature of our institutions. Our censors are the idols of the marketplace.

For this reason our form of censorship is unusually fluid and changeable; one should never feel sure one has defined it. Suppressions occur before one is aware of them; they occur behind one's eyes.

We have no Zhdanov saying, "You must not criticize the Government; you must not write about unhappy things. You must write about brave soldiers of the Fatherland and happy workers in the hydroelectric plants. You must be a socialist realist, and you must smile." There are no such orders, no absolute standards, either positive or negative. The only standard, in the marketplace, is *Will it sell?* And that is inherently a broad, and constantly changing standard.

Where the market reigns, fashion reigns. The fine arts, like the arts of costume, cooking, furnishing, etc., become subject to a constant pressure to change, since novelty, regardless of quality, is a marketable value, a publicizable value. It is, of course, a very limited kind of novelty. The skirt up or down two inches; the lapel half an inch wider; the novel's dead this year, but fictionalized journalism is big; in science fiction, Holocaust is out, but Environment is in. Pop art, so called, was the pure essence of art as commodity: soup cans. Genuine newness, genuine originality, is suspect. Unless it's something familiar rewarmed, or something experimental in form but clearly trivial or cynical in content, it is unsafe. And it must be safe. It mustn't hurt the consumers. It mustn't *change* the consumers. Shock them, *épater le bourgeois*, certainly, that's been done for a hundred and fifty years now, that's the oldest game going. Shock them, jolt them, titillate them, make them writhe and squeal—but do not make them think. If they think, they may not come back to buy the next can of soup.

The almost limitless freedom of form available to the modern artist is, I think, a function of this trivialization of art. If art is taken seriously by its creators or consumers, that total permissiveness disappears, and the possibility of the truly revolutionary reappears. If art is seen as sport, without moral significance, or if it is seen as a self-expression, without rational significance, or if it is seen as a marketable commodity, without social significance, then anything goes. To cover a cliff with six acres of plastic film is no more and no less "creative" than to paint the Creation of Adam on the Sistine ceiling. But if art is seen as having moral, intellectual, and social content, if real statement is considered possible, then, on the artist's side, self-discipline becomes a major element of creation. And on the audience's side, the middlemen begin to fret. The publishers, the gallery owners, the entrepreneurs, the producers, the marketers become uneasy. Insofar as they are in the business for money, they are happier if art is not taken seriously. Soup cans are much easier. They want *products* to sell, quick turnover, built-in obsolescence.[1] They do not want large, durable, real, frightening things.

At moments I find the most frightening man now alive to be Aleksandr Solzhenitsyn. I have lived in the same world with Stalin and Hitler, and in the same country with Joe McCarthy and G. Gordon Liddy, and they have all scared me. But none of them so much as Solzhenitsyn does, because none of them has had his power: the power to make me ask myself, *Am I doing right?*

I wonder if the reason why we have no Solzhenitsyn in this country (and no Pasternak, no Zamyatin, no Tolstoy) is that we do not believe in the possibility of having one. Because we do not believe in the reality of art. The strange thing about the Russians is that they do believe in art, in the power of art to change the minds of men. That is why they censor it. It is also why they have a Solzhenitsyn. It has been said that every country has the government it deserves. I would add that every people has the artists it deserves.[2]

SKETCH FOR A NATURALISTIC NOVEL

Our hero, X., was a mathematics teacher in high school, who wrote stories on the side. He sent a couple off to science fiction magazines; they sold, and he began to meet some SF fans. The more he saw of the writer's life, the better he liked it. So he decided, Enough of teaching math, I am a writer, capital *W*.

But he had to eat.

So before he got to work on the big novel he planned, he did a potboiler, sword-and-sorcery, since that was selling well, called *Vulg the Visigoth.* It was successful, and the publisher asked him to make it a series. So he did. And eight years later, he is still writing about Vulg the Visigoth. The latest one, #14, is called *The Rape of the Eldritch Ichor.*

Revised ending. He started to write his big novel, but a friend told him what good money there was in porn while the boom was still on, and offered to agent his stuff for him. Eight years later he is still writing porn. The latest one is called *Deep Armpit.*

Revised ending #2. It was not porn, but comic book continuity. Or true romances? Or international spy thrillers? However, he is still going to write that serious novel, as soon as he has paid for the air conditioner and the electric can opener.

Revised ending #3. He wrote the novel. It was good, and it sold well. But reading it in print he realized that it was not quite the book he had wanted it to be. It was a first novel, and he realized he had a lot to learn; but he knew he could learn. The next book would be better, and the one after that, if he learned his trade, would be the best SF novel yet. But this first one got picked up by a movie studio. They offered him fifty thousand dollars for the rights. When he came to, he packed up and went to Hollywood. And now, eight years later, he is a successful scriptwriter for films and TV. What he writes gets changed a good deal, almost emasculated you might say, before it is produced, but does that matter to a man who makes sixty thousand a year? He has never got around to writing the next novel, but he is going to, after he's paid for the heated swimming pool and the ninth wife.

So after a life of fame and fortune, he dies.

Thirty-six years later, fifty-two years later, his great novel has never been published in his own country. Or in any other country. It never will be. He never wrote it. He accepted the judgment of the censor. He accepted, unquestioning, the values of his society. And the price of unquestioning acceptance is silence.

PRIVILEGE, PARANOIA, PASSIVITY

The saddest thing about Mr. X. is that he was a free man. We are all free. We are free not only to write fuck and shit, and to spell America with a *k*; we are free to write what we please. This freedom was won for us by artists and by just men of law and government during the first half of this century, insofar as it was not already established in the Constitution of 1783. It exists. We are free, freer perhaps than any writers or public have ever been.*

Recently I read in Giovanni Grazzini's fascinating book on Solzhenitsyn the following passage:

> The cultural industry, vanity, the resentment felt by intellectuals at seeing power slipping from their hands, have so obscured the vision of Western writers as to make them believe that not being persecuted by the police is a privilege.

I am very slow indeed. I puzzled over that sentence for three days before I understood what Grazzini meant. He meant, of course, that it is not a privilege, but a right.

The Constitution, which is a revolutionary document, is absolutely clear on that point. It does not grant us, permit us, allow us freedom of speech. It gives the government no such authority. It recognizes freedom of speech as a right—as a fact.

A government cannot grant that right. It can only accept it, or deny it and withhold it by force.

Ours mostly accepts it; Russia's mostly denies it. But we do not have any privilege that Zamyatin did not have, or that Solzhenitsyn does not have. We have, simply, the same inalienable right.

But they have used theirs. They have acted. Have we?

A story of mine once appeared in the magazine *Playboy* with the

---

* Note (1989). The problem with our freedom, of course, is who "we" are. The freedom "won for us by just men," for example, was to a large extent freedom for men, not for women. Fortunately, freedom tends away from exclusivity, toward mutuality; as all tyrants know, the more freedom there is the more people want. There couldn't have been woman suffrage, historically speaking, if there hadn't been male suffrage. And as women continue the struggle initiated by just women of the past century to win and hold freedom for ourselves, men will find themselves further liberated in that measure.

byline "U. K. Le Guin." This is because after the fiction editor had accepted the story, someone else in the firm wrote me asking if they could use the initial of my first name only, saying rather touchingly, "Many of our readers are frightened by stories by women authors." At the time this struck me as merely funny, and I agreed, even furthering their obfuscation by writing, in the biographical form they sent me for their about-the-authors page, "The stories of U. K. Le Guin are not written by U. K. Le Guin, but by another person of the same name." I don't think I thought any more about it than to feel slightly amused, slightly scornful, and to decide, vaguely, that since they paid writers so well they had a right to their little whims. So my work appeared censored. That is, my first name, in other words my sex, was suppressed. The suppression of this single, though rather significant, word is the only instance I know of direct Market Censorship in any of my works. There are certainly other effects of Market Censorship in my works, but I think no direct ones. That is why I mention this one. It was so obvious. And yet I accepted it. To be sure, these things are more obvious now; our consciousness have all been raised. But I was a feminist in 1968 . . .*

Why couldn't I see that I was selling out?

When there are no formal rules, no thou shalts and thou shalt nots, it is difficult to notice, even, that one is being censored. It is all so painless. It is still more difficult to understand that one may be censoring oneself, extensively, ruthlessly—because that act of self-censorship is called, with full social approval, "writing for a market"; it is even used by some writers as the test and shibboleth for that most admired state of being, "professionalism."

Indeed, to distinguish free enterprise from self-censorship takes

---

* Note (1989). Well, I was beginning to be one, anyhow.

a most uncomfortable degree of vigilance. And that so easily becomes paranoia.

After all, a book may be rejected simply because it is a bad job. Editors have taste, skill, and standards. The defense of countless utterly inept writers is "They're afraid to print my work!" It is very easy indeed to join that crew, and start seeing conspiracies in every rejection slip. How can you be sure?

I know many rumors of books being refused by publisher after publisher because the subject matter was considered dangerous; but I know no facts. Until I do I cannot discuss these cases. I can only hazard a guess concerning certain such cases within the science fiction field: that the books were not "subversive" or "shocking"— whatever that could mean now—but that they were serious, morally, ethically, socially serious, and that this quality of seriousness struck the publishers as a very unsafe investment.

"Serious" is an inadequate word. I wish I could find another, but "sincere" has been murdered by President Nixon, and "authentic" by the fancy critics, and there is no adjectival form of "integrity," which is the quality I am talking about. Integrity, plus intelligence. An author who thinks out a major subject thoroughly, who feels the subject intensely, and who talks about it clearly, that is what I mean. The word "clearly," of course, does not imply logic, expository prose, naturalism, or any other specific device; clarity in art is achieved by means that suit the end in view, which may be extremely subtle, complex, and obscure. The skilled use of such means is the artist's art. And the use of them involves considerable pain.

The recent fantasy bestseller *Jonathan Livingston Seagull* is a serious book, unmistakably sincere. It is also intellectually, ethically, and emotionally trivial. The author has not thought things through. He is pushing one of the beautifully packaged Instant Answers we specialize in in this country. He says that if you think you can fly very fast, why, then you can fly very fast. And if you smile, all is well. All the world is well. When you smile, you just know that that man dying of gangrene in Cambodia and that starving four-year-old in Bangladesh and the woman next door with cancer will feel ever so much better, and they'll smile, too. This wishful thinking, this callous refusal to admit the existence of pain, defeat, and death, is not only typical of highly successful American writing, but also of the Soviet writers who "succeeded" where a Zamyatin "failed"—the Stalin Prize winners, with their horrible optimism. Once you stop asking questions, once you let Stalin into your soul, you can only smile, and smile, and smile.

The smile, of course, may become the grin of despair, the rictus of the skull, an expression fashionable among more sophisticated readers. Recent science fiction, for instance, is full of edifying and hideous pictures of terrible futures—overpopulated worlds where people eat each other in the form of green cookies; post-Holocaust mutants behaving in approved Social Darwinist fashion; nine billion people dying various awful deaths by pollution at the rate of a billion per chapter, and so on. I have done this myself; I plead guilty. And I feel guilty. Because none of this involves real thought or real commitment. The death of civilization, the death of a species, is used the way the death of an individual is used in murder mysteries—to provide the readers a cheap thrill. The writer holds up a picture of overpopulation, or universal pollution, or atomic war, and everybody says, *Ugh! Agh! Yecchh!* That is a "gut reaction," a perfectly sincere one. But it is not an act of intelligence and it is not a moral act.

Man does not live by gut alone. Reaction is not action.

Novels of despair are intended, most often, to be admonitory, but I think they are, like pornography, most often escapist, in that they provide a substitute for action, a draining-off of tension. That is why they sell well. They provide an excuse to scream, for writer and reader. A gut reaction, and nothing further. An automatic response to violence—a mindless response. When you start screaming, you have stopped asking questions.

Despite all disclaimers, it is only when science asks why, instead of simply describing how, that it becomes more than technology. When it asks why, it discovers Relativity. When it only shows how, it invents the atomic bomb, and then puts its hands over its eyes and says, *My God, what have I done?*

When art shows only how and what, it is trivial entertainment, whether optimistic or despairing. When it asks why, it rises from mere emotional response to real statement, and to intelligent ethical choice. It becomes, not a passive reflection, but an act.

And that is when all the censors, of the governments and of the marketplace, become afraid of it.

But our censors are not just the publishers and editors and distributors and publicists and book clubs and syndicated reviewers. They are the writers, and the readers. They are you and me. We censor ourselves. We writers fail to write seriously because we're afraid—for good cause—that it won't sell. And as readers we fail to discriminate; we accept passively what is for sale in the marketplace; we buy it, read it, and forget it. We are mere "viewers" and "consumers," not readers at all. Reading is not a passive reaction, but an action, involving the mind, the emotions, and the will. To accept trashy books because they are "bestsellers" is the same thing as accepting adulterated food, ill-made machines, corrupt government, and military and corporative tyranny, and praising them, and calling them the American Way of Life or the American Dream. It is a betrayal of reality. Every betrayal, every lie accepted, leads to the next betrayal and the next lie.

Let Yevgeny Zamyatin, who understood something about truth, have the last word.

A literature that is alive does not live by yesterday's clock, nor by today's, but by tomorrow's. It is a sailor sent aloft: from the masthead he can see foundering ships, icebergs, and maelstroms still invisible from the deck.

In a storm you must have a man aloft. We are in the midst of a storm today, and SOS signals come from every side. Only yesterday a writer could calmly stroll along the deck, clicking his Kodak; but who will want to look at landscapes and genre scenes when the world is listing at a forty-five-degree angle, the green maws are gaping, the hull is creaking? Today we can look and think only as men do in the face of death: we are about to die—and what did it all mean? How have we lived? If we could start all over, from the beginning, what would we live by? And for what? What we need in literature today are vast philosophic horizons—horizons seen from mastheads, from airplanes; we need the most ultimate, the most fearsome, the most fearless "Why?" and "What next?"

What is truly alive stops before nothing and ceaselessly seeks answers to absurd, childish questions. Let the answers be wrong, let the philosophy be mistaken—errors are more valuable than truths; truth is of the machine, error is alive; truth reassures, error disturbs. And if answers be impossible of attainment, all the better! Dealing with answered questions is the privilege of brains constructed like a cow's stomach, which, as we know, is built to digest cud.

If there were anything fixed in nature, if there were truths, all this would, of course, be wrong. But fortunately, all truths are erroneous. This is the very essence of the dialectical process: today's truths become errors tomorrow; there is no final number.

Revolution is everywhere, in everything. It is infinite. There is no final revolution. There is no final number.[3]

NOTES

1. My qualifier, "insofar as they are in the business for money," clearly exempts many publishers—at least in their fiction and poetry departments—from this accusation. But for the perfect example of what I am talking about, one might look at the creation of a "bestseller" through promotion; or at the publication and distribution habits of several major SF publishers.

2. (Author's note, 1978): This was written in the early 1970s, before Solzhenitsyn left the Soviet Union.

3. The Zamyatin quotation is slightly condensed and rearranged from the essay "On Literature, Revolution, Entropy, and Other Matters," in *A Soviet Heretic: Essays by Yevgeny Zamyatin*, edited and translated by Mirra Ginsburg (Chicago: University of Chicago Press, 1970).

THE STONE AX AND
THE MUSKOXEN

(1975)

I want to thank you all for having me here—specifically, I want to thank the Literature Board of the Australian Arts Council for bringing me here, and the workshop and Robin and the rest of the con-committee for looking after me—and, most of all, John Bangsund, for thinking of the whole silly idea in the first place.

I have a question, a serious question to ask you. What on earth are we all doing here?

Well, I think we have come here to celebrate. This is a celebration; this is what the word means—the coming together of many people, from all kinds of weird places, away from their customary life and ways, often at some trouble and expense, maybe not knowing very precisely why they come, but moved to come, to meet together, in one place, to celebrate.

And a celebration needs no cerebration, no excuses or rationalization. A celebration is its own reason for being, as you find out once you get there. The heart has its reasons which reason doesn't know, and a celebration such as this has its own reasons, its own strange laws and life span; it is a real thing, an event, an entity, and we here, long after, in our separate ways and places, will look back on it and recall it as a whole. And if there were bad moments in it, if some of us got drunk and some of us got angry, and some of us had to make speeches, and others of us got horribly bored by the speeches—still I think the chances are that we'll look back on it with some contentment, because the essential element of a celebration is praise; and praise rises out of joy. When you come right down to it, we've all come here to enjoy ourselves.

We aren't going to accomplish anything, you know, or establish anything, or sell anything. We're not here in order to make a new law, or declare a war, or fix the price per barrel of crude oil. No, and thank God we're not. There are enough people involved in that sort of rubbish.

We are here, I think, simply to meet each other, in hopes, and some confidence, that we'll like each other. We're here to enjoy ourselves, which means we are practicing the most essentially human of all undertakings, the search for joy. Not the pursuit of pleasure—any hamster can do that—but the search for joy. And may I wish to you all here that you find it.

But what it is that brings us, this particular us, these particular peculiar individuals from unearthly places like Canberra and Oregon, together here, all standing on our heads in Melbourne? What is that we're here to celebrate? "Joy" is a bit vague, after all; we have to specify, and narrow it down, and put our finger on it. I put out my finger, here, tonight, and what is it that I touch?

Science fiction, of course. That's what brought us here. It does seem a rather bizarre motive, but it's certainly no odder than the motive that brings together International Conventions of Manufacturers of Plumbers' Supplies, or Summit Conferences of Heads of State discussing how to achieve parity in overkill. Science fiction is the motive and the subject of our celebration. That's the one point where all our different minds and souls touch, though on every other subject they may be utterly different, light-years apart. Each of us here has a button somewhere in his soul, like a belly button, but a soul button, and it is labeled science fiction. Many people do not have a soul button, they only have belly buttons, but each of us does. And if you put your finger out and touch that button, the whole spiritual console lights up and goes Zzzzzt Blink All Systems Go, All Systems Go.

I am your guest of honor, and deeply honored to be so. As such, I think I am to speak not only to you, but for you: to be the Oracle, the Leader of the Celebration, the Priestess of the Cult. When the last orgy is over, I understand I am to be led forth and thrown into the nearest volcano, to propitiate the Fertility Gods of Melbourne. But never mind that. So long as I'm here, my job is to speak for you. To celebrate what we are celebrating. To speak in praise of science fiction.

Well, that's something I don't mind doing a bit. I like science fiction. And I have reason to be grateful to it. For the past dozen years or so, SF has added money to the family pocket, and confusion to the family income tax returns, and books to the family bookshelf, and a whole sort of Parallel Universe dimension to the family life—"Where's Ma going this month?"—"Australia"—"You mean I have to wash the dishes for a *week*?"—"No, we get to come along"—"Can I have a pet koala, can I? I promise I'll feed it myself!"

Do you people realize, by the way, that to my three children Science Fiction is not a low form of literature involving small green men and written by small contemptible hacks, but an absolutely ordinary, respectable, square profession—the kind of thing your own *mother* does? We, you and I, most of us, those over twenty-five anyhow, read SF when young, and hid our copy of *Galaxy* inside a copy of *Intermediate Algebra*, in order to appear respectably occupied. We asked children's librarians for SF and they said, "Oh, we do not allow children to read escapist literature." We asked adults' librarians for it and they said, "Oh, we do not carry children's books on this side of the building." We had to put the books down face down because of the cover, which showed a purple squid carrying off a fainting maiden in a large bronze bra. We had the difficulty and the pleasure of doing something which, if not actually illicit, was sneaky, eccentric, addictive, and splendidly disreputable.

Now, you know, our kids—not just my kids, but all our kids, and everybody here that's too young to have any business having any kids yet—the rising generation, shall I say, is almost entirely missing this experience? The poor things have nothing disreputable left but sex and marijuana, and sex is getting respectable all too fast. They're getting *taught* SF in the *schools*. Some of them for all I know may be hiding their copy of *Intermediate Algebra* inside a copy of *Again, Dangerous Visions*, and solving marvelous irrelevant equations in secret while Teacher thinks they're reading Meaningful Literature.

I gather this coopting of SF into the curriculum is less usual in the Commonwealth than in America; but I was in England earlier this year, and got stuck on a tele spot with five beautiful Cockney kids from a Marylebone school who had read more SF than I had, and done a whole school session reading and writing it. So it's coming, fans. In the States, it's come; and from St. Pancras Station to the farthest sheep-station, it's coming. Science fiction is being taught, by teachers and professors, in schools and colleges. Science fiction is being seriously discussed, by futurologists with computers and by literary critics with PhDs. Science fiction is being written by people who don't know Warp Five from a Dyson sphere, and being read by people who don't read science fiction. I am here to proclaim unto the assembled faithful that the walls are down. The walls are down, we're free at last. And you know what? It's a big cold world outside there.

I can't really blame those of my generation and older who don't want to see the walls come a-tumbling down, and who cling to their ghetto status as if it were a precious thing, making a religion of SF, which the touch of the uninitiated will profane. They were forced into that attitude by the attitude of respectable society, intellectual and literary, toward their particular interest; and it was perfectly natural for them, like any persecuted group, to make a virtue of their necessity. I can't blame them, but neither can I agree with them. To cling to the posture of evasion and defense, once persecution and contempt has ceased, is to be not a rebel, but a cripple. And what I want is to see SF continue to rebel. I want to see SF evade, not those who despise it, but those who want it to be just what it was thirty years ago. I want to see SF step over the old, fallen walls, and head right into the next wall, and start to break it down, too.

One of those walls is the labeling of books by publishers as SF—labeling, packaging, and distributing. At the moment this is pretty much a necessity of the publishing trade. It is sensible, and I don't expect an immediate rejection of the practice. Public librarians, school librarians, and booksellers want to shelve and display SF so that those who want it can find it. It's convenient for us addicts, and profitable to the booksellers and publishers. But the practice does considerable wrong to the innocent nonaddict, who is prevented from picking up an SF book by chance; he has to go to Shelf 63, between the Gothics and the Soft Core Porn, and look for it. And of course the SF label perpetuates a dichotomy that no longer exists, between SF and Mainstream. There is a spectrum, now, not a chasm. The SF label is a remnant of the ghetto wall, and I'll be glad to see it go. Oh for the day when I can go into my library and find *The Man in the High Castle*, not shelved next to *Barf the Barbarian* by Elmer T. Hack, but by the author's name, Philip K. Dick, right next to Charles Dickens—where it belongs.

And another day. The day when the *Times Literary Supplement*, or the *New York Times Book Review*, or the *East Grong-Grong Sheep Rancher's Weekly* reviews a major new SF novel along with the other novels, not in a little column set apart and headed Sci Fi or Spec Fic or what have you. In which columns, by the existence of which columns, it is implied that however highly praised the work reviewed may be, it's not to be placed in the same category, of course, as the other novels reviewed throughout the paper—the *real* ones.

There's lots of walls yet, you see, to be reduced to rubble.

But all this is a bit external. The worst walls are never the ones you find in your way. The worst walls are the ones you put there— you build yourself. Those are the high ones, the thick ones, the ones with no doors.

See, here we stand, Science Fiction, a noble figure among the ruined walls, chains dropping from our giant limbs, facing the future with eagle eyes, and all that. But actually, who are we? And exactly what future are we facing with our eagle eyes? Now that we're free, where are we going?

From here on I have to speak as a writer. I've been trying to speak for the community of SF writers and fans, and enjoying it, but I can't keep it up. I'm faking. I'm not a fan. As you know, many SF writers are, or were; they started as fans. It was a phenomenon of the ghetto which is now called the Golden Age of Science Fiction.

Well, I came along just late enough to miss the Golden Ghetto, in ignorance that it even existed. I read SF as a kid, but knew nothing about fandom. I wrote SF first, and discovered that it was SF second, when the publishers told me so, and then finally, third, I discovered the existence of fandom. That was in Oakland in 1964, the first big Worldcon, I guess. I heard there was this Science Fiction meeting going on, and I'd published three or four SF stories and was crazy about Phil Dick and Cordwainer Smith, and so I went down to Oakland to see what was going on. And there were about 5,000 people who all knew each other and absolutely everything about SF since 1926. And the only one I met was Barbara Silverberg, who was so incredibly gorgeous that I instantly went home and put my head in a paper bag for a week.

That was the last Worldcon I attended. Until now. You see, I am an outsider, an alien, for all you know I come from a whole different galaxy and am planning the overthrow of the entire Australian Ballot System. But all the same, I do write SF. And that's why you asked me here. And so I think it would make sense if I went on and spoke as what I am; a writer. A writer of SF. A woman writer of SF.

Do you know that I am a very rare creature? My species was at first believed to be mythological, like the tribble and the unicorn. Members of it survived only by protective coloration and mimetic adaptation—they used male pen names. Slowly, timorously, they began to come out of hiding. Looking around warily for predators. I myself was forced into hiding just once, by an editor of *Playboy*, who reduced me to a simple, unthreatening, slightly enigmatic shape—a U. Not Ursula, but U. I have felt a little bent, a little bit U-shaped, ever since. But we kept creeping out; it took a while, and there were setbacks, but gradually my species took courage and appeared in full mating plumage: Anne, Kate, Joanna, Vonda, Suzy, and the rest. But when I say "the rest," please don't get alarmed, don't feel threatened or anything. There are very few of us. Maybe one out of thirty SF writers is a woman. That statistic is supplied by my agent, Virginia Kidd, a very beautiful member of my species; the ratio is a guess, but an educated one. Do you find it a rather startling ratio? I do. I am extremely puzzled, even embarrassed, at my own rarity. Are they going to have to lock me up in pens, like the Whooping Cranes and Duckbilled Platypuses and other species threatened with extinction, and watch eagerly to see if I lay an egg?

Why are women so scarce in SF—in the literature, among the fans, and most of all among the writers? A good many historical reasons come to mind—American SF as action pulp fiction during the thirties, Campbellian SF written for adolescent engineers, etc.—but all of them are circular. *Why* was Golden Ghetto SF a males-only club? Is there really something in the nature of the literature that doesn't appeal generally to women?

Not that I can see. *Analog* and its school did certainly follow one minor element within SF to the extreme, to a point where only those who enjoy either wars or wiring diagrams—preferably both at once—can enjoy it much. Most women in our culture are brought up to be rather indifferent toward military heroics and wiring diagrams, so they're likely to be bored or irritated. They're used to this; juvenile males in almost all cultures tend to be afraid of women, and to form clubs that cut them out, exclude them. And similarly a good deal of sword and sorcery leaves most women cold, because it consists so largely of male heroics and male fantasies of sexual prowess, often intensely sadistic. But those two minor provinces set aside for Boy Scouts only, all the rest is left—all the broad, beautiful countryside of grown-up SF, where anything can happen, and usually does. Why have more women not moved in and made themselves at home?

I don't know. My trouble is, I was born here, I didn't move in, so I can't figure out what the problem is. Year by year I see more members of my species, young ones mostly, coming and building temporary nests, or boldly trying out their wings above the mountains. But still not enough. Twenty or thirty males to one female is not a good ratio for species preservation. Among domestic fowls, in fact, it goes quite the other way, half a dozen hens to one rooster; but never mind that.

I just want to ask the men here to consider idly, in some spare moment, whether by any chance they have been building any walls to keep the women out, or to keep them "in their place," and what they have lost by doing so.

And to ask the women here to consider, idly or not idly at all, why are there so few of us? We can't blame it on prejudice, because SF publishing is in general a quite un-sex-biased field. Have women walled themselves out, through laziness of mind, fear of being seen using the intellect in public, fear of science and technology, fear of letting their imaginations loose—and above all, perhaps fear of competing with men? That, as we all know, is an unladylike thing to do.

But no art is ladylike. Nor is any art gentlemanly. Nor is it masculine or feminine. The reading of a book and the writing of a book is not an act dependent in any way upon one's gender. (In fact, very few human acts are, other than procreation, gestation, and lactation.)

When you undertake to make a work of art—a novel or a clay pot—you're not competing with anybody, except yourself and God. Can I do it better this time? Once you have realized that that is the only question, once you have faced the empty page or the lump of clay in that solitude, without anyone to blame for failure but yourself, and known that fear and that challenge, you aren't going to care very much about being ladylike, or about your so-called competition, male or female. The practice of an art is, in its absolute discipline, the experience of absolute freedom. And that, above all, is why I'd like to see more of my sisters trying out their wings above the mountains. Because freedom is not always an easy thing for women to find.

Well, all right, so we've established one fact about who and what science fiction is. It's very largely male, but seems to be tending always a little more toward androgyny—at least I hope so. And what else is it? As one Theodore Sturgeon once remarked, it's 95 percent trash—like everything else.

I'm in an heretical mood. I dare to question Sturgeon's Law. *Is* 95 percent of everything trash? Really? Is 95 percent of a forest trash? Is 95 percent of the ocean trash? It soon will be if we go on polluting it, but it wasn't to start with. Is 95 percent of humanity trash? Any dictator would agree, but I don't agree with him. Is 95 percent of literature trash?

Well—yes. It probably is. Of the books now published in the world in a year, 95 percent probably aren't even trash, they're just noise.

But I revert to my speaking as a writer, not as a reader, and inquire, How many books, *while they are being written*, are conceived of by their authors as trash?

It's really an interesting question. I have no idea of the answer. It's not zero percent—far from it. There are many many authors who deliberately write junk for money, and I have met others who, though less cynical, spoke of their own works as "moneymakers" or as "mere entertainment"—a little defensively, to be sure, because the ego is always involved in the work, but also honestly, realistically, in the full knowledge that they had not done, and had not tried to do, the best work they could do. And in art, from the artist's point of view, there are only two alternatives: the best you can do—or trash. It's a binary system. On/Off. Yes/No. But not from the reader's point of view, of course. From there, there are infinite gradations between the best and the worst, all degrees of genius, talent, and achievement between Shakespeare and the hack, and also within each work, even Shakespeare's. But from the writer's point of view, while writing, there are just two ways to go: to push toward the limit of your capacity, or to sit back and emit garbage. And the really unfair thing is that the intent, however good, guarantees nothing. You can try your heart out, work like a good slave, and write drivel. But the opposite intent does carry its own guarantee. No artist ever set out to do less than his best and did something good by accident. You head for Perfection and you may very well get trash. But you head toward trash, and by gum, you always get it. The Quest for Perfection fails at least 95 percent of the time, but the Search for Garbage never fails.

I find this repetition of the trashiness of most SF too easy— both defensive and destructive. Defensive: "Don't hit me, folks, I'm down already." That's the old, ingratiating, self-protective ghetto posture. And destructive: because it is cynical, it sets limits and builds walls. It says to the SF writer, of all people, Why shoot for the moon? The chances are 19 to 1 that you won't get there. Only a tiny elite gets there, and we all know that elite people are snobs anyhow. Keep your feet on the ground, kid; work for money, not for dreams; write it like the editor says he wants it; don't waste time revising and polishing; sell it quick and grind out the next one. What the hell, it's a living, isn't it? And so what if it's not art, at least it's entertainment.

That "entertainment" bit really burns me. It hides a big lie behind an obvious truth. Of course an SF story is entertainment. *All* art is entertainment. That's so clear it's fatuous to repeat it. If Handel's Messiah were boring, not entertaining, would thousands of people go listen to it year after year? If the Sistine Ceiling were dull, would the tourists troop there endlessly to get cricks in their necks? If *Oedipus Rex* weren't a smashing good show, would it be in the repertory after 2,500 years? If *The First Circle* weren't a gripping, powerful, highly entertaining story, would the Soviet government be so terrified of Aleksandr Solzhenitsyn? No! If he was a dull hack, they'd love him. He'd be writing just what they want, writing to the editor's specifications, weak tea, perfectly safe. He'd probably be a People's Artist by now.

Of course, some art is immediately attractive, and some is difficult, demanding intense response and involvement from its audience. The art of one's own time tends to be formidable, in a time of change like ours, because we have to learn how and where to take hold of it, what response is being asked for us, before we can get involved. It's truly new, and therefore truly a bit frightening.

I'm easily frightened myself; I was afraid of the Beatles, at first. People are easily frightened, but also brave and stubborn. They want that entertainment that only art can give them, that peculiar, solid satisfaction, and so they do keep listening to the weirdest electronic music, and staring at big ugly paintings of blobs, and reading queer difficult books about people on another world 20,000 years from now, and they say, I don't really like it, it's unsettling, it's painful, it's crazy . . . but you know I kind of liked that one bit where something went *eeeeoooooo-bwangg!*—it really got to me, you know?

That's all art wants to do. It wants to get to you. To break down the walls between us, for a moment. To bring us together in a celebration, a ceremony, an entertainment—a mutual affirmation of understanding, or of suffering, or of joy.

Therefore I totally oppose the notion that you can put Art over here on a pedestal, and Entertainment down here in a clown suit. Art and Entertainment are the same thing, in that the more deeply and genuinely entertaining a work is, the better art it is. To imply that Art is something heavy and solemn and dull, and Entertainment is modest but jolly and popular, is neo-Victorian idiocy at its worst.

Every artist is deeply serious and passionate about their work, and every artist also wears a clown suit and capers in public for pennies. The ones who put on the clown suit and the painted grin, but who don't care about performing well, are neither entertainers nor artists; they're fakes. They know it, and we know it, and though they may indeed be briefly and immensely popular, because they never frighten anyone, or move anyone, or make anyone really laugh or cry, but just reassure people by lying to them—all the same, that popularity is meaningless. The name dies, the work's forgotten, and what's left? A hollow place. A sense of waste. A realization that where something real might have been done—a good handsome clay pot, or a really entertaining story—the chance was lost. We lost it. We accepted the fake, the plastic throwaway, when we could have held out for the real thing.

I'm not one of these antique-lovers, but do you know how moving it can be to use, or just handle, some object—a piece of pottery, or a tool—that has been used by several generations of people, all strangers, all dead now? I keep a stone ax on my desk at home—not for self-defense, but for pleasure. My father used to keep it on his desk. It makes a good paperweight. It's New Stone Age, but I don't know how old, anything from a few centuries to 22,000 years. It's partly polished and partly left rough, though finely shaped. It is well made. You think of the human hands patiently polishing that granite. There's a sense of solidity and of community in the touch, the feel, of that ax to me. There's nothing sentimental about it, quite the opposite; it is a real experience, a rare intimation, of *time*, our most inward dimension, which is so difficult to experience consciously, but without which we are utterly disoriented and astray in the seemingly so familiar external dimensions of space. Well, that's what I mean about the real work of art. Like a stone ax, it's *there*. It stays there. It's solid, and it involves the inward dimension. It may be wonderfully beautiful, or quite commonplace and humble, but it's made to be used, and to last.

Hack work is not made to be used, but to be sold; and not made to last, but to wear out at once and be replaced. And that's the difference, I believe, between art-and-entertainment on the one hand, and trash on the other.

Ted Sturgeon, when he made his Law up, was simply responding to contemptuous and ignorant critics of SF who scarcely deserved so clever an answer. But his Law has since been used as a defense and an excuse and a cop-out, and I suggest that we in SF stop quoting it for a bit, at least if we're using it in a resigned and cynical fashion. I'd like us not to be resigned, but rebellious; not cynical, but critical, intransigent and idealistic. I'd like us to say, 95 percent of SF is trash—Yecchh! Let's get rid of the stuff! Let's open the windows and get rid of this garbage! Here we have Science Fiction, the most flexible, adaptable, broad-range, imaginative, crazy form prose fiction has ever attained—and we're going to let it be used for making toy plastic rayguns that break when you play with them, and prepackaged, precooked, predigested, indigestible, flavorless TV dinners, and big inflated rubber balloons containing nothing but hot air? The hell we are, I say!

You know what our statue of Science Fiction needs to do? To use its eagle eyes to look at itself. A long, thoughtful look. A critical look. We don't have to be defensive anymore. We aren't children, or untouchables, or cripples anymore. Like it or lump it, we are now adult active members of society. And as such we have a challenge to meet. *Noblesse oblige.*

We've got to stop skulking around playing by ourselves, like the kid everybody picks on. When an SF book is reviewed, in a fanzine or a literary review, it should be compared with the rest of current literature like any other book, and placed among the rest on its own individual merits. When an SF book is criticized, in print or in a class, it should be criticized as hard as any other book, demandingly, with the same expectations of literacy, solidity, complexity, crafts-manship. When an SF book is read, it should be read as a novel or a short story—that is, a work in the traditions also employed by Dickens and Chekhov—not as an artifact from the Pulp Factory.

The reader should expect to be entertained, but should also ex-pect to travel on unfamiliar ground. Experimentation, innovation, irreverence, complexity, and passion should make the reader rejoice, not run away whimpering, "But it wasn't like this in 1937!" And the science fiction writer really should be aware that he or she is in an extraordinary, enviable position: an inheritor of the least rigid, freest, youngest of all literary traditions: and therefore should do the job just as well, as seriously and entertainingly, as intelligently and passionately, as ever it can be done. That's the least we can ask of our writers—and the most. You can't demand of artists that they produce masterpieces. You can ask that they try.

It seems to me that SF is standing, these days, in a doorway. The door is open, wide open. Are we going to just stand here, waiting for the applause of the multitudes? It won't come; we haven't earned it yet. Are we going to cringe back into the old safe ghetto room and pretend there isn't any big bad multitude out there? If so, our good writers will leave us in despair, and there will not be another generation of them. Or are we going to walk on through the doorway and join the rest of the city? I hope so. I know we can, and I hope we do, because we have a great deal to offer—to art, which needs new forms like ours, and to critics who are sick of chewing over the same old works, and above all to the readers of books, who want and deserve better novels that they mostly get. But it will take not only courage for SF to join the community of literature, but strength, self-respect, the will not to settle for the second-rate. It will take genuine self-criticism. And it will include genuine praise.

If you think, secretly or openly, that you're second-rate, that you're 95 percent trash, then however much you praise yourself it won't mean much—to you, or to others. That's like adolescent boasting, which so often reveals a terrible sense of worthlessness and weakness.

SF is pretty well grown up now. We've been through our illiterate stage, and our latent or nonsexual stage, and the stage when you can't think of anything *but* sex, and the other stages, and we really do seem to be on the verge of maturity now.

When I say I'd like SF to be self-critical, I don't mean pedantic or destructively perfectionist; I mean I'd like to see more SF readers judging soundly, dismissing the failures quietly, in order to praise the successes joyfully—and to go on from them, to build upon them. That is maturity, isn't it?—a just assessment of your capacities, and the will to fulfill them. We have plenty to praise, you know. I do think SF during the past ten years has produced some books and stories that will last, that will be meaningful and beautiful many years from now.

It seems to me that we can grow and change, and welcome growth and change, without losing our solidarity.

The solidarity of the SF community is a really extraordinary thing. It makes the lives of fans much richer and a great deal more complicated, and for the writers, it can be an incredible boon—the support, the response, science fiction writers get from their readers is unique. Most novelists get nothing like that, they are quite isolated. Their response comes mainly from the paid reviewers of the review services and journals. If they are bestsellers, they're totally isolated from genuine response by the enormous mechanisms of salesmanship and publicity and success. What fandom, the SF community, gives the SF writer, or at least this is my own personal experience, is the best modern equivalent of the old small-scale community, city-state or the like, within which most of the finest art forms developed and flourished: a community of intensely interested people, a ready audience, ready to discuss and defend and attack and argue with each other and the artist, to the irritation and entertainment and benefit of all.

When I say the ghetto walls are down and it behooves us to step over them and be free, I don't mean that the community of SF is breaking up, or should break up. I hope it doesn't; I think it won't; I don't see why it should. The essential lunacy that unites us will continue to unite us. The one thing that's changed is that we're no longer *forced* together in a mutually defensive posture—like a circle of muskoxen on the Arctic snow, attacked by wolves—by the contempt and arrogance of literary reactionaries. If we meet now and in the future, we writers and readers of SF, to give each other prizes and see each other's faces and renew old feuds and discuss new books and hold our celebration, it will be in entire freedom—because we choose to do so—because, to put it simply, we like each other.

ABOUT THE AUTHOR

Ursula K. Le Guin (1929–2018) was the celebrated author of twenty-three novels, twelve volumes of short stories, eleven volumes of poetry, thirteen children's books, five essay collections, and four works of translation. Her acclaimed books received the Hugo, Nebula, Endeavor, Locus, Otherwise, Theodore Sturgeon, PEN/Malamud, and National Book Awards; a Newbery Honor; and the Pushcart and Janet Heidinger Kafka Prizes, among others. In 2014, she was awarded the National Book Foundation's Medal for Distinguished Contribution to American Letters, and in 2016 joined the short list of authors to be published in their lifetimes by the Library of America. Le Guin was also the recipient of the Association for Library Service to Children's May Hill Arbuthnot Honor Lecture Award and the Margaret A. Edwards Award. She received lifetime achievement awards from the World Fantasy Convention, *Los Angeles Times*, Pacific Northwest Booksellers Association, and Willamette Writers, as well as the Science Fiction and Fantasy Writers of America's Grand Master Award and the Library of Congress Living Legend Award. Her website is UrsulaKLeGuin.com.

TEXT PERMISSIONS